THE FOOTBALL THUG WHO DIDN'T GIVE A FUCK

THE INSIDE STORY OF MANCHESTER CITY'S NOTORIOUS MAYNE LINE SERVICE CREW

ANTONY SULLIVAN

EMPIRE PUBLICATIONS

EMPIRE PUBLICATIONS
1 Newton Street, Manchester M1 1HW
© Tony Sullivan 2008

ISBN 1 901 746 53 4

Cover photographs © Ashley Shaw
Cover design and layout: Ashley Shaw

Printed in Great Britain.

CONTENTS

Acknowledgments

I'd like to thank the following individuals: The girls in my solicitors office (Kaufman's) - don't worry girls, I don't blame you for the final 18 months inside! Tracy Ralston, Tracie Farnsworth, Nicola Farnsworth, Lianne Camp, Carrol Miller, Stuart Kaufman, Joanne McNulty, Kathryn Harrop and Colin Rowley RIP.

Some of the above wrote me letters whilst inside and that really kept me going, others I apologise for driving you mad! Stuart's Angel's will never let you down.

To Dave E who sorted out my visiting orders for my girlfriend and friends Pete, Den, Bren and Colin. Also to John Berry who took my daughter to City games when I was inside and Mary Carr, Rest in Peace, thanks for the memories of Southport.

To Chris from Prestwich - one of the gamest lads I have met - and his son James who it was a pleasure to meet. The trip to Belgium was one of the funniest times I've had in my life. James was a real funny lad and I hope he remembers my words. 'Go for your goals and keep out of trouble, go the right way not the wrong way.'

Thanks to Ashley Shaw and John Ireland at Empire Publications for agreeing to publish the book and to P Hill for spending hours and hours typing up my hand written memoirs and putting up with me on the phone each week asking 'when will it be ready'!

Finally to my girlfriend, Lizzie, for putting up with me and my daughter Chloe, who has been brave throughout my time inside and who I treasure spending every minute with on civvy street.

INTRODUCTION

I am the sweet and tender hooligan
And I swear that I'll never, never do it again
(And of course he won't,
Well, not until the next time)

SWEET AND TENDER HOOLIGAN
THE SMITHS

L et's get this straight from the start. I was never one of the leaders of a football firm and I do not pretend to be, I'm just one of the lads who ran with the gang, yet after chatting to fellow inmates during my last stretch in Strangeways about my experiences, one or two suggested I wrote the details down and had them published and that is what I did, this book was completely written inside. I also decided to write it after reading a few similar books by lads from other firms - in particular one certain Munich who wrote a pile of shite about City fans always hiding in Fallowfield at derby games. Every firm at one stage has been run ragged or smacked all over the place. Reading some of these books makes you think they were all SAS material and invincible. What a load of bollocks! Some books are like sociology lectures and fashion catwalks. The wankers wearing all the labels and Stone Island crap wouldn't be seen anywhere near a fight - they'd be too scared of ruining their shirt, jacket or trainers. Wankers.

Throughout the book you will read about so-called hooligans who talked the talk but couldn't back it up by walking the walk - wannabee hooligans on the fringe of the action, watching (and running when it gets a bit too near them) and then telling their mates all about it later, with a slightly exaggerated version to impress their mates eagerly listening to the story and being impressed by the narrator.

And it is the same with a book. If you are going to write a hooligan book, simply tell the truth, do not over-inflate your ego filling page after page with fantasy fighting that never took place and the book being an exercise in bullshitters simply going on with themselves to impress their mates.

Writing this book, I have set out to explain how I got involved in my early teens - not just into football hooliganism, but robbing, gang fighting, running away from kids homes and ending up in prison on a number of occasions on different charges, not to mention ending up in hospital on a regular basis! There were also lots of funny stories to tell and hopefully the humour involved in some of the activities I got involved in will come across whilst you are reading this.

I apologise to no one for what is written. It happened so it is included. The language used is strong at times, but then again it is a real language that we used all the time.

I originally wanted to put the book in chronological order from start to finish, but although the games and incidents are fresh in the memory, in many cases the dates are just a blur (due to too many cracks on the head!). Some are obvious to recall like specific derby games or cup games, but the rest are just one big memory with no dates attached. Therefore chapters in the book concentrate on particular geographical teams such as Yorkshire clubs and Cockney clubs etc.

This book concentrates solely on my times as a Manchester City hooligan - I am in the process of writing a further book on my experiences watching England home and away and hope to have that book published in the near future. In the meantime, you have this one to read, I hope you enjoy it,

Tony Sullivan

'MUNICH'

Before we get into the book, I would like to comment as to my repeated use of the word 'Munich' - referring to Manchester United fans. This word has been common currency among City fans for sometime but as far as I'm aware it has never been used in print before - other than once by accident in the official City Programme!

Many United fans, indeed football fans in general, maybe appalled by its liberal use in this book, referencing as it does the Munich Air Disaster of 1958 that claimed the lives of Manchester United players and staff and, lest we forget, the life of former City goalkeeper Frank Swift.

But let's be honest here. City fans use this word in reference to our rivals all the time. Walk into a City pub when a United game is on or before the derby and the word will be heard many times by all sections of our support, in the same way that United fans refer to Liverpool supporters as 'Murderers' in reference to the Heysel Stadium Disaster of 1985. To deny these words exist as part of modern football culture is to stick one's head in the sand.

My advice, should you be offended by the word and think it wrong, is to put the book down and read something else instead. These words, and other epithets bandied about between rivals, are just that. As the saying goes 'sticks and stones... '

MISSPENT YOUTH

I grew up in Blackley one of five kids (three brothers and two sisters). Now my old man was a blue through and through and there was no debate whether you were City or United in our family – you were a blue, plain and simple! I went to my first football match when I was just three months old. Obviously I was too young to remember the details but my old man reckoned it was against Spurs.

I used to go to all the home games with my dad, but my main memory of this period was the fighting between my mam and dad and my brothers and sisters taking sides. I remember trying to stop my elder brother trying to have a go at my younger brother – I jumped in to stop it and one of my brothers gave me a crack. I turned to him as if to say 'Is that the best you can do?' as he's having another go at me. I was surprised that I wasn't knocked out by his punches and before I knew it we were having a full-on fight.

Then he dissappeared into the kitchen – I thought he'd run off but all of a sudden, as he returned, my dad knocked him to the floor and he was holding a pair of scissors. The old man started having a right go at our kid, saying 'Why did you want to stab your brother?' My dad might have been a fighter but he didn't like weapons – he used to say 'If you can't fight, you shouldn't start one'. It's not nice to witness things like that as a kid but things got worse. One day my sister told me that my dad had been nicked - he was a bit of a villain and about two weeks later mum and dad sat us down and told us they were separating – it wasn't a surprise.

As time went on I was getting into trouble: nicking cars, missing school, shoplifting and getting into gang fights. I wasn't even eleven! I went to stay with my dad because mum couldn't cope with it any longer but that lasted two months.

My dad was a card player, he was mad for it. Anyway one night he'd gone out playing cards and our kid was looking after me and there's a knock on the door. It's a our kid's chick, Tracey – anyway, I let her in and she sits down next to our kid but you know what it's like when your younger brother is hanging around when your bird's there and you can't get up to anything. Anyway I went into the kitchen to make a brew and when I came back in they're having a kiss and a cuddle. Suddenly he starts bribing me to get lost – finally, losing patience, he says, 'haven't you got any homework to do'.

So I go over and turn the telly on – Z cars was on I remember. He jumps up but I can't stop laughing because there's this big bulge in his pants that he's trying to hide. Luckily enough there's a knock at the door just then and my friend answers.

'Are you coming out?'

Before I can answer our kid pipes up, 'Yeah, he's going out but be back by ten', because he can't wait to get rid of me. So we went round the corner, gave it ten minutes, sneaked back in and caught them both bang at it. So I crept upstairs and got my catapult and passed it to my mate who fired this stone at my brother's arse, then we ran off with their clothes and put them in the front garden and hid round the corner. When our kid thought the coast was clear, he came out with nothing on. The neighbours were watching by now, the nosey ones looking out of the window and a man and his wife walking home from the pub.

By now our kid's face was a picture and someone shouts out 'it's that shag bag Tracey, she was at it with the scoutmaster last night!' – what an embarrassment. Mind you, I don't think she was the type to get embarrassed. Anyway, after that our kid never bothered to come round to dads – every time he did he got loads of grief and I don't think he ever forgave me for setting him up.

Later, he grassed me up to dad for nicking a car and I certainly paid for that - I had a sore arse for a week but you know what it's like, after a few days you've forgotten the beating and you're back doing it again for the buzz. It was great living at my dads because he was never in, so he never knew what I was up to – my school wasn't bothered (in fact they were probably relieved) that I didn't turn up so I had a great time.

So there's my childhood: a broken home, brothers and sisters who didn't give a fuck and me, the youngest, left to fend for himself - it's enough to make a social worker weep. In truth, I had to learn fast and think on my feet to survive. I was already a cocky little shit who didn't give a fuck!

*   *   *

I can always remember a kid called Timmy, he was a buzz. Apart from nicking cars he liked to fight and there was one time he called round to the house to tell me of some shit he was having with some lads who lived on Monroe Road, Blackley. Clearly, it needed sorting so we planned to go down there that night.

Anyway, I knew dad wouldn't be back 'til late so I was alright and my sister didn't care as long as I was in before dad. Everyone was due to meet at 6.30pm on the hill-top. There was a nice firm (about 50 lads) and we started to go over the hill - it would only take us ten minutes so we split-up - we knew they'd be at the youth club.

We crossed over the road and some went the back way with the rest taking the front as we all picked up stones for catapulting. Anyway we were round the back when all of a sudden you just heard someone shout 'come on', it was Ged leading the way forward and, as we made our way to the front, there were some of the Monroe gang backing off towards us. This kid just let loose with a catapult and whacked this kid on the head with everybody just steaming in - it was going off for about 15 minutes. Suddenly, the dibble came and everyone was trying to hold the line. In the end I was trying to stop people getting nicked and sure enough I got nicked myself and wound up in the back of a black Maria.

I can remember my mam and dad coming to get me out. My dad turned round and said 'you'll have to go to your mams', and then my mam saying '1 don't want him he's nothing but trouble, he's just like you'.

After all the arguing I went back to my mams but that didn't last long (about a week if that) before my mam said to me 'I'm fed up, all you do is bring trouble'. I promised her I'd change my ways but you know what it's like after you've had a telling off, your like 'yeah I'll be good' knowing as soon as she's gone into the next room you start giggling like fuck to yourself.

Anyway the next morning I got up ready for school looking like an ultra bright kid, sparkling like mad. 'Right mam, I'll see you later' and she gave me some dinner money. Next thing, my mate is knocking on the door and we're walking to school, or rather legging it past the school so no one noticed because my mam lived right round the corner from school. We legged it for the bus, sometimes we might have to go three stops down until we found a queue so you could successfully jib on. The bus fare was only 2p but you'd jib it anyway and hope that the blakey wouldn't get on. Then it was straight into town and a go on the amusements - then you'd be starving, go into the sandwich shop, rob the butties and crisps and try and eat them in the Arndale, looking round to make sure you've not been followed before trying to work out what you're going to do for the next five hours... believe me missing school was fucking hard work!

So we headed back to the arcade. One scam was to kick each other in the bollocks and tell someone we'd just been robbed of our dinner money, someone would always help you out. We'd be like 'cheers mister' and then you'd be thinking 'silly bastard fell for it again' and we'd try it on with the next person - this was a buzz and it rarely failed - I was the younger one so I always had to do the poor boy act. Then we'd go into the shops, a personal favourite was Debenhams - the jeans were near the door and there were no alarms back then. We'd always do it at dinner time because the staff would change and sometimes there was no one near the till where the jeans were.

Anyway I bunked school all week and then it was the weekend. On the Saturday my mate called for me and my mam gave me some money for the match, City v Brighton, and I headed out at about 9am. I was buzzing like mad as I'm going out of the gate, I shouted 'don't worry I'll be back for 7pm, I'm going with Gary'.

My mam shouted back 'two lads knocked on, Darren and Jay, they'll meet you at the bus stop'.

'Nice one mam', my mam liked them two so I knew it was

okay. My mam was a bit funny if she didn't like you she'd let you know but Darren and Jay were older than me, (I was 10, they were 13 and 14). I always knocked around with lads who were older because most of my school mates were still into action men and none of them would dare go to the fair as their mams' would shout. I couldn't imagine my mam shouting at me, it was more a case of giving me money and telling me to get lost and don't come back for a good few hours. At the time I thought it was because I was her blue eyed boy!

Anyway we set off to the match. Got the bus, usual thing - jib the bus, get off in town, cut through Debenhams and as we were walking through we couldn't believe our luck, there was no one near the jeans so we grabbed a couple of pairs of jeans and walked out with them and sold them in town to a woman near the underground market. I got £20 for 5 pairs. Now I'm thinking '£20 I'm only 10 years old it's a lot of money'.

We went to the bakers – as usual riffle Gregg's for sandwiches and a drink and then go to the amusement arcade. Then we'd get the match bus which was an easy jib because everybody's getting that. It was hammered at the turnstile so we'd try and double up with other fans, it was easy to get in. There was always a gap somewhere or something left open and we'd be in, making our way to the top of the Kippax and we stood there looking at the away supporters. On this day, City won 1-0 and I can always remember the chant going up on our way out, directed at the small band of Brighton fans, of 'You've come all this way - and you've lost, and you've lost'! As we were coming out of the Kippax we could see some lads hanging around and their number was getting bigger by the minute. I could sense something was going to happen and the next thing the gates for the away fans opened up and all I could hear was 'come on' from the City fans running towards Brighton.

Me, Gary, Jay and Darren are buzzing shouting 'Come on lets have it' and the police start steaming in on their horses like the cavalry whacking out with their truncheons and charging everyone. It was going on for ages, I was loving it. I was ten years old and this buzz was like something out of a movie. Eventually they cleared everyone away and we went to get the bus from near the Parkside pub on Lloyd Street.

As we were waiting you heard 'come on then' and there was a group of Brighton fans on the other side of the road. They came over and grabbed me, kicking and punching and then a group of City fans came to the rescue from out of nowhere. I started fighting back and a blue cracked this Brighton fan who had been attacking me and as he was on the ground, I followed up with a few kicks to his balls. I could see Darren, Jay and Gary chasing these two lads away but then Darren stopped and turned round and also started steaming into the lad who had jumped me.

I remember saying to him, as I delivered another kick at him 'Don't fuck with Blackley'! He must have thought 'who the fuck is Blackley'? Eventually the dibble came and everyone was running to get out of the way. We made our way to the bus stop, got on the bus and went home laughing at what had gone on. I'd just caught the bug at the age of 10. The bug and the buzz that was to remain with me for many years to come…

*　　　　　*　　　　　*

I can always remember Timmy calling for me late on night and my mam telling him 'He's in bed. What are you doing calling for him at this time of the night?' Anyway I climbed out of the window, down the drain pipe and met him round the corner.

'What are you doing knocking on at nearly midnight'. Now Tim wasn't the brightest of lads, but he apologised and then said 'Come on I've got a car, you right?'

'Yeah anything for a buzz'. I couldn't nick them but I'd always go for a spin with him. Anyway he took it on the grass and rallied it around for a bit then I climbed back up the drain pipe and it was the same the next night.

A few days later we got chased and I legged it up the drain pipe got undressed and into bed, just as I got in bed the door went and it was the car's owner. I could hear my mam say it couldn't have been me as I was in bed fast asleep, anyway I heard my mam come in the room and then go back downstairs, she said 'go and have a look if you don't believe me'. I could hear my mam come back up with this bloke, the door opened and then shut; I could hear them go back down and I started giggling to myself.

The next day we did the same again. As I'm climbing in the window I just got in and the light went on it was my mam. She started screaming and shouting like mad hitting me with her shoe, 'I knew it was too good to be true, I've given you a chance, but not this time, I'm ringing up social services tomorrow I can't cope with it anymore'. I knew she meant it this time, I was going to be put in care.

After that I sat on the bed thinking how can she put me into care - why me? Anyway can you imagine what it was like, a ten-year old kid being told he's going away - my head was up my arse and I was shaking like mad. I just kept thinking over and over again until I made a decision.

I jumped off my bed and got my bag and started packing. I wanted to cry but couldn't get any tears out. Eventually I made my way downstairs, packed some butties and made my way out of the door. I walked down the hill towards the motorway. That was the worst feeling I've ever had. As I'm walking along I decided to get my head down under a tree. I soon fell asleep and when I woke up it was daylight, I didn't know what time it was. I started making my way to the bus stop and as I'm walking I found £10 in my pocket - it must have been some of the money I had left over from the jeans I'd sold. I carried on walking, eventually I found a bus stop that was pretty packed, I waited for the bus and jibbed it as usual. As I sat down I heard someone shout 'Sully', it was Tracey. I told her what had happened and she gave me some money.

'Where are you going' she said.

'Blackpool' I answered. As the bus reached Piccadilly I got off and told Tracey 'don't say a word'. I started walking to Piccadilly train station and watched the trains. I saw on the screen Blackpool and made my way to the platform, someone said it'd be here in ten minutes, so I thought I'd nick some crisps, coke and chocolate for the journey. I came back to the platform with my head still up my arse.

The train came in; I jumped on it and sat by the toilet in case the blakey came round so I could hide in there. In those days it was easy to jib the train, a lot of the conductors never bothered coming round - you might get one if the train was small but a lot of them were long enough to hide in.

As I was sat there, I heard someone call out my name. I looked up and it was Tracey. She came down and sat next to me – we just started laughing and talking about the time I'd tricked her and my brother when they were at it on the sofa. As the train pulled away from the station I asked, 'How come you're going to Blackpool?'

'Well I couldn't let you go all on your own, could I?'

At some point I went to the toilet and when I came back Tracey was nowhere to be seen. So I started wandering up and down the train. As I passed through First Class I saw two people bang at it in the carriage - it's Tracey and one of the conductors! I thought 'nice one' so I went back to our seats by the toilet. Half an hour later Tracey comes back and she says 'It's ok, I've paid the conductor for our tickets' and I started laughing.

'What are you laughing at?' she asked innocently.

'You silly twat, I've seen you bang at it with the conductor!'

She tried to say it wasn't her but we both knew different. Anyway, I thought, Tracey's a free ticket to anywhere.

As the train pulled in at Blackpool she said, 'come on, let's get something to eat'.

After we had eaten, we had to find somewhere to stay.

'Don't worry, we'll find somewhere,' she said and, well, she sorted it – although the first night was in a shitty hotel, by the second night we'd upgraded to a better one.

We covered the hotel bill by shoplifting. Tracey was streetwise as fuck and she knew the script backwards. She even banged the bloke who owned the hotel so we got a week out of it on the house. When he'd had his way she came out with, 'I'm not sixteen yet' and to keep her quiet the landlord gave us the complimentary room so he could keep an eye on her. Tracey may have looked seventeen or eighteen but she was only fifteen years old!

One time I went out on my own and I came back with jeans and T-shirts and I was buzzing. Tracey had shown me the ropes and she was mustard at the game. At the time Blackpool was a bit behind the times in terms of security - we would go into cafes, have something to eat and leave without paying or go to the toilet and jump out of the window.

After a while we jibbed the train to Birmingham – I don't know why we went there, I suppose it was for the buzz and to see how far we could get but it was probably Tracey's idea and deep down inside I felt safe with her.

When we got there it was the same old trick from Tracey. Some old git would cop for the 'I'm only fifteen' line. We'd only been there a few days when I went out on my own to do a bit and I was caught with a pair of jeans dangling underneath my coat. Anyway the police took me to the station asking, 'how did you get down here' and I just looked at them as if to say, 'shut the fuck up you silly bastards'. Eventually I told them I was from Manchester, I'd lost my sister and I was just holding the jeans for someone.

Anyway they eventually worked out who I was and told me 'your mam's coming down'. Sure enough eight hours later me mam shows up. I was too young to be charged and we went back to Manchester. When I got back a woman from Social Services turned up – after a brief chat she says, 'you're coming with me' and without another word I left with her.

*   *   *

I got in the car and the woman is going on about this kids home and I'm looking out of the window paying no attention. My ears pricked up when I heard the kids home was in Southport. 'Won't be there long', I thought, they've tried to send me as far away as possible so I can't get back to Manchester. Anyway the place was called Beech Mount and as we pulled up it just looked massive.

'There are a lot of kids your age in here,' said the social worker, 'but you have to do chores'. I just smiled. Eventually I was shown to my dorm and all the time I was thinking I was looking for an escape route. After Social Services had gone all the kids started coming up to me asking me what I'd done and where I was from, one kid even tried to shake my hand. Needless to say I ignored the silly cunt.

My first night in there reminded me of the final scene from The Walton's - 'Good night John Boy, good night Jim Bob' and every fucker's name you could think of. Then this lad comes over, I'll never forget him, he looked like a long streak of piss. Anyway he comes over saying 'I'm the Daddy in here' and asks my name, adding that I am to address him as 'Sir'.

As he's waiting for a response I look him right in the face and ask him 'What do you think my name is, you silly twat?' and before he can answer I jump off the bed. He went to punch me and as I moved out of the way he went smack into a wall. He was going that quickly that he cracked his head open and started screaming. I ran back into the dorm to get a sock to shove in his mouth when the staff came running to his rescue. Still I tried to get at him and the staff are pulling me back so I whacked one of them and as I've done that the carer reaches for the red panic button. Then they're all on top of me whacking me all over the place and eventually I was carted off to some lock-up, a bit like a prison cell.

As they were leaving they cracked me again and the last one out says, 'Sullivan, you've been here a couple of hours and you've already started. You'll learn anyway'. After that I lay on the floor. I wanted to cry but couldn't so I just lay there thinking of all things I had done – I wasn't even eleven years old yet. From the night mam and dad told us they were splitting up I had been in nothing but trouble: fighting, nicking, running off to Blackpool and Birmingham with Tracey and then being brought back by the dibble.

I didn't sleep that night because before I knew it, it was daylight and I heard the door open, it was three of the care assistants. They were telling me how I should be sorry because that lad was in hospital and I just said, 'Ok, just close the door on your way out'.

Then one of them grabbed hold of me saying, 'Don't be a cheeky bastard' and I said, 'Don't you mean I'm going to be a hard little bastard'. Well he was fuming at that and I could tell he just wanted to leather me – everything he said I had an answer for.

Eventually I said, 'You're forgetting that I come from a family of five kids and I've had more kickings and belts across the arse from my old man and my brothers than you can imagine. So a kicking off you lot is a piece of piss compared to that and before you start again, that fucker,' I pointed to one of them, 'Yeah you in the middle, you hit like a tart you fat fucker'. Well, you can imagine his face. I knew they wanted to give me a kicking but they couldn't because it was daylight and there were more staff on.

When they'd gone out and closed the door I could hear them saying, 'There's only one place that fucker is going and it's prison'.

Half an hour later the door opens and a woman enters with my dinner. I just looked at it and said 'no thanks' and she notices the bruise on my face and asks my age.

'Ten and a half'

'I've got a son your age' she says and I could see her thinking 'poor little thing'.

Then she's asks me more questions. I thought to myself 'is she dibble, I better not say anything', I knew the script I'd been in the dibble shop that many times.

After she left three care staff came to get me, 'Social Services are coming to see you' and they made me have a shower. As I'm walking about the place I can see all the different rooms and all the kids are doing different things in them. In one room they were cooking, in another they were playing table tennis or snooker. At the end of the corridor I was told to wait, they opened the door and there she was sitting with a smile on her face asking me how I was. I didn't answer. She didn't seem to notice the bruise on the side of my face – some social worker she is!

When she'd gone I asked one of the careworkers if I could have a breath of fresh air and he says 'fair enough'. They took me outside and as I was sat there I clocked this hole in the fence. All of a sudden there's a voice in my head shouting, 'go, go, go'. So I made a run for it. I got through the fence and carried on running, glancing back to see if anyone was following. I saw the fat fucker trying to get through the fence and reckoned that now was my chance to get my own back. He was never going to get through the hole and by now he was stuck so I ran up to him and twatted him and shot off over the grass.

When I thought I had run far enough I slowed down to catch my breath, keeping an eye out for any chasers before I spotted the train station sign. The station itself was off the road and I was glad to get away but then I realsied that this would be one of the first places they'd look, so I went to hide. As I was walking along I saw this old house and took cover in there but just as I was about to hide, a car pulls up with this fat fucker and two others in it. I climb on to the flat roof of the house and put my head down. They came sniffing around right next to where I was but luckily they couldn't see me. I heard them say, 'He's not here' and they carried on looking down the road. I stayed on the roof for a bit longer, it seemed like ages.

Soon after a train pulled in and I got on it and sat, as usual, near a toilet. It seemed to take ages for the train to pull away but soon I was on my way. When it pulled into Manchester I decided to have a walk around looking at the shops. I didn't lift anything and as I was walking through the Arndale there were a couple of lads I recognised. I didn't let on or anything and went to look in a shop window. As I've turned to walk away I felt a tap on my shoulder, I jumped, one of them said 'didn't mean to scare you' – it was then that I realised that it was Roy and Chalkie - lads a little older then myself I had met hanging around the Arndale all the time.

Anyway I told them what had happened and they both said I could stay at their house because my mam's house would be the first place they'd look. I stayed at Roy and Chalkie's for a while but I knew, deep down, that I couldn't stay there forever. I was soon back robbing to make a bit of money – Roy and Chalkie were both at it as well and while I was hanging about with them I got to know a few lads and girls who knocked about in the Arndale but I was always on edge, looking about – it was hard.

Roy and Chalkie were going to Crystal Palace on the Saturday and said if I could get some money together I could come along. On the Friday I went into town as it was the last chance to make a bit of cash and that night I stayed at Roys, buzzing – I couldn't wait for the trip to London.

We went on the football special train. There were loads of City fans. Chalkie said the blakey wouldn't come round because there was no way he'd get past everyone. Everybody was singing and dancing, having a laugh and before long we pulled into Euston – there was dibble everywhere as we headed towards the ground following these City fans. Time was getting on and we needed to get to the turnstiles pretty quick as to not miss the start of the game.

As we were walking round the ground Chalkie spotted this gate half-open. As we got closer we saw there was no one guarding it and we dashed in. A few of us got caught but the rest of us made our way into their end – it wasn't hard in those days you could just walk around the ground.

When we got there we spotted Billy and Jay. Billy turned around and said, 'it's just like walking into Tesco's'. We all laughed but then people started clocking us, Billy pointed out some blokes staring at us. No one was bothered, we all knew that if anyone got a crack, we were all there for one another. Anyway they started edging closer and all of a sudden there was a shout of, 'Come on Mancs' and that was it – everyone just ran at them and it went off. We got the better of them before the police moved in to separate us. They formed a line and everyone was trying to get at each other again, buzzing like mad. Then City scored and we all jumped up and no one gave a fuck because we were in their end. I can always remember a copper looking at me as if to say, 'you cheeky little bastard'. All the lads were older than me and I couldn't believe how no one got nicked.

The game finished and we had to stay in for an hour. Then they marched us all back to the train station, we were buzzing that we had taken their end. The dibble held us up for fifteen minutes at the station before we were allowed on the train and when we got on everyone was singing, 'number one is Colin Bell'. As the train pulled into Manchester there was loads of dibble waiting but we went to the amusement arcade and Roy came back with a burger for me and said there were loads of Geordies in McDonalds.

Chalkie went to scout it out and sure enough there they were. We went to the bus stop over the road and there were others in the Gardens where they could see everything as well. Eventually they came out and Eammon said, 'we'll follow them over the road'. They were heading towards Piccadilly and as they approached Hurleys sportswear we started falling in behind them in twos and threes. As they got closer Roy turned around and whispered, 'get ready' and soon we hit them from the side and then everyone was laying into them from all over the place – they were in disarray, hitting them from the side came as a complete surprise. We started to chase them as they ran for the safety of the station, then one of them shouted, 'fuckin' hell – they're only kids'. With that Billy twatted this guy and he went down, 'not bad for a kid' said Billy.

Then the dibble came and they were nicking all of us. Well we were kids and we didn't give a fuck – one gets nicked we all get nicked. The lads I was with trusted each other but I was thinking, as I sat in the back of the Black Maria, I couldn't help thinking that I wouldn't end up back at the kid's home.

*   *   *

Eventually I was bailed and when I came out I was expecting Social Services to be there but was buzzing to see my auntie who assured me that everything was ok saying, 'I'll explain it all in the car, let's go'. My auntie was as scouse as they come – she was funny and she used to call me a 'little alarse'. As I got in the car she starts telling me what had happened. I could tell she'd been crying.

'How did you know I was here?' I asked.

'The police rang me. I was at your mams and your dad told me what happened and then the bizzies came to your mams to let her know. I was sorting out with your mam to take you to Liverpool. She said, 'take him if you want' and she rang up Social Services. It was hard work at first but eventually they agreed. Your dad's been put away for eighteen months'.

'Can I see him'

'Not just yet but soon'

Then as we got back in the car I gave her a hug and a kiss and told her what happened in the kids home, my auntie just looked and gave me a massive hug – I was buzzing and told her she was the only one that cared about me. Which was true.

'Your Uncle Dan and everyone in Liverpool is buzzing and can't wait to see you' – this was the first time I'd ever heard anyone say that to me.

I told her that I was going to come to Liverpool anyway but thought that she might turn me in. She said, 'I'd never have let them take my little alarse away'. I smiled, my auntie and uncle's family were great, I used to go up and see them a lot. I know my auntie didn't like my mam and even more now for what she'd done to me.

When we got to Liverpool, I couldn't wait to see everyone. She told me that my Uncle Dan had taken the day off work and my cousin George hasn't been to school and my other cousin Glen not been to work and my Auntie Jean had come up from Widnes. As you can tell, my auntie had a big family and they all seemed to have come up to see me!

When we arrived, George was the first out of the house he gave me a dig in the arm and then a hug – me and George were like brothers, he used to come up to Manchester a lot. He was another one who didn't like my mam but put up with it because of me and my dad – he was glad when my mum and dad split up. George didn't get on with any of my brothers or sisters and neither did Glen. I was like the blue-eyed boy to this side of my family. I could do no wrong, which made a bit of a change from doing no right.

Everyone gave me a hug and a kiss and I felt like a bit of a pop star, I'd never been fussed over so much in my life. My auntie had made cottage pie with Jam sponge for afters and I sat and ate the lot. After eating all that I thanked everyone and told my uncle thanks for having me. He gave me a hug and that night I just sat in with everyone. Then Glen and George's mates came round, I knew them all because they used to call me the 'mad Manc'. It was as if I'd come home to my family.

*   *   *

I always remember being sat outside this pub called 'The Nook' and I was talking to this lad, one of Glen's mates. He used to live in Manchester, in Crumpsall he said and he'd been down in Liverpool for six years after his mam married a Scouser.

The next thing I remember he looks across the road and says, 'I'm sure that's Lee Park over there' I could see a few lads having a look at us. Then I heard someone shout 'come on then' and I can remember this bloke about to take a swig out of his pint pot. I nicked it off him, poured the contents on the floor and took off after these lads shouting, 'come on then'.

We chased most of the lads off but there was one that fell on the floor so I started hitting him, then he started to shout 'don't hit me', I thought 'you've come down here for a battle and now your screaming "don't hit me"' so I cracked him again and let him go. As I turned around I saw my uncle coming toward me and I'm expecting a crack or a lecture, so I went over and said, 'go on then give me a crack' and he just looked at me and said, 'don't be daft'.

Anyway he comes out of the pub with some crisps and a glass of coke for me and my uncle says, 'I wish our George was like that, you've only got to say "boo" to him and he runs a mile. He's probably inside now changing his strides!'

I went back to sit on the wall and this bird came over and started chatting. Anyway the next day we're at my aunties and this girl calls round for me. So I'm sitting next to her in the lounge and when my uncle comes downstairs, clocks the girl and gives me the wink. Then he says, 'George, did you see our little alarse running after them lads last night. Oh, you probably didn't 'cos you were changing your keks at the time!' and me and this chick are laughing.

A bit later we were sat outside and George says he's going to Everton the next day to watch the game with Brighton. Well I was well up for it, I couldn't have given a fuck about Everton, it was getting after Brighton that I was more interested in. I said, 'I'm not that bothered whether I get in the Everton end or the Brighton end', George is like 'fuck me'. Anyway me and George are talking about it and I bet him that I can get in without paying. I was buzzing and this bird is just looking at me like I'm daft... she wasn't far wrong.

Now I couldn't wait until Saturday, and when the day arrived John came round with three others and I went with Glen and our George and got the bus to Liverpool and then onto Goodison. We got off at Stanley Park. Glen said he'd got me a ticket, I said 'You'd better sell it, I'll either get in or get taken in a Black Maria'.

So we were walking round the ground and I spotted an open gate but didn't go in. 'I need to get in their end' I said to Glen, he just looked at me as if I was mad. Anyway I ask, 'who's coming to have a go at getting in their end?'. There was no response. 'Ok, Glen, you go in with George and I'll meet you at the pub afterwards'. Just as I said this a gate opened and I dived in. John and three of his mates followed me and there were a few other lads. We were in Brighton's end and I was buzzing like mad.

Half way through the first half Everton scored and we jumped up and everyone is looking at us – these lads were giving us daggers so I went, 'let's go over, if they want it, let's do it'. We went right over to them. At half-time Glen's mate got whacked and we were outnumbered but everyone went in. Then the dibble came over and marched us around the ground to the Gladys Street end. I couldn't believe it, the Scouse coppers weren't like the Manchester police, they weren't bothered about the away fans, they took sides.

I was buzzing and after the match we met Glen and George at the pub and we were telling them what went on but Glen had seen it and said, 'why did you want to go in their end?' So I told him about the Palace game when we got in their end, well Glen's mates couldn't believe it – 'you game fucker' one of them said.

On the way back in the bus we were sat there chatting about what had gone on and these guys were staring at us. So I said, 'what you fucking looking at?' Still they were staring and I couldn't help myself, I just went over and lamped him one in the kipper and we start scrapping. We were quickly pulled apart.

As time went on I was getting into trouble: fighting, shoplifting, missing school and I can always remember my 11th birthday as I spent most of it in the dibble shop as I'd been caught trying to break into this shop and I was trying to tell them it wasn't me.

Then this copper comes out and as I'm saying it wasn't me he just says 'save it' and sticks me in the cell. They ring up my auntie to come and get me and this kept on happening.

In the end there was a bad fight in which two lads got slashed and I got roped in for it and I ended up at a Young Offenders Institute. I can always remember the first night, it was miles worse than the children's home – these lads coming up to me, giving me shit, telling me to clean their shoes. I just looked at them and said, 'alright, I'll have them sparkling like mad'.

Anyway the next day I've gone to get something to eat thinking 'this is a bit of a shit hole but there's no chance of getting out' when these lads came up and asked me where I'm from. When I said 'Manchester', they said they were too, but one said 'you sound a bit Scouse'. I explained that I'd lived with my auntie in Liverpool for a while. They told me that everyone tries it on in here so don't worry and I told them about the fat twat wanting me to clean his shoes. The next thing the fat twat and a friend came over saying, 'don't forget about the shoes'.

As he said that I picked up a tray and whacked him in the face with it. He started screaming and went down on his knees I whacked the other one quickly as well, his nose was gushing with blood and then I turned and cracked the fat one as he hit the floor again.

'You'll be doing my chores and cleaning my shoes from now on, you fucking half wit!' I said. The next thing I was nicked again and I shouted, 'any other twat that wants it, I'll give it them'. Anyway they walk me down to the cell and it was freezing cold and pitch black.

I was in there for three days until they eventually let me out and when I got back on the dorm I started making friends. I even went to school and only had a few fights – I thought fuck me, I haven't got a choice here, I'll just have to go with the flow. The next time I was released I was put into care – there was nothing my auntie could do about it.

*　　　　　　　*　　　　　　　*

Eventually, I ended up back in Blackley – my mam had already moved from there, not that I gave a shit about her anymore. I was put into foster care with this couple who had three kids of their own and another three that they'd fostered while I was in the Young Offenders Institute – I went to visit them twice and then I stayed there. I couldn't believe it, I knew the other two in care but not to talk to, so I settled in well. They were City fans and I started going to the matches with them.

One time we went to City v Wolves and we were stood near

the away end that was segregated off with a huge fence. I saw Chalkie, Roy, Billy and Emmon and I told them what I'd been up to and that I was back in Blackley. Billy reckoned I was lucky to end up where I had and as I was introducing one of the other foster kids to them it was going off – some Wolves had got in our end, so we just rushed them and they were getting it from all angles. The dibble came and got them out, some of them were leathered to fuck, another was on a stretcher.

Anyway we were all buzzing like mad and I started knocking about with Billy, Roy and Chalkie again – we'd be in the Arndale Centre in the day and then in the Amusements at night – looking for fights with others lads and robbing shops.

When West Ham played City at Maine Road we were all up for it. There were about thirty of us milling round the Arndale and then we went up to the train station. It was mid-day and we hung around Piccadilly Gardens for a bit when we heard the unmistakeable East End song, 'I'm forever blowing bubbles'. As a group we started moving towards the noise - there were about 60 or 80 of them. We met them at the bottom of the ramp near the train station and just steamed into them. It was going on for about fifteen minutes before the dibble came and separated us. There were a few other lads there as well that I recognised and eventually the West Ham fans went to the Brunswick pub, the nearest pub to the station while we went over the road near the gardens.

At about 1.45pm we could see them getting ready, there weren't many dibble with them as they started towards the ground. We followed them towards Oxford Road, some of the lads went the back way near where the Imperial is now – we kept behind them, then, as they turned the corner you just heard 'come on' and everyone steamed into them from all directions. They were completely taken by surprise and strung out all over the place – they split up and some ran up the steps to Oxford Road station – they were getting it all over, it was happening all the way to the ground.

After the match we all met up at the Parkside to have another go at them. We got the bus into Piccadilly and while we were hanging around the Gardens we saw these lads – one had an afro and was wearing a polo shirt. He looked at us, we looked back at him so we go over to him, 'come on then'. He just smiled at us and said, 'you cheeky little twat, we're City'

As we were sorting all this out we heard West Ham going towards the station – so we chased them back, giving it them all the way up to the station.

On our way back we came across the guy with the afro again. He told us his firm was called the Cool Cats, a firm that everyone knew about. A few of them recognised us from the underground market and in the Arndale and we were getting a bit of a reputation. We were given the name, 'the Arndale boys' and I went home that night buzzing because we'd met the Cool Cats and they respected us – they knew we were game and didn't give a fuck.

As time went on we would meet everyday in the Arndale by Alley Square – we were also getting a reputation with the older heads who hung around in the Brunswick. We might have been too young to drink but I always remember going in there to sell some jeans and meeting Donald Francis and a lad called Vinny who had blonde hair. Donald bought the jeans off us and said 'anything you get, we'll buy it'. Then he said, 'we're playing Liverpool next week, do you want to come?' Obviously we were up for it, so then Donald says, 'fuck the train, we're getting a coach from the Brunswick – be there 10am Saturday – we're leaving dead on 10 so don't be late'.

I was buzzing for the rest of the week, I couldn't wait for the weekend to come around – on the Friday we bumped into Donald, he was with another lad called Charlie and he was telling this lad about our exploits against West Ham.

'Do you think these lads are up for it?' asks Charlie.

'Without a doubt' says Donald, 'don't forget lads 10am tomorrow'.

That night I stayed at Roy's house buzzing like mad and the next day we jibbed the bus into town and met the others at the Arndale, had a quick go on the Space Invaders and then went to the Brunswick. We met Donald there – 'are you right lads? We've got four coaches going – everyone bin their scarves, we're not wearing colours today.'

Then there was a bit of a set to with some others who were there. So Chalkie pipes up, 'we'll have it with you if you want' before Donald intervened saying, 'we're all City, there'll be plenty of that going on when we get there'.

So we made tracks to Liverpool. We left the coach at a pub near Stanley Park and I gave everyone a bit of inside info, 'Liverpool will come from Stanley Park, I know Everton always come through there and try and snipe from both ends'. Everyone just stared at me, thinking 'shut up you twat, we have been here before' and I had to explain about living at my aunties in Liverpool and that I had been to see Everton a couple of times.

Sure enough, as we approached Stanley Park, the scouse welcoming committee greeted us. We held our line and it was like that all the way to the ground with Donald shouting 'forward'. They kept charging, we kept charging back and the dibble were helping them push us back at the same time. Eventually we made it to the ground and the dibble shoved us into the Anfield Road end through an open gate.

We got beat 2-0 but most didn't give a fuck as it just geared everybody up for another fight on the way back. We knew it was going to be tough when we were kept in for forty minutes because we still had to walk back across Stanley Park. We knew they'd be there and as we were walking past we heard 'come on Manc bastards'... It was the same again, they charged us, we charged back and there were bricks and bottles flying. Eventually the dibble split us up and marched us back to the coaches. Some of the lads got nicked but there was one thing I noticed about Donald, he would never leave you there, he just turned around and said 'if one's nicked, we're all nicked'. They ended up letting the lads they'd nicked out of the van and we set off with everyone on the look out for missiles that might come through the window. When we got back to Manchester four of the lads ended up in hospital, one of the lads had been stabbed, two had fractured arms and another a head injury.

Donald was buzzing though and when Chalkie asked him what he thought of our young firm, Don said that we had the respect of the Cool Cats because we'd stood our ground. Then everyone started chanting 'Cool Cats... Cool Cats... Cool Cats...'.

When it stopped I reminded the guy who was having a go when we set off that we still had one fight left 'The Arndale Boys versus the Cool Cats – what do you say?' There was laughter all round, which only went to show that we had the respect of everyone!

We got off in town and Donald says, 'right everyone in the pub'. We made to leave and Donald called us back 'come on I'll get you lot in the pub'. Everyone looked older than me in our firm so we were OK. I was buzzing now – some lads from the first train from Liverpool came in and they had been battered, they looked a mess.

That night I got in at 2am and just went straight to bed – I was knackered. The next morning June (my foster mum) said 'it's for you' - Donald had phoned. He explained to June where I'd been the night before and she said, 'it's OK as long as he's back, that's all that matters'. It was half-term so I wasn't supposed to be at school anyway.

*   *   *

One of the next big games was at home to those other Scouse twats, Everton. It was an evening kick-off and we met with our gang at the Arndale as usual early on, whilst Donald turned up at about 2pm. We sent some scouts out to Victoria Station to give us a bit of advanced warning when they were coming in and eventually Everton fans started to arrive. There were about twenty five of them on the platform and Billy said, 'right, let's give them a reception'.

We didn't make a big fuss about it we just approached them and started laying into them, they were screaming like mad and backing off. We heard the dibble coming to their rescue and we told one of the lads to keep an eye on them. We watched them come out of the station towards the Ducie pub where we got them again and this time we did give it to them proper – I can remember at least two of them who were game as fuck as they just kept coming. Then a couple of our lot sneaked up behind some of them and twatted them with a brick. They went down like shit, we just left them there and made our way up to where Donald was. We were buzzing now, on a real high – I went up to the leather shop to see Pete, a lad I knew - he said there was loads of them up by the station.

By this time their numbers had grown to more than one hundred and we met a few other lads around town and we marched down to Victoria again. We staked out their mob and waited to see which way they would go.

Eventually we decided to split up, some went around the other side and by this time it was about 5.30pm and we were all itching to get started. Donald commanded our unit, telling us to wait on his signal – then he raised his hand and we ran at them. It seemed to take them by surprise, they were dropping like flies and most of them moved back towards the safety of the station. They were trying desperately to regroup by now and we must have been at it for a good twenty-five minutes when the dibble arrived with sirens blaring and dogs barking.

Eventually the dibble took control and started nicking people. Both sides retreated and we set off for the ground – we had a few battles near Oxford Road with a few Mickies that caught another train. There were about 80 or 100 of them and a couple of them were saying 'we don't want trouble'.

When we got to the ground we made our way over to where the Cool Cats stood – from there you had a good view of the away end. After the game we waited for them to come out down the side streets about an hour after the match had finished. As soon as the gates opened we just let loose with bricks and bottles, anything we could lay our hands on. They took a hell of a bombardment and battering, cut heads and hands everywhere, the alleyways were awash with blood.

Soon after that Donald told me that the Cool Cats had finished – I was only glad that I had a brief chance to run with them.

*   *   *

After a while I got fed up with hanging around town at night. During the week I stuck closer to home because there was a bit more going on. A black lad I knew had got a bit of beating in Blackley – it was a National Front area at the time. Some people assume that because you are a 'football thug' and you like a fight you are going to be National Front. This is bollocks - as far as I was concerned I had a lot of top mates from the Arndale who were black so because I'd grown up with them, race wasn't an issue with me and I never get involved with that crap.

I don't go to Blackley much these days, but did recently and as I pulled up at the Kwik Save car park, it brought the memories flooding back. We had some right set-to's with Langley on that car park. I can always remember sitting on the wall with seven other lads. This kid came up to one of us and asked for a light and as he's getting his lighter out, the kid smacks him – then all these lads steam in and, I have to admit, we took a bit of a kicking that night - we didn't run, though maybe if we had we wouldn't have received such a kicking!

After that word got about that Langley had come to Blackley and taken liberties, so it was payback time as far as we were concerned. We met up at the Lion and Lamb before hand, there were about thirty of us. Then a lad turned round and said we'd get killed if we went down to Langley looking for revenge and someone said, 'OK, we'll all get killed together – if you don't want to come, fuck off'.

Anyway this time it was our turn to give it to them and we jumped on the bus down to Middleton and split up into two groups. My group walked up the hill towards some shops, Langley is full of hills and you don't want to get trapped at the bottom of a hill. Almost as soon as we got to the top of the hill we heard this roar from this pub called The Moonraker – well most of the lads did a runner back down the hill which left about five of us. We were shown up if truth be told – I wasn't used to people running off to be honest. One of the lads, Wayne, turned round as these lads were running down the hill and shouting 'why the fuck did you come up here if you're going to run?' The worst thing about it was the time it took to walk up that bastard hill but just two fucking minutes to run down it!

This kind of thing carried on for two or three years – one week they'd come down to Blackley, the next we'd go to their area. Obviously we always had the better of it on our patch and sometimes we'd track them down somewhere else – I remember going down to Alkrington Youth Club where we gave them a good hiding and smashed the place up.

In the end though it was only me, Wayne and this lad

Sheeney who had any bottle. One time we got off the bus and they were waiting for us – they stood there and laughed, 'it's the same three again!' In the end we got to know them and started to knock about up in Langley and sometimes we would go back into Blackley and then we would often find ourselves fighting against Moston. We had a good record against them as by now Blackley's mob had grown from thirty or so to about a hundred of which there were some older hands and a few top lads from City. I reckon when we were at our best no one could take on Blackley – Moston tried it but failed, whenever they did get a result against us it was probably because we were short of numbers.

Crumpsall was another firm we had a few rucks with – they had a few lads that could go a bit, we used to meet them every now and then but it was mainly against neighbouring Moston that we fought with. Boggart Hole Clough is a huge park with lots of space to fight in without anyone knowing about it and there were no phone boxes and mobile phones to call the dibble!

As I got older we started going in the pubs near Crumpsall Hospital, there was a pub where all the nurses went after their shift, it always went off. I remember one night I was chatting this nurse up and I really wanted to shag her so I couldn't really be arsed with a fight. Anyway we were walking out of the door when all of a sudden this bottle whizzed past me and smashed on the wall – I turned around to see who'd done it when this kid whacked me in the face, it was a bit of a shit punch to be honest so I started laughing at him. I turned round and went outside when this lad comes running over and he's not spotted that the dibble have parked up opposite the pub. As I'm walking away he runs up to me and I stick my elbow out and he sort of half falls to the floor. Then I say, 'hang on a minute' to this nurse and give him a couple of cracks.

'That's him parked up for the night' I said with a wink and as we were walking up the hill towards her flat a Black Maria van pulls up and the dibble says 'Can I have a word with you?'

I just looked at them and he was just about to give me a lecture or start asking questions when he sees it going off at the bottom of the hill – there's a fight in the middle of the street and the dibble in the van are massively outnumbered. So the dibble breaks off his questioning and shoots off down the hill - a good night all round!

Sometimes we used to go to the Tudor Lodge, that was always good for a fight and the birds were top as well. One night we were in there and I've copped for this bird and she lives near the Ben Brierley pub in Moston. I hadn't been down there for years as I always got a slap whenever I went anywhere near the place. Anyway I was in there and these lads are giving it the big one. There were only three of them so I slapped this kid and chased the other two off. I felt great as usual, just gave it the wink and a smile.

We always had a problem with Damhead – this is a part of Blackley we didn't like as when we asked for their help against Moston they would say they were going to turn up at such and such a place and without fail they would never show.

Anyway it was the night that Moston came down and so did Cheetham Hill and Crumpsall. It went off at the bottom of Blackley Village and carried on all the way up past the Lion & Lamb. It went mental – everybody seemed to turn out, apart from Damhead. There were hundreds of lads there from all over Blackley and the dibble didn't know where to start – I reckon it was the best battle I've seen in the area for gang fights, I saw many lads from City down there as well.

The fights started when Cheetham Hill and Crumpsall tried to take Blackley – they might have been able to do that before the gang wars started but once word got round it became an impossibility, so Cheetham Hill were run out of town, as were Crumpsall and Moston.

Anyway after the no-show for the big one we went on to the Damhead estate and we saw a load of them by the shops. There were only eight of us but we just wanted it and we picked up anything we could lay our hands on and ran behind the shops. Then we came at them from behind, whacking into them, we were outnumbered but we weren't going anywhere. We gave it them like mad and a load of them ran off – we waited for the others to comeback but they never did. We carried on going up there for a few nights and eventually a few nights later there were more of them but we still kicked them to fuck. The scared bastards even got Moston up there to help them out, but they were sent packing once again.

As time went on I started drinking in Blackley village, I was only fourteen but I could get in most of the pubs - apart from the Lion & Lamb. It used to be like the Wild West in the Red Lion especially at the weekend. There'd be chairs and tables flying about and people flying through windows. Great stuff.

THE MAKING OF THE MAYNE LINE

I used to knock around the Arndale with a few lads and recall Donald Francis coming over and telling us he was looking at getting a new firm together and for anyone who was up for it to meet at the Underground market (which was situated below what is now Tesco's on Market Street) on Saturday as City didn't have a game. So we all met up and spent most of the day discussing the forming of a new firm. Some of the lads were that keen they wanted to attack a group of Mods who appeared in the market! Donald managed to calm them down and tell them that their time would come soon – but at a football game, not outside his shop.

The first game we all went to as a firm was Blackburn away on a coach. Donald stood at the front of the coach and says 'Right lads, no thieving'. There was a huge roar of laughter as practically the biggest bunch of thieves in Manchester was on that bus! Everyone wound him up by getting off the coach. 'Where the fuck are you all going?' he asked. Someone replied 'Well you just said no thieving so we're getting off to go on a bus where we can thieve!'

Donald shook his head. 'Fuckin' hell, I knew one or two of you were robbing, but no idea the fuckin' lot of you were at it!' As far as Donald saw it, we were only going to fight. We saw it differently, we were there to fight but anything that wasn't nailed down was coming back to Manchester! We all piled on the coach and off we went, stopping off at Darwen for a pre-match pint and a bit of 'work'. The landlord was so pleased to see so many people in there that he couldn't see us taking the pictures off the wall and passing them along to each other. By the time we left, the cash register was full, but the walls were bare! On the way to the ground some of us wanted to go back and get the cash register after the match. It was one of those places that were so open and welcoming, they trusted everyone and wouldn't know they were being robbed unless it was pointed it out to them.

At the ground there was nothing happening at all, we couldn't even be bothered going into the game we were that anxious to do something on our first day. After the game it was just the same so we eventually got on the coach and headed for Darwen but ended up in Rawtenstall. We were going from pub to pub and our final one was one of those pubs that when you walk in the place falls silent and everyone turns around and stares. There were a few local lads in there and one of our lot knocks into a local lad as he's walking from the bar with a fresh pint, causing him to spill it. There was a bit of a stand off and the next thing it's kicking off in the pub.

Not a problem at all we thought but then from out of nowhere the doors fly open and a whole mob of locals steam in. Fuck me, how the hell did they get a signal to turn up so quickly? They were like the Lancashire Hillbillies, there was a farmer and a couple of girls joining in too, it was mad. It had nothing to do with football, it was just one of those occasions when a village gets all parochial and protective against outsiders and join together against 'The Townies'. Eventually the dibble turned up in a couple of Land Rovers and attempted to control the fighting and ordered us back onto the coach. As we were getting on, one of the coach windows was put through. 'That's it'! someone shouted, 'through the rear exit'. Everyone piled out of the back door and it kicked off all over again, the dibble were calling for reinforcements, there were just too many of us for them to handle and we just going wild with the locals. The extra dibble arrived and soon we were back on the coach. We all had a whip round for the driver and gave him enough money to cover the cost of the window. Donald described the event by saying 'Well we didn't have any action with the big town Blackburn, but we certainly did with little Rawtenstall!'

We continued to meet up daily in the Underground to plan the next few trips - some only wanted to go to home games or just the big away games and some of us didn't care where it was, we just wanted to be there. I was in with the latter lot. As time went on, more and more lads would turn up and want to join, but I'd look around at some of them – in fact more than just some of them – and I just knew I wouldn't want any of them near me when we were looking to make a stand against a top firm. I said to Donald that if he is putting a coach on for games, I only want to be on it with lads who I grew up with, lads who I knew and could trust my life.

This was summed up for me when we played at Wolves – my first time there. There were three coaches that day and as we arrived and found a pub, a mob of Wolves arrived and we went out to front them. It had only just started when a good number from our coaches turned and ran. Those of us at the front had no option but to retreat, regroup and then have another pop, which is what we did. But as I'm looking around to see who was with us, it was the original lads from the Arndale and only a handful from the other two coaches – the rest had vanished, wannabee hooligans who could tell their mates they're in a firm to impress them but are nowhere to be seen when the action gets going.

We managed to stand our ground as Donald was leading the line well, it seemed to go on for ages until West Midlands' Finest arrived and escorted us to the ground and back to our coaches after the game. On the way back I had another chat with Donald, telling him we could have got hurt had we not regrouped and had a go back, those raggamuffins who ran let us down for the first and only time. Our coach arrived back in town and we waited for the other two coaches as some of us wanted to teach some of these fuckers a lesson. The other two coaches came in together and we all walked over to Piccadilly Gardens as if nothing had happened. But how can you honestly forget about it? We were dependent on each other to stand firm and fight, if you are likely to crap yourself and run at the first sign of trouble then don't turn up – it's as simple as that. Don't pretend or play at being a hooligan, it's for real.

Halfway across the gardens the signal was given and we started slapping a few of them, none of them even fought back and true to form they all ran off at the first opportunity. One of us shouted 'Don't come back again, if we see any of your faces you know what you'll get'. The name Mayne Line service crew was soon created, due to the coach company being used to carry us to games being Mayne's Coaches. On Mayne Line we wreaked havoc across the country but first we had to earn a reputation - this is how we did it.

*   *   *

I knew this lad who worked at Wimpy's burger restaurant in the city centre and when West Ham were playing at Maine Road he was put through the window by the East End mob. They also kicked off at us big time at Maine Road. It was clear that for the return game later that season we had to go down there and show our faces. For the two weeks leading up to it, this game was the sole topic of conversation. In the end, it was a lot of the younger lads who went down, a lot of the older heads threw in 'sickies' a few days before which pissed me off.

In the event, Donald called a meeting in the Brunswick for the Friday night, the day before the game. The place was heaving with around one hundred of us in there. Donald gave a briefing as to what was going to happen and for once everyone actually took it all in – we were well up for this trip. The time given for the coaches to leave was 7am so we were told to be at the pub for 6.45am. Most of us went home after that – I certainly did and went to bed immediately, setting the alarm clock for 5.30am. I was so up for it I kept waking up every hour or so to check the time. The alarm went off and I got ready and caught the bus to Piccadilly Gardens. As I walked towards the pub, Chalkie, Roy and Dave were coming off the bus from Moss Side and cutting through the gardens. At the pub, it was the usual 'back door job, curtains shut, no lights or jukebox on' - the place was chocker, it took us ages to get served! When we did, we ordered extra bottles to drink on the coach.

The coaches arrived and we piled on. Donald wanted to get there early and take the Hammers by surprise so we only stopped at two service stations - we managed to get a bit of a kip on the way down before we hit London. Once there everyone was like a kid at Christmas time what a buzz. We stopped off at a huge pub a few miles from the ground that Donald had visited before, the plan was to have a quick drink there and move on to the ground. As we were getting off, there were a couple of young lads sat outside, they quickly legged it inside and announced our arrival!

Within seconds a hundred or so were running out to front us. They started coming towards us, one lad threw a bottle and that was it, the start of a mass brawl. They were backing off when a few of us pulled out blades and a couple of them got stabbed, one lad was on the floor with a bottle in his face his faced was badly mashed up. We carried this on all the way to the ground, more Hammers were coming at us around each corner but we stayed together. It was unbelievable – even the dibble couldn't control us that day. They tried to put us in an escort but failed miserably, one copper was kicked to fuck while another had blood pouring from his head.

Eventually they got us into the ground, we watched the game but with a few minutes to go we just went mental. The two sets of fans were jumping up and down trying to get at each other and they were doing the same on the other side. We were kept in for an hour and given an escort back to the coach - all along the other side of the road the cockneys were flinging bottles at us while we kept chanting 'MCFC, Mayne Line'.

The coaches had had their windows put through and we refused to get on them, in the end the Old Bill called for more back up and marched us to the station, they wouldn't let us go on the tube so we had to walk to the nearest over-ground station. We could see a mob of a hundred waiting for us, gesturing for us to have a go at them. We quite fancied taking them on but before we were able to do that, from behind us we heard 'you facking Norven monkeys' and smack! - they hit us from behind, breaking up the escort as the dibble could not cope with the size of their attack. After the initial hit, we held tight together and stood our ground, going toe-to-toe with them, backing off and then hitting them. They were dropping like flies, getting kicked all over the place.

It was going off for around 30 minutes until even more dibble arrived and cornered us - they were about four deep keeping us back. They couldn't wait to see the back of us. They finally put us on a train and as it pulled off we gave a big roar as Donald told us we had 'given it to those Cockney bastards!' The older lads with us were coming up to us saying 'respect lads, well done' and this made us feel seven feet tall hearing it from them, they were top lads with great reputations.

We got back to town completely knackered. The following week's game was at home against Norwich yet everyone was still going on about West Ham. We walked into the Clarence and were being greeted by more of the older lads, those that didn't go, who were shaking our hands and congratulating us as they had been told the full story by those who were there. All we could hear was 'you young lads are game as fuck, not one of you ran, nice one'. The word was out – the Mayne Line Service Crew were here and had earned respect.

*   *   *

The next away game was at Chelsea but as I made my way to the coaches I didn't seem to have the same buzz – maybe West Ham was still too fresh and I was still on a high from that? However, once on the coach, I soon became excited by the prospect of a bit of action! On the coach Donald read out a message he had received from a West Ham source. It said that 'We can't wait to play you at Maine Road, we've met some firms over the years but Mayne Line was one of the best we have faced'. Donald then told us that he had sent a message back – 'You've just been tuned in by MCFC Mayne Line Service Crew'!

Arriving in London, we used the same trick as at West Ham by pulling short of the ground by a mile or so and going in search of a drink along the way. We had a good firm, not as many as against the Hammers, around two hundred or so on four coaches. After a while we decided to go to another pub, although some of us who had just got another round in stayed behind. It was 6.30pm and we were wondering where Chelsea were, maybe they had only just finished work and were on their way!

We were in this second pub for about 30 minutes when all of a sudden Danny comes running in, his face cut, telling us how it had all gone off in the first pub. They had tried to get out but there were just too many cockneys on top of them. At the time he was sat there next to a window with a pint, when the window just shattered around him and within seconds all of the other windows followed suit. Eventually the dibble came and escorted all the City fans to the ground. Donald had been listening to all of this and his anger was growing. He stood up saying, 'right, come on, let's go looking for them' and we left our drinks in search of Chelsea. It wasn't long before kick off and as much as we looked we couldn't find any Chelsea fans anywhere.

Finally, as we neared the ground we saw a large mob standing on a street corner. We continued towards them, then the call went out and we just charged at them – we knew after the West Ham game that we could handle it, we were so confident and self-assured, everyone knew we would stand our ground. As soon as we hit them I ended up being decked on the floor and those around me were helping me up. We had them on their toes and backing off, pushing them into a side street, where they were joined by more Chelsea who were coming up that way. They were throwing bottles and bricks and we retreated in order to regroup.

'Let's just run at them again, they'll run out of things to throw' one lad shouted. He was right, after we charged and a few more missiles came our way they had nothing left, no ammunition at all to use against us, only their hands and feet. Those of us at the front either had blades (or pretending to!) and that sent the cockneys off like Linford Christie! We just went wild – one lad was slashed across the face, another was holding his throat as blood poured around his hands as he ran around screaming. The game had kicked off and we could hear the crowd chanting and singing whilst all around us mayhem was unfolding and Chelsea had become the second set of cockneys in successive away games to be tuned in by the MCFC Mayne Line!

Not before too long the dibble came to their rescue and after one copper was kicked to the ground and a police dog kicked in the head, we finally ended up being taken to the ground. After the game we were given a strong escort back to the coaches. Naturally we expected them to be all window free but were pleasantly surprised to find every window intact! Between the ground and the coaches Chelsea were still around but all they were doing was acting hard to no effect, offering plenty of 'Come On's' but doing very little else.

Once on the coaches, we were three short. What a result, two hundred lads and only three nicked. They weren't even charged, just given a kicking in the back of a police van and set on their way. I've said this before, despite getting a kicking by the dibble, it was much more preferable to ending up in court the following morning and getting a record. The dibble knew that we'd get let off or fined peanuts anyway so they preferred to administer their own form of punishment. That's just the way it was back then.

On the way back we stopped at a service station and a coach full of Ipswich Town came in. We could see straight away they were not a firm, just a bunch of straight heads with scarves and shirts. They looked like they were shitting themselves once they clocked us, so one of the lads went over and told them that they were OK and we weren't going to be let loose on them! One of the rules of Mayne Line was if you smacked anyone who was not looking for a fight then the rest of the lads would give you a good kicking. Besides, who wants to fight a bunch of Ipswich Yokels when there was a shop to be pilfered!

The thing with the Mayne Line was that it wasn't just about violence, to many of us it became a way of life and some of the incidents were comical rather than dangerous, here are a few skirmishes that illustrate the point...

PORTSMOUTH

During the 1984/5 season we played Portsmouth at home and we were in the Platt Lane stand. Pompey scored and a little roar came out from the Main Stand as a small group of around thirty had somehow got tickets in there. It was piss easy to get into the Main Stand from the Platt Lane so me, Roy, Chalkie, Eamonn, Bill and a few others made our way towards them. We came up the stairs and onto the aisle where they were sat and just launched into them, using umbrellas, fists and feet. They had nowhere to run and were getting leathered, even those City fans sat around them felt confident enough to join in because we were there. The dibble arrived and took them out, walking them round to the safety of the segregated away end in the corner of the Kippax terrace. Afterwards the Pompey fans were really wound up by what had happened and it was going off all over the place - nothing major, just kicks and punches here and there all the way to the coaches, with City fans coming at them from the side streets and back alleys. The away fans coaches used to park half way down Princess Parkway on Hough End Fields – a good twenty minutes or so walk from the ground, if not further. When you are being followed by a mob trying to attack you, that walk would seem even longer I imagine. We were battling all the way back to the coaches and credit to them as they did have a go back but were simply outnumbered.

It would be a different scenario for the return match later in the season on the South coast. We piled down in a van, which was always my preferred choice of transport. A coach driver wouldn't pull into all of the service stations along the way, where as in the van we were in control as one of us was driving. That's the reason it always took forever to get there! We always left at 2am when the clubs shut. The services were always best and easiest to rob in the middle of the night as hardly any staff were around at that time. So after helping ourselves at a few services, we arrived at the ground and parked up nearby. We were there when the players arrived and Donald convinced the door staff that he was Daley Thompson (there was a resemblance!) and he blagged his way in, taking a few of us with him – me included. We ended up with free seats in their Main Stand, yet nothing happened that day, we thought we'd be in for it after what happened earlier in the season at Maine Road but they were just not interested.

On the way back we pulled in at another service station and were up to our usual tricks. I remember seeing two lads walking out of one shop wearing Peter Storm jackets and after that we just took the piss. Everyone was just walking in, putting clothes on and walking out, some were trying on Hush Puppies and leaving their old shoes on the shelf in their place. It was one of the best service stations we ever turned over! Then Roy started having an argument with someone (not one of us) about a fucking sandwich! This then spills over into the small amusement arcade and it kicked off. One lad came at me and I grabbed his head and smashed it on the side of a slot machine twice and gave him a kick in the bollocks as he went down. Apparently they were Norwich City fans coming back from wherever they had played

– about twenty of them on a small coach. I'll hand it to them, they were game fuckers, we never knew Norwich had a firm, we always considered them and Ipswich to be country bumpkins but these lot turned out to be tasty. Other users of the area were scattering around getting out of the way as we had it out with them around the arcade area. The police have their own little building at each services so it wasn't long before the arrived and broke it up, putting us on our way. Thankfully they didn't get to see inside the van, which was full of the day's takings!

BRIGHTON – VIA THE BIER KELLER!

Brighton away was always a good trip – lots of service stations to graft in and a trip to the seaside too! In November 1984, we set off on the Friday night after Tropicanas on Oxford Street had shut. We made our way to the Brunswick where we were to meet Donald who had the van. Just as we were arriving there, one of the lads came running round the corner out of breath. Eventually he was able to tell us that a mob of Cockney Reds were in the Bier Keller just a hundred yards away, this lad reckoned there were about 60 of them – we did a head count and there were 14 of us, without hesitation we carried on to the club.

As we arrived at the door we heard 'Come on! Come on you cunts!' and turned round and there was Donald crossing over the road coming towards us pissing himself laughing. He asked us what we were up to and when we told him he said 'right, back off for now, I'll just move the van around the corner' and off he went and drove off. On his return we were within yards of the door and Donald said 'when I say "GO" we all just steam in past the bouncers and straight down the stairs'. We were buzzing, my heart was pounding like fuck. 'Three, two, one, GO' and we just whacked the bouncers who were crapping it and eager to get out of the way, ran down the stairs and cracked anyone in our way, picking up their drinks and bottles and throwing them at them.

Someone whacked me with a stool on my back, I turned around and it was Chalkie! Fortunately I had a thick coat on so it didn't hurt as much as it might have done. We just continued to fight, tipping tables over and eventually someone called 'get out now' but no one wanted to go, we had United backing right off but then the call to leave was made again and we went back upstairs and outside. This gave the reds a bit of time to get themselves together and soon they were coming up the stairs looking for us. We let a few out and just wasted them, one lad had a large umbrella and thought he was 'Zoro' lashing out at us as if it was a sword. The stupid twat just got leathered with everyone sticking the boot in. Other reds were trying to get out and at us but the bouncers had shut the doors and locked them in. The next thing we could here were the meat wagons coming towards us – thanks for the warning you thick twats!

'Make your way to the gardens, I'll pick you up in the van', Donald announced and we scarpered in different directions taking different side streets, to make sure no one was following us. Donald arrived soon afterwards with the van and a quick head count saw that no one was missing, we'd all made it safely and in one piece. We jumped into the van and off we went, down Princess Parkway where Donald stopped to fill up the van whilst we all piled into the shop and robbed it to fuck, we just didn't care, we were all on such a high! Back in the van, I turned around and thanked Chalkie for cracking the stool across my back. Everyone was pissing themselves as Chalkie denied it, blaming Eammon. I said, 'it was you, you daft twat, Eammon's white, I can tell the difference between you two!'

Donald then passes around the new calling cards, saying that he will buy a pint for the first person that tunes someone in at Brighton. We looked at the cards – 'You have just met The MCFC Mayne Line Service Crew'. Everyone was well impressed and people were making bets as to who they thought would be the first to 'deliver' a card. Eventually people were just starting to crash and try and get their heads down. It was around 3 – 4am and we were stopping every two hours or so to give Donald and Mick a break from driving. We finally arrived in Brighton about 11am and parked up around the back of the station. We had a look round but couldn't see anything of any note from Brighton fans but we did bump into a City firm called 'The Under 5s' (so called because they all used to travel on Family Railcards) who said they had a little ding-dong with a group a short while back.

We decided to go and find somewhere to eat – without paying, of course – and made or way back to the station. Just as we got there a train full of City pulled in but the dibble were in control and put everyone into an escort so we did one quickly before they put us in there too.

We still couldn't find anyone anywhere, not even around the ground. Some of the lads were getting very itchy, 'we've come all this fucking way for nothing, where are these soft bastards?' The game was shit, a 0-0 draw and afterwards we went to a pub near the station. As we were in there, this City fan comes in saying that there is a women outside in the bus stop giving free blow jobs! Well, we couldn't get out of there fast enough and sure enough, there she was with a queue of City fans waiting in line, there were two blues with their pants down and she was wanking them both off together, we thought she must be a right ugly fucker but she was actually quite fit! We soon retreated back to the pub and after a while those on the train were leaving so we thought we'd give it one more pub and head home. Just as we were about to leave the Under 5's came running in. They had found Brighton's boys hanging out in an amusement arcade and as they told us that, two City fans came in and said they'd just been smacked by Brighton in there. We set off for the amusement arcade with the Under 5's leading the way and as we got closer we could see there were around 40 or so of them.

We started chanting whilst walking towards them – 'Mayne Line, MCFC, Mayne Line, MCFC' over and over again and then the walk became a run and we're shouting 'come on' by which time they'd legged it. We were chasing them as one Brighton lad turned and lobbed a bottle, which hit Mick on the head and that made us even more determined to get them. They carried on running, we are shouting at them 'come on, this is your fucking turf you twats'. We were getting pissed off with running, we hardly ever ran after firms, we stood and fought them, that's the whole fucking point of it. Then, two Brighton lads turned to see if we were still after them and they tripped over each other and hit the deck. The Under 5's were in there like a shot, kicking them both all over before they could get up. We all joined in – it wasn't the normal Mayne Line way of fighting but we were so wound up having had nothing all day and then when it did have the chance to kick off, the twats ran away.

Later on in the evening we passed by the arcade again and the shit houses were in there, but they spotted us and managed to shut the doors. They were quite good security doors for obvious reasons so we couldn't do anything about it. We ended up taking Mick to the hospital as his head was cut quite badly from the bottle that hit him, the nurse said it would be around an hour so we said we'd be in the pub near by. The dibble caught up with us and tried to run us out of town but we told them our mate was in the hospital and no way were we leaving without him. Whilst Mick was being treated we went to the van and Donald was the only driver left but he was too knackered so he asked if anyone else could drive. I said I could drive but I hadn't passed my test - that was enough as far as Donald was concerned!

I got in the driver's seat and after stalling a few times – much to the amusement of everyone in the back – I managed to chug it along, jerking forward all the time until I got used to the gears and clutch. Somehow I managed to drive all the way back to Manchester and dropped the first lad off on the hard shoulder of the M56 just before the slip road round by the Royal Thorn pub in Wythenshawe. He asked if I could drop him off on the roundabout at the end of the slip road, I took one look and said 'are you winding me up? I can hardly fucking drive on a straight road without having to go round a fucking roundabout with cars coming at me from all angles!' He took that as a 'no' and got out of the van. Donald said he would take it from here and he drove the rest of the way into the city centre.

NOTTS COUNTY

There were two games left of the 1984/85 season and one win would take City back into the First Division after a two year absence.

The day before Notts County away, a few of us met up in the city centre and went over to Donald's shop in the Underground for a drink. Donald asked a daft question. 'How many of you have got suits?' Only two replied that they had and Donald tells them to wear them at the game the next day. We all left the shop around 11am and then Roy suggests that those without suits go and acquire one from either Lewis', M&S or C&A. In those days, without CCTV and trained security on the doors it was a piece of piss to walk out with gear - no wonder Mancs and scousers made a regular habit out of looting shops!

So five of us walk into one of the stores and five waited outside keeping a lookout. We come across the suits but there was a shop assistant working at that spot. The next thing Roy goes over to the assistant and says something to him and the next thing the assistant is walking quickly across the floor and starts working near the shoe department, adjusting misplaced items - anything to not be near to Roy! Within a few seconds, we are forcing suits into a bag and Roy calmly walks out with the bag. We all head off to the Arndale toilets to try them on. Every suit was black - the jacket would fit but the trousers would be too short or too long, or the trousers were fine but not the jacket, so every one was swapping around - except Roy who had the perfect fit from the start and couldn't hide his pride in this fact and kept going on about it all day! But we were all buzzing in the end. We ended up in a pub, chatting to some birds who were under the impression Roy was loaded, sat in his suit! It certainly made him look the part but I didn't find a match that fitted perfectly.

The next day, we went to the back of Victoria Station to get the coach to Nottingham - we always changed the location of the meeting place to dodge the dibble. It looked like a fucking fashion parade! Around ten of them rolled up in suits that they had either borrowed off their dad or brother or - like Roy - had nicked the day before. One lad turned up and looked awful - he was a small lad and his jacket was too big, the pants looked even bigger despite having a belt on yet he thought he was the dogs bollocks! Even more comical was when he asked what time we would be back as he was taking his girlfriend out in his suit to impress her! Another lad had his trousers up at half mast and when he put his arms up in the air, the underneath ripped and everyone cracked up.

As it was, me, Chalkie, Eamon and Billy had arrived without suits - we were wearing shoes and cords - Donald looked at us and let on, saying if he was going to have a bet on who would have worn a suit it would have been us. Within minutes the Mayne Line coaches set off for their destination - those with suits on were sat together on the 'Mayne Line Executive Coach', the rest of us non suits were sat in the 2nd class coaches! On arrival in Nottingham, and getting off the coaches, everyone watched those suited up, marching off towards the ground - it was like the scene in Reservoir Dogs! Donald had decided to go into County's main stand, using a unique approach to get in. He approached the player's entrance and produced a letter to the steward which stated that they were all Manchester City youth team players and the next minute me and the others were watching the suits being led through the underneath of the stand and into the ground. Donald had pulled a similar trick just a few weeks before at Portsmouth. At the time he looked a lot like the athlete Daley Thomson, who of course was a huge superstar at the time. At Fratton Park, Donald had managed to blag his way in to the players' changing room. A couple of City players who grew up around Maine Road knew it was Donald, but the other players were taken in! That was the thing about Donald, he looked the part and had the balls and confidence to pull it off. Anyway, as Donald led the suits into the stand, the rest of us made our way on to the away terrace.

Inside the ground there must have been 12,000 City fans in a crowd of 17,000. blues were everywhere. Unfortunately, the game didn't go as planned and by half-time we were three-nil down and that's when the trouble started. City fans in the stands started to snap off the seats and were throwing them onto the pitch. A few County fans tried to have a go at the blues in the seats but they soon got a hiding. Then City fans aroud us behind the goal were trying to pull the fencing down and get onto the pitch. There were police horses on the pitch trying to control fans but there were just too many of us all over the ground, the second half was delayed by almost 40 minutes. The County chairman, Jimmy Sirrell, made a plea for calm over the tannoy but that just inflamed the situation - who the fuck is Jimmy Sirrell!

Eventually City's manager Billy McNeill made a similar

plea and that calmed things down. County fans were then asked over the tannoy to leave the Main Stand and go behind the goal for their own safety! This was an 'end' of the ground where there weren't really seats or much standing but the back wall of a sports centre facing Nottingham Forest's ground! The embarrassment of it all for the County fans - their ground was completely overrun by City!

The second half got under way and despite a decent comeback, we still lost 3-2 and were still a win short of promotion. Due to the huge amount of City fans there, the police had no choice but to let us out at the end. We knew they didn't have a firm of any standing, maybe about forty or so lads, who had been battered in the Main Stand at half time, so we knew they wouldn't be bothering us. We headed off to a nearby pub for a few drinks to let the traffic clear up before leaving.

When we headed back toward the ground a bit later, we could see a coach outside the ground with a few people getting on - it was the City coach! We ran over and as the last two players got on, steamed up the steps and started giving them verbals about the first half performance. Billy McNeill gets up at the front, he is a big bloke I can tell you!

'Look lads', he says, trying to calm the situation, 'I know you are upset...' someone shouts 'upset, you're taking the piss, we follow you everywhere and you don't give a shit about if you win or lose'. After a few minutes chat, McNeill says he will sort some tickets out for us. Donald calmed us all down and everyone got off the coach except Don. When he finally came back he says we are all sorted for tickets for the final game of the season against Charlton. As the coach pulled away, we are chanting 'MCFC Mayne Line' repeatedly. The players looked stunned, except for the local players who knew the script.

Mayne Line FC

As well as travelling all over the country watching City, Donald decided we should form a Sunday League team and play the game ourselves. He arranged for an initial trial at Hough End fields one evening and loads of us turned up... way too many in fact!

Some had boots, some had trainers, other had shorts and tracksuit bottoms, others wore jeans. It didn't take Donald long to decide who was decent and who wasn't up for it and after another session, the number was whittled down to 16 - one of whom was me!

We trained hard all summer and even had a few friendly games - if you could call them that... One team fucked off at half time as they felt very threatened after receiving a few (illegal) challenges! Donald was going mad as lads who were not even playing were coming onto the pitch and smacking the opposition!

We kicked off the season in the Manchester & District Sunday League in the bottom division and for our first game everyone turned out to support us, there were dozens of lads lined up along the touch line where as normally it would be four men and a dog watching the game. It didn't take long before we were being reported by the referees for our behaviour on the pitch. In one game, we scored a goal and the ref disallowed it for offside. Roy had put the ball in the net and wasn't too pleased that his effort was ruled out and as a result he smacked the ref. Nice one Roy! In another game, Chalkie broke an opponents leg off the ball! The league were getting a bit pissed off with us for being reported each game and Billy Fox didn't help matters during another game when as a spectator, he ran on the pitch and thumped the opposition goalie for saving a penalty! Once the league sussed out we were not paying the fines for all the bookings and sendings off, they kicked us out of the league. We reformed a while later under the name 'The Brunswick' but that didn't last long either. We were playing one game and on the next pitch a team were playing wearing a Munich strip. We ran onto their pitch and kicked them to fuck! The cunts ran off the pitch screaming all the way to the changing rooms!

It goes without saying that we looked the business in our sky blue and white strip - cool as fuck!

STOKE ON THE SERVICE STATION

One of the best battles we had as Mayne Line took place miles away from a football ground, at Rothershorpe service station on the M6 in Northamptonshire in 1984. We were on our way back in three coaches from a game down south in the capital and pulled into the services. There were a good number of coaches already in there and we could see they had a Stoke-on-Trent address on the back of them so we were on red alert, hoping for some action as they'd been playing in London that day. I was one of the last to get off and as I was walking towards the shops, a few of our lads were spilling back out having been smacked inside by Stoke. All you heard next was our lads shouting to us 'Come on, Stoke are here' gesturing towards the shops. We charged right in at them, as regular punters were scattering out of the way. There were running battles throughout the shop and this spilled out into the car park and it was getting nasty. Coach windows were getting put through by lads using fire extinguishers, while others were knocked to the ground and whacked. This was proper hardcore stuff, not for the faint hearted. Donald got cracked on the back of his head by a brick and hit the deck, we were trying to get him up, two of our lot were whacking this one lad all over the place with a brick and a bottle, he was one of quite a few on both sides who got badly hurt that night - including Donald, who was taken to hospital. It was a good old-fashioned toe-to-toe battle, there was nowhere to run so you had to stand and fight.

The police turned up and took ages to get it under control, as they stopped one skirmish another battle started elsewhere. They just had to nick a few, bang them in a van and come back and start again. Eventually I was one of those nicked. I had blood pouring down my face – I didn't even realised I'd been stabbed! We were battling like mad and on such a high you tended not to feel any obvious pain - the cut was at the top of my nose, just under the eye. I was taken from the police station to hospital and given butterfly stictches across the top of my nose and then returned to the police cells for the remainder of the weekend.

Five of us then appeared in Northhampton Magistrates court on the Monday and I knew I was going down given my previous record. It looked quite grim as the dibble told the judge what had happened at the services, yet amazingly we were all bailed and told to come back in two weeks time. In between all this the media gave it loads of coverage, pictures in the papers and the

TV showing the damage caused to coaches and shops. Everyone was talking about the scale of violence. The return date came and the five of us returned together on a train. My face was still swollen and bruised during the second hearing. Again I had said my goodbyes to everyone expecting to be sentenced, yet once more we were bailed and the case went to Crown Court.

So there I was sat outside Crown Court room with my brief as they dealt not only with the five of us, but around eight Stoke fans. The first group of Stoke came out celebrating as the charges had been dropped, they were buzzing. I said to my brief, 'What the fuck is the judge up to? How did they walk?' We eventually got into the court, where it was just the five of us left of us left, everyone so far had walked free. Again I asked my brief what was going on. He said it looked like we were going to cop for the lot. I asked him how long he thought I'd get and he replied twelve – eighteen months, but he was going to ask for an adjournment for a pre-sentence report from probation. This he did and to my amazement the judge agreed. Two days later I received a letter from a probation officer asking me to meet with them so they could do the report. I turned up on time and asked for a woman named Val. We went into the room and she was full of questions, questions and more questions. We discussed lots of things, including my background and family life with mum and dad and the kid's home. I was giving her a right sob story and telling her I hadn't been out of jail for long and didn't want to go back in there and how my head was burnt out and there was no escape from it all. Eventually she said she had enough information to complete the report and asked if I had any questions. I asked her what my chances of walking free were. She said she was going to recommend that I be placed on a combination order which is probation, community service and undertaking a re-offenders course. I said I'd be happy with that and thanked her. The following week I was back in Northampton. My brief was confident as he said the report was favourable. As my defence were pleading for another chance, the prosecution wasn't having any of it.

'Your honour, it is clear from his record that it is not a first occasion, he has only just served a 12 month sentence for similar offences and he hasn't learnt his lesson.'

The judge looked at me. 'Mr Sullivan, don't you think it is about time you grew up a little and stopped causing trouble? You are aware this is a very serious offence.'

I bit my lip. Inside I was screaming at him 'Fuck you, it's what I get a buzz out of doing, what the fuck do you know?' I imagined the judge having the perfect life... boring as fuck!

'Mr Sullivan', I broke off from my daydream and looked up. 'Come on you cunt, just get on with it and bang me up' I thought.

'I have heard all the evidence and read your report and I'm going to give you a chance. You've not had many in your life so I am going to give you a combination order'. I nearly fainted. I was speechless as he strongly recommended that I stuck to the order or face the consequences. I shook the hand of my brief and legged it out of court before the judge changed his mind. It was a very close shave indeed. The judge had a point about me not catching many breaks in life - so I suppose this was one of the bigger ones. But did his decision stop me from pursuing my favourite hobby? Did it fuck! The buzz was just too strong.

Anyway that was a summary of the MCFC Mayne Line - a scary bunch of fuckers who rampaged through city centres, service stations, pubs and council estates at will for a fair chunk of the 80s. I've sorted the rest of the highlights of my travels (some with the Mayne Line some not) into regions so supporters of the clubs we 'tuned in' can easily find recollections of the full extent of the kicking they received...

East Midlands

Derby County

On the way to Derby we often stopped off in Bakewell for a drink and 'work'. This one time, a few of us were sat outside the pub having a drink when Roy comes running out of the pub with a picture under his arm. The next thing a few others run in and come out with other pictures. The dibble were called and everyone threw the pictures over a wall and we were lined up outside the coaches as they went on board to search for stolen goods. Just as they are doing this one lad comes round the corner with a handful of gear but someone tripped him up before he came into sight of the police and disposed of his loot before being spotted. We tried not to piss ourselves. After about an hour and a half all four coaches were given an escort to the Baseball Ground.

We had missed most of the first half by now and a few at the front were kicking off with the turnstile operator as he was asking for the full price. The police just wanted us inside as soon as possible so they could get off, so they weren't too bothered about many of us jumping the turnstile! Inside we were chanting 'MCFC Mayne Line' for ages and Donald then showed us the latest 'calling card' he had made. This was a slight variation on the last one and read 'You have just been tuned in by The MCFC Mayne Line Service Crew'. Everyone was going mad for one, just so they could smack someone and leave it on their chest as they lay on the ground. On the way back we stopped off for a drink – not in Bakewell, the dibble were waiting for us there and made sure we soon left town – and one of the lads hung up one of the cards on a wall for a laugh.

A few weeks later we were in London and at Euston station on our way to Crystal Palace, we had arrived early and bumped into a few Chelsea who were away at Birmingham. We caught a couple of them and gave them a good hiding, it was hilarious, there we were, kicking the crap out of a few lads whilst at the same time flicking calling cards at them as they were cowering on the floor – we certainly think they got the message! I get annoyed when you read books by other hooligans and a lot of them claim to be the first firm to do it and it's all bullshit. I hate to disappoint you boys, but I can tell you now that MCFC Mayne Line were the first to dish out the cards to victims. FACT.

NOTTINGHAM FOREST

Promotion to the First Division in 1985, meant not only a return of the big boys on the pitch, but also with the big boys off it. Although there were some handy fans in the second division, (Portsmouth to name one) there was nothing like getting back to the familiar grounds of London, Liverpool... and Stretford. Yet there is one club's fans I always heard were quite tasty. Nottingham Forest had won the European Cup a couple of times in the late 70s and had Brian Clough as manager and they regularly attracted crowds of over 30,000.

We played them one Tuesday night and met up in the Underground market early in the morning. Donald informed us something important had come up and he couldn't go to the game but he was still running the coaches. Once the rest of the lads turned up and heard Donald wasn't going, Roy made a move and said he was taking charge. There were a number of lads who didn't like Roy and people started to drop out of the trip, before Chalkie stepped in. Now Chalkie didn't give a shit who was leading the firm - like he said on that day, 'It doesn't matter who's leading, we are all one unit' and he was right. Eventually there was enough to fill one coach - just - which was a major disappointment as normally we would be taking up to four coaches, yet without Donald we could barely fill one.

So after all the messing about throughout the day, we finally set-off but there was an atmosphere on the coach, no one was saying much and eventually Dave got up to says he was getting off unless everyone cheered up. I manage to convince him everything was OK, but Dave wasn't convinced, particularly with Donald not being there. He was right on that score, of course, but he calmed down enough to stay.

As we approached the ground, we could see it was going off and saw a City firm running down the road, looking as if they were being chased. We decided to get off there and follow what was going on, but unknown to us we were now being followed by a large Forest mob. They just steamed into us and we were soon getting whacked everywhere. There were hundreds of them and we were legging it all over the place - back one way and then another. It was one of those occasions where we just needed to start pulling together but we were lost without a leader. It was the first time I have ever seen the Mayne Line run like fuck and when I say run, I mean run! We were getting slapped from all angles.

At no point did we turn and stand our ground and that was a mistake - no matter what happens, you always stand your ground. It makes it worse when one or two go, you know then that more will follow and then the rest are left behind and have no choice but to go too. Inside the ground, everyone was smarting like fuck, blaming each other and pointing the finger. Roy reckoned that it was the first time we had been hit like that and that we had to stick together and regain our respect. That appeared to rally everyone and we couldn't wait to get out of the ground at the end of the game. However, we had to wait longer than expected as the police kept us in for an hour.

When we were eventually let out, Forest came at us and had a right good go again. However, this time we stuck together and moved forwards. When you end up being with people you don't know there's no way of knowing if they will stand and fight or run - at least with your own mob you know you are going to stand your own ground. It was all about pride and that is one thing we had whilst walking up the road. We came up to a canal bridge and could see Forest holding the bridge and City fans being slapped all over the area - in fact, some blues were jumping off the bridge and into the river to escape a beating!

The next thing we see is a mob of about forty coming towards us, in the dark we couldn't recognise them at first, but as they got closer, we realised that they were City and joined up with them as there was only one way out and that was over the bridge! We got to the bridge and just steamed in. It went off big time, bodies were flying into the river, it was one of the worst fights I've witnessed. We stood our ground, but we got licked in the end. Everywhere you looked, City fans were getting slapped and thrown into the canal. As mentioned, we only took one coach that night, had we taken more it may have been a different story, but for those that did go, we won't forget that night! We made our way to the train station - we had to as our coach had been smashed to fuck. It was still kicking off - lads were soaking wet, crammed onto a train and were taking the light bulbs out and throwing them in the faces of Forest fans - the police just had no control over what was happening.

After we returned to Manchester, it was the talk of the boys for days and revenge was definitely on the cards when Forest came to Maine Road later in the season.

When that day eventually arrived, everyone was ready and waiting. It was a wet Saturday afternoon and we all met in the Arndale Centre. It was soon obvious that this would be a special gathering as faces appeared that had not been seen in years - even a few of the now defunct 'Cool Cats' came out of retirement for the occasion - and no one was going to stop us that day. We had the 'scouts' down at the station waiting for the trains from Nottingham to arrive - which they did at 1.30pm.

As the Forest fans came down Piccadilly Approach, escorted by the police, we waded into them, smashing straight through the police - the poor dibble didn't know what had hit them and neither did the Forest fans who got slapped all over the place on their way to and from Maine Road. Their coaches were also targeted and smashed up in the melee.

Immediately after the game, we all headed for the forecourt around the ticket office waiting for the Forest fans to be let out. The police were trying to move everyone on using their dogs. One copper was about to set his dog on to a few of us when one lad just ran up and kicked the dog in the mouth - it yelped like fuck and fell to the floor! Then we heard Forest were being escorted down Claremont Road and we all legged it there whilst all around us the sirens on the meat wagons were going off. Two vans pulled up next to us and they got smashed up. Further up on Upper Lloyd Street near the Ducie Arms another van was over-turned. The police appeared to back off at one point and let us get on with it as we were just so overpowering that day. Forest were screaming like fuck all the way to the station where there was no respite from our attacks either.

Sadly - and once again - City were relegated at the end of the season, so it would be another two years before we got to play Forest again.

*   *   *

Another such visit to Trent Bridge before The Mayne Line wound up was one Saturday afternoon when we took four coaches and this time Donald came with us. We decided to park the coaches north of Nottingham, in Mansfield, have a few beers and then get a local train into town, arriving just before kick off. We split up, going into different pubs and arranged to meet at the station at 2.15pm. We expected to be sussed out by the local dibble, gangs of strange lads in town centres always seem to attract unwanted attention, but that didn't happen. Donald told us that we were to say we are on a stag party. At one stage the police did come into the pub but as we weren't singing football songs they soon left.

In one pub there were some attractive girls and we were all trying our best to kop off with them, it was a right laugh and then one of the girls amazes us all and decides to give us a private strip in the middle of the pub! She was down to her knickers and we are all going wild and then fuck me - from out of the blue comes Chalkie into the middle and starts stripping too and in no time is giving her one over the pool table!

Not surprisingly we ended up missing the train and subsequently the game itself. Donald told us it was time to go and off we went to the station - it was 4pm and luckily enough a train appeared and off to Nottingham we went - arriving just before the end of the game and heading for Trent Bridge, taking the bridge over. Forest fans were nowhere to be seen around the bridge so we headed off for the town centre in search of them. Everywhere we walked, we just took the piss. They tried to have a go but they were nothing and we ended up running amok in the centre around the shops that were just closing. Some of us went on a looting spree. Eventually the police rounded us up and took us back to the station and on the train back to Mansfield where we finished the night off before taking the coaches back to Manchester.

*   *   *

My final trip to Nottingham quite a few years later in 1998, was also eventful - for all the wrong reasons. I went to the game with two blues - Barry and Tim - who I had met after I moved to Collyhurst. They were not hooligans, they just liked a beer or four! We went down in a car and as we were approaching the city centre, it brought back memories of the previous battles. Another reason for going to the game with these two lads is because I was in court in Chesterfield on the Monday and as they were not into the fighting scene, I imagined it would keep me out of trouble too. I was wrong.

We were walking towards the ground and a few blues started chanting City songs and Barry and Tim naturally joined in. The next thing that happens is that I get a smack in the mouth and I turn round and am about to thump this lad when he apologises to me! He thought we were Forest fans setting a trap by chanting City songs and seeing who joins in... it seemed that he and his mates had had a bit of trouble further up the road. I looked around and could see a group of lads on the other side of the road and they were definitely Forest fans. They watched us with their arms folded. I told Barry and Tim to keep an eye on them but Barry kept on singing and it looked like they were going to pick him off. Tim looked at them and then me and said 'you're right' I told him I *knew* I was right and that I know how they work.

They started to follow us, crossing over one by one and mingling in with us. The next thing I see - thankfully - was a City firm walking behind us just as we've got to the ground and both groups are stood there giving it the 'come ons' when I get another crack on my face. I turn round and give the lad a thump back and off he runs to join the Forest crew. I wasn't ending it there so off I ran towards them on my own, followed by another Blue. I lashed into them but before I knew it I was on the deck with my arms up my back and handcuffed. As I was pulled up, a police dog bit me on the stomach, the wound was pouring with blood as they took me to a cell inside the ground.

I was soon joined by a friend who had stuck up for me whilst I was being arrested. I was screaming like mad at them to get a doctor to treat the bite and eventually they patched me up and transferred me to a cop shop where they held me over for two days. They soon discovered I had a charge against me in Chesterfield on that Monday and then one copper said 'you were down here the other week using a stolen credit card' as he was reading all of my previous convictions, 'you seem to be involved in a lot of things Mr Sullivan. You seem to go along way to commit crimes.'

Monday arrived and I ended up getting sent down. I was lucky - I only got nine months for fraud. I ended up at a prison in Lincoln - it was full of Nottingham lads!

LEICESTER CITY

For a while, I stayed at my auntie's in Liverpool after being released from prison in 1984 but of course Manchester was only 35 minutes away so meeting up with the lads or going to a game was no problem. The Friday before onea game at Leicester I stayed over at Donald's with my girlfriend. The plan was for Donald's girlfriend to entertain my girlfriend on the Saturday whilst we went off to the match. In the morning we walked from Donald's house to the Sherwood, just up from Maine Road. We went round the back and there was a good number already there waiting with a beer in their hand. As we walked in it was heaving and lads I hadn't seen for ages were coming up and shaking my hand and asking how I was doing.

I finally got a pint in and was about to sup it when I got a tap on my shoulder – it was Jimmy and I hadn't seen him for over a year! Whilst I was doing bird he was in Spain flogging timeshares. We sat there for the rest of the time chatting as Donald went round collecting the coach money off everyone – he just winked and passed by when he came up to me. Then it was everyone on the coaches and off we went to Leicester.

I sat next to Dave, he was telling me how he had to 'disappear' for a while, as the dibble were onto him. In turn they were all keen to hear about my stretch inside. We were so busy catching up with each other that the journey went quickly and soon the three coaches were on the outskirts of Leicester. Once at the ground and off the coaches, we could see a firm of around 80 stood on the other side of the road, looking at us. One of our lot went over and asked if they fancied it – he came back and said they would do but not until after the game. As he told us that, some of our lot couldn't be bothered waiting that long and started walking over to where they were stood. They shit themselves and moved nearer to the dibble for protection.

The police sussed out what we were up to and started moving us away, using horses to back us off. We tried to stand our ground but they pulled their batons and beat us back. We ended up having it out more with the Leicester dibble than we did with Leicester's "infamous" Baby Squad. After the game they tried to have a pop at us at the back of the coaches, but they always made sure they were never too far away from the dibble so they could go running when things got a bit too hot for them and as a result nothing much happened. There was this one lad that we were all laughing at – stood behind the dibble shouting his mouth off. He was a right scruffy twat, skinny with long red hair and freckles – he looked like a fucking raggamuffin!

On one occasion at Maine Road, they did bring a decent crew with them. They were being escorted down Cambridge Street and Upper Lloyd Street and we were waiting for them at the Ducie Arms. As they passed by the pub we just hit them with beer glasses and bottles. As I ran in, one Leicester fan threw a glass back in my direction, just missing me, whilst a Leicester fan went down from a brick hitting his head. The police pushed us back into the pub car park and held us there whilst they carried on with the escort towards the ground.

After the game we were walking back into town when we heard that around thirty Leicester were knocking around near Piccadilly, we made our way over there. There were about thirty of us too, so we knew it wouldn't be a problem. We checked all the pubs in the area but couldn't find them so we presumed they had fucked off home so we went into The City pub on Oldham Street. After a while, a lad came in and told us Leicester were in The Bulls Head. Fuck me, that must have been the only pub we didn't check! We sent the scouts off to check it out as we made our way there behind them. They ran back to meet us and said there was no one in. We made our way via Back Piccadilly heading for The Brunswick and as we passed a side street we clocked a group of around 30 – 40 lads coming our way. They didn't see us so we kept tabs on them until we definitely knew they were Leicester and at that point we came from out of the side street and ran at them.

They were bouncing around and trying to make the effort as we were laying in with the punches but it just seemed they were lost and didn't know where to run. They finally realised they had to stand and fight. We were battling with them for 10 minutes, they were handy but were on the wrong side of a beating - they were just too inexperienced to handle us, they were smacked and kicked around the place, I grabbed one lad and with his head in an armlock and rammed his head into a lamp-post, blood spattered all over my jacket and he was semi-conscious as I left him on the floor to crack another lad fighting Chalkie next to me.

Finally the dibble finally came along and got the Baby Squad up against a wall and tried to disperse us but they had no chance as they were too short-handed to control both sets of fans. They escorted them back towards Piccadilly and we kept close by looking for opportunities to jump in and have a pop but the dibble had it all sussed and they waited with Leicester at the station until the Sheffield train came in.

SMOG HEADS & GEORDIES

MIDDLESBROUGH

Some authority figures seem to think that being a football hooligan, or at least taking part in violence in and around football matches, was an optional extra for me. Well unfortunately, as this tale will show, it wasn't - especially if a firm tries to take the piss on your territory.

I was released from Lincoln prison, following a spell inside for fraud, on the Thursday and two days later City were at home to Middlesbrough, I wasn't going to miss it. I had a lot of respect for 'Boro as a firm. They had a bit of a reputation in the 80's, but in the 90's they got together a tasty bunch. By then there about eighty of them and they always stood together. They were all brought up in the same area and that is a big help - you know each other from back to front. There was a few firms like that - especially the London clubs like West Ham and Spurs, but also Sunderland and Birmingham. With City in the 90's it was different, we came from all over Manchester and barely saw each other away from match days. In the 70's and 80's with The Cool Cats and Mayne Line, we all knocked around together in town most days, but those days had long since gone.

Anyway there I was sat in The Clarence, wondering where all the lads were, when a recognisable face arrived. It was Nick and we were having a pint when Little John came in and told us the others were at McNally's. We drank up and got a bus down there. The stop before the pub we saw a big firm walking down the road. We sussed out they were 'Boro and quickly jumped off, crossing over to the lads were having a drink outside. Just as we reached them, to let them know what was happening, 'Boro came flying over onto the grass fronting us. The three of us are in the middle of it, trying to back them off, but we could see a lot of our lot fighting their way back into the pub. If that had happened ten years before with the Mayne Line, they would have received a good kicking from within - and deservedly so! There were a small number with us on the grass but all we could do was dodge the bricks and bottles that were aimed at us by other blues! One of the lads, Martin, got a brick in his head and another, Phil, ended up with a broken arm.

All of a sudden, one of the 'Boro fans caught a brick on the side of his head and went down, just as the police arrived and started to charge at us. Nick shouts 'Sully, run!'. I didn't want to but had no choice - if I'd have stayed I'd have been nicked. Having just been released two days previously, there was no way I wanted to be back in court on Monday morning or get remanded, so I did one sharpish! The police didn't let up and chased us all the way to Maine Road.

After the game we re-grouped outside the bookies on Claremont Road and made our way to The Sherwood where we managed to run at 'Boro, but it didn't kick off as the dibble beat us back. At one point it looked as if 'Boro were chasing both the police and City as they were following the police chasing us! However, we did manage a small ruck in Whitworth Park. Somehow two lads had managed to mingle in with 'Boro - fuck knows how they managed that and this confused them, but again, the cops were onto us straight away so it didn't last long. Later on I found out that Rangers and Hibs had joined up with Boro and they had been at the park.

That time was a cup game and we still had to play them again in the league at Maine Road later that season. As kick off approached, there was not a 'Boro fan in sight - shithouses we thought, too scared to come down twice in a season, so off we went into the ground disappointed. The game was nearing the end and the stewards opened the exit gates as normal. But rather than let City fans out, a mob of about 20 'Boro ran in. They had not bothered with the game at all and had sat in town waiting for three-quarter time when the gates opened. They flew into the North Stand, whacking anyone within reach. The stand immediately split into two halves - those trying to get out of the way and those trying to have a go back. We were jumping from row to row to get at them, one City fan cracked this lad who ended up rolling down a few rows on the gangway as others waded into him with their feet. They were certainly game but we outnumbered them and were getting the upper hand when the police - who took a few minutes to get into the stand as they had left the ground waiting for the end of the game - finally arrived lashing out with their truncheons at us, separating the two factions and rounding up 'Boro and escorting them away from the ground.

We met up outside on the forecourt planning what to do. Word had got out that 'Boro had smashed up The Clarence shortly after 3pm and also that they had parked their coaches at the back of the MEN Arena, which was a smart move, parking well away from the ground and the usual away coach park so you can go about your business away from the police escorts. We headed off ahead of them towards the MEN Arena using the back streets to avoid the dibble and sure enough their coaches were parked up as we'd been told. We left a couple of spies nearby as a lookout and went into the pub built onto Boddingtons brewery around the corner. Eventually the spies reported that they had returned and we ran out after them but the police escort was just too tight and we couldn't get at them. In the meantime, the 'Boro boys were laughing and shouting at us, boasting that they had taken the North Stand and taken the piss. And of course they were right and we had no reply for them.

*　　　　　*　　　　　*

The next time we went up to Middlesbrough was the following season, for a Friday night game. A lot of the old school turned up, seeking revenge for that last visit to Maine Road - it would prove to be a frustrating day and highlighted modern police methods of dealing with hooliganism.

A few of the old boys were talking on the way up. They couldn't understand how 'Boro had got away with strolling into the North Stand the previous season - with CCTV all over the place. A decade before that Mayne Line and Guvnors were getting picked up on camera on a regular basis and ending up in court for doing the same thing! It was because of an increase in security measures that many of the boys gave it up. Where was the fun in fighting if you were going to get nicked every other week and end up doing time in Strangeways?

We arrived early at The Riverside and we were enjoying a quiet drink nearby when who turns up out of the blue but the Manchester Dibble! Where they came from and how they knew where we were remains a mystery. We left from a different place than normal and hadn't seen them at any time on the journey - yet here they were in front of us ordering us to finish our drinks and escorting us into the ground, taking pictures of us all one at a time stood up against a wall. Bastards!

While this was going on, I heard someone shout out my name but with lots of people milling around and the police keeping us against the wall I couldn't see who it was. My name was shouted again and this time I recognised a 'Boro fan I had met a few times with England. I tried to get over to him to have a chat but the dibble were not having any of it and pushed me back against the wall and then put us straight into the ground. Fuck me, it was an hour before kick off and we were in the ground! The whole trip was a disaster. We came for a bit of action and end up being dumped into an empty football ground. After the game it was just as bad as we were escorted straight to our coach and given a motorcycle escort out of Teeside.

GEORDIES

During Kevin Keegan's 'first coming' as a player at St James Park in 1983, the Geordie 'faithful' had shot up from around 14,000 a week, when they were near the bottom of the Second Division, to full houses. Loyal fans, my arse! By the time City played them in the north east that autumn, both teams were in the top four.

We travelled up by train and there were about four hundred of us. As the train pulled into the station all we could see out of the windows was bar codes – black and white replica shirts. Then one by one the windows on the train were put through, we all took cover on the floor, covering our heads from flying glass and whatever was coming through the windows. The sound of 'Toon Army' was echoing through the cavernous station. We tried to get off the train but the police were forcing us back on, whacking us with their truncheons – it was as if we had been the ones trashing the train! They were setting the dogs onto us, we couldn't believe it, it was bad enough having to face the Geordies but now we had to take to their dibble on too, we were on a hiding to nothing.

When they finally allowed us off, some lads had cuts to their heads. One lad stepped onto the platform, saw he was badly cut and fainted. We were trying to help him and asked the dibble for help but they took no notice and just pushed us on and told us to 'move it'. That was it, we started going mental and lashing out at them as they wielded their truncheons and set the dogs on us. One lad just kicked a dog in the head and it was yelping to fuck as it went down. It was wild as coppers came flying in and having a go back. One thought he was a clever bastard as he let his dog off the lead and the stupid mutt ran away as we stood there laughing at the prick who let it go. Eventually reinforcements turned up and they controlled the situation and we were being escorted to the ground.

Outside the bar coded fuckwits were waiting for us – all big bastards and not kids either, beer monsters with their bellies sticking out of their shirts. They were following us and waiting for an opportunity to break the police line. On one occasion they had a pop and got through for a few seconds until the police got their act together again and sorted it. It was like the whole of Newcastle had come out to get at us. Once in the ground we were hearing from lads who had come up on coaches and they'd had a rough time of it too. Some coaches had been bricked and the drivers were not hanging around after dropping them off and had turned round and gone straight back leaving lads having to jib the train home. At the moment that was the least of their worries – getting to the station after the match was a major concern.

The segregation was non-existent - it was supposed to be an all-ticket match but there were Geordies in our end in small groups, kicking off and eventually getting escorted out by the dibble. Newcastle scored their first goal (in a 5-0 win) and both sets of fans were up against the small fence separating us, bouncing around, throwing coins and gesturing to each other.

Some blues tried to get over the fence but were knocked back by the dibble. At the front, a bit of the fencing gave way and we were able to get through into their end and it kicked off whilst the game was going on. I was cracked on the head with something and ended up on the floor, with one eye open and the other one closed. I was trying to get up but was too dazed, I could feel hands picking me up off the deck, they took me to the front and I passed out.

I recall being in an ambulance but I could barely keep my eyes open and just felt faint, as blood ran down my face. I felt something go in my arse and I heard a voice say 'don't worry, its just a needle, something to help with the pain'. The next thing I remember was waking up in hospital and a nurse asking me 'Are you alright, Pet'? I had one eye open and she asked if I could open the other eye and also if I could hear her. Fortunately I could and opened the other eye. She asked me what happened and I said I couldn't remember. I tried to sit up, I hadn't got a clue where I was and other than it being light outside I didn't know the time of day – come to think of it I didn't know what day it was! I was unable to sit up, my head hurt the more I tried. The nurse fetched a doctor and he asked me if I remembered anything. I told him I was standing at the match and the next thing I got whacked on the head and I woke up here. I also told him my head was banging. He gave me an injection which quickly – and thankfully – put me back to sleep for another night. The following morning I woke and I was still in pain but nowhere near as much as before. They kept me in hospital for a full week. On my way out, I passed a City fan in bed, lying there with his leg in a plaster, his head bandaged up and his arm in a sling. He said there had been lots of blues in here after the game – but made my day when he said there had been more Geordies admitted than City!

So that was a trip to Newcastle in the 80s, it looked like we'd visited a war-zone, and the following February, when we played them in the return fixture at Maine Road, we were determined to return the compliment. Not one of us needed a reminder about the date of this game, it was clearly marked (in my case on my head!). Everyone was buzzing about the revenge we were going to take on the Geordie cunts.

On the day itself we met up in Piccadilly Gardens quite early and went over to the station to catch the first train coming in from the north-east. We went around in small groups, going onto the platform their train was due to arrive on, as if we were waiting for the train ourselves. As the train pulled in the doors opened and they piled out, around three hundred of them. As they walked off the platform, we mingled with them, walking up the stairs and making our way out of the station.

As soon as we got outside we started, those with knives were jibbing them, moving quickly to jib as many as they could. They were confused as fuck as they didn't know where we had come from as we were all around and within them. One they realised what was going on we just smacked them, they were getting whacked to the floor. The dibble came running out of the station but there were too many of us and not enough dibble to be able to stop it - they had cut faces and bleeding noses. One group of Geordies ran up Market Street towards Piccadilly Gardens which was the worst thing they could have done as a group of jibbers were waiting for them there. As we got there all you could see were Geordies legging it around the gardens followed by young lads trying to slash them. It was going off all over the city centre as the Geordies panicked and went off in small groups whilst we were mingling in with them and smacking them, taking them by surprise every time. From Oxford Road all the way down to Maine Road it was like a battlefield as the dibble tried their best to escort them in one piece but they were helpless as we jumped them at every opportunity.

After the game the dibble kept them in for ages so we had running battles with the dibble. One copper on horseback was dragged off and kicked to fuck on the ground and for each lad who was nicked there were more waiting in line to take their place. Once the Geordies were let out they were hit by flying bricks, bottles, rocks, dustbin lids – we had been given almost an hour to stock pile our ammo! The side streets and alleyways were our advantage – the dibble were always at a disadvantage around Maine Road as we could jump out of nowhere and then disappear just as quickly.

Eight lads came walking down the side street towards me and Billy, they had jumpers on and showing no colours, apart from one lad who had not tucked his black and white shirt into his jeans properly. You could tell they were absolutely shitting it, just walking and not saying a word to each other. A young lad asked them the time honoured question – 'you got the time'? One of them showed them his watch and they continued on their way. I said to them 'You're Geordies'? they were close to tears, one lad begged us not to jump them and they were just looking for their car and not there for trouble. I asked them where their car was parked and they said 'near a pub called the Parkside'. I looked at them and said 'It's your lucky day and a good job it was us who picked you up and not some of the others'. I told them to walk with us and they'd be OK and I'd get them to their car safely. We walked round the back of Platt Lane and across Maine Road, passing a few firms on the way who all sussed out they were Geordies with me, I reassured them they'd be ok as long as I was with them and eventually we got to their cars and they shook our hands. 'I know how you feel' I told them, telling them the story of when I was outside Sheffield United and going to get jumped when a United fan gave me his scarf and told me to walk with them and helping me get away safely.

We got the bus back into town from outside the Parkside and we passed loads of blues around Oxford Road walking back but we decided to carry on and get off at the Gardens. There were small gangs of City moving around in dribs and drabs, looking to pick off any Geordies passing through. Then word came out to head for the station as the escort was getting near. We all moved along via the side streets and passageways going around the back of the station. It was like Fort Knox in there with dibble crawling all over the place. Fortunately a few lads had taken souvenirs from their Geordie victims – hats and scarves – and these were spread around as much as they could be and wearing these 'colours' we slipped passed the unsuspecting dibble and moved onto the platform. I looked around and could see the group of lads from Blackley – who were National Front - on the platform too, so I knew there were going to be a few stabbings.

The train was actually in before the escort arrived, so we

all jumped on board and waited for them to arrive. It was about 15 minutes before we could hear the noise of the police dogs barking and the sirens on the meat wagons from outside the station. As they came onto the platform, we ducked down by the seats and doors, one lad produced a massive knife – even I was shocked by the size of the blade, it was like a machete. They were yards away from the doors and you heard the whisper go down the train 'let them get on first' - we couldn't wait to jump them. The doors opened and I heard 'Welcome to Manchester' and a scream coming from a Geordie who had been slashed across the face, they were getting it from the very moment the door opened, I'd never seen so many City fans with blades in all my battles, there was blood and screaming faces along the train.

As they turned around to get off, we followed them and continued hammering them. It was chaos as everyone was running around the platform - including the dibble - who had no control over what was going on as regular members of the public became involved. I got a crack on my head, fortunately it was a fist not a knife and as I turned around to see who it was, I heard a voice call out 'that's Sully you stupid twat' and I looked at the lad who had thumped me - a City fan stood right behind me, blade in hand! The police were trying to get us off the platform and set the dogs onto us. The jibbers were on the ball though, they would do the business, discard the blade under the train and move away from the scene before the dibble were on top.

A fair few lads were nicked that day and fortunately I wasn't one of them. Monday's media was full of it – the *Manchester Evening News* reported:

'Serious clashes between City and Newcastle fans, 18 officers had been injured, lots of fans taken to hospital including a good number of stabbings.' The local TV news described it as one of the worst incidents of trouble at a game for years...

*   *   *

In 2000 the Geordies did a 'Boro' when they turned up at the Clarence just before kick off and trashed the place. They came through the back door and it was ten of us against forty Geordies. Supposedly there were boys in our firm who remained there having a drink. In the days of the Guvnors and Mayne Line this would never have happened. If it did, they would have got a good hiding - this was the difference between firms of the 80's and firms nowadays, back in the 80's, we were mates, it wasn't just the football, we knocked around with each other every day, meeting in the Arndale or Don's shop in the Underground. We'd be living off our giros and robbing big shops for our clothes and other stuff to pay for our away trips and ticket money. And if we didn't have the money then we blagged our way around the country or into grounds. You learnt how to survive and if you didn't then you either got caught by the dibble or whacked by the other team's fans. We kept an eye out for each other and looked after one another, this bred trust. We all came from run down areas such as Blackley, Moston, Langley, Moss Side, Rusholme and Fallowfield. Day-to-day life was all about survival in these areas so going to the match was just an extention of that.

Now I look around at some of the boys, from good homes from places like Timperley or Chorlton, who only see each other for a day a week and there is no way I'd trust them with my life. These lads watch a couple of football hooligan films - Football Factory or Green Street for example - and think they're Danny Dyer acting the part but when it comes down to it, they don't fancy the reality of violence, the pain of getting hit and they tend to run when the odds are against them.

City were drawn away at Newcastle in the FA Cup the year after the Clarence incident. I hadn't planned on going, but I bumped into an 'old head' who said some old heads were turning out. Now with it being the cup, you always had more tickets available so I thought this sounded plausible and might provide an opportunity for a ruck with the old boys - perhaps we could show the younger ones how it's done! I also met one of the main lads from years ago and told him about it and he was up for it too. All week he was coming, even on the day before the game he said he would meet me in town in the morning. I hadn't met him in years, apart from a brief encounter with the Boro fans as mentioned outside the Sherwood, he was about to get stabbed and I whacked the lad with the knife with a cosh. I pulled him away from the area and then we both disappeared away from the scene in different directions. See what I mean about looking after each other?

On the day of the game I called him and told him the coach was leaving at 11am from the Waldorf pub, across the road from the bottom of Piccadilly Approach, on a nice quiet side street. He said he'd be there for 10.30am. Off I went to a café on Piccadilly Approach and some of the younger lads were already in there having a brew. A few of them let on to me, I recognised about two of them and that was only because they were from Blackley. Then one of the lads I went to the Forest game with when I was bitten by a police dog came in. He was waiting to see who was going before he would commit himself to join us. 'Sully', he said, 'I'm not from your time, but what I do know is if we don't take a good firm we will get fucked over'. I tried to reassure him that a few of the older lads would be with us. He then told me about how recently he had gone to Liverpool, got off the train, looked around Lime Street and there was not a Scouser in sight, so he jumped back on the returning train and came home. I had to explain that those days are gone, the days of jumping off trains and straight into a fight like something from the wild west were over. The firms have gone, the dibble are wiser - and there are cameras everywhere. That's why the trouble now takes place away from the train stations and football grounds.

Eventually we made our way to the Waldorf and a few lads were there - but not the old heads. I telephoned this lad who was supposed to be meeting us and he says he is on his way, hold the coach. So we wait for thirty minutes and the lads are kicking off, so I call again and he says his wife is giving him grief for wanting to go, so he isn't going now! Bollocks.

I looked around, there was a coach just over half full of young lads, although a few others had gone up in cars and we had arranged to meet them in Whitley Bay. We were playing in the Cup and this is the best we could do. I looked at this kid - aged fourteen maybe fifteen at the most. 'I hope you're ready for a battle, lad?' I told him. He just laughed back. I thought back to some of the scraps we'd had with the Geordies, home and away, and reckoned they would have laughed at us if we had turned up with this lot ready for battle.

We got to Whitley Bay at 2pm as planned and there were a small number of blues there - some had arrived the night before. It was an early evening kick off, live on TV and whilst we were having a drink, I kept looking at this 'crew' expecting us to get well hammered by the Geordies. An hour later we headed for Newcastle by train. On arrival, the old bill were nowhere to be seen, so we made our way into the city centre. We walked past one pub and a scout went in and it was half full of Geordies in their replica shirts. We looked around for items to use as ammunition and put the windows through, moving on quickly to a second pub and doing the same thing there. We reached a third pub and just as we were taking aim, the Geordie dibble appeared - and in retrospect it was a good job they did as a big mob from both pubs we had bricked arrived on the scene at the same time!

The police had us all against a wall and they nicked about twenty of us. I was lucky, I managed to mingle with the crowd and slip away from the area with another lad. It was very dodgy walking to the ground, we kept our heads down and mouths shut. We bumped into a few lads from the Parkside and they - like ourselves - didn't have a ticket for the game. We got to the turnstiles and just doubled up with this other lad, said a few words to the operator and he just let us through and we moved quickly to the bar area before the stewards could clock on to what was happening.

After the game (which we lost!) we had to make our way back to Whitley Bay via the train station, passing small gangs of Geordies along the way. A car suddenly pulled up along side us and it's Mark, we jump in and he's telling us how two of his friends were arrested in the city centre.

'We know we were there!' I tell him. Mark dropped us off at Whitley Bay so we avoided the train station. One by one the others arrive back whilst we are having a drink, but quite a good number had been arrested. A group of lads in a mini bus found out that those arrested would be let out in around two hours and said they'd wait.

COCKNEYS

CHELSEA

Over the years I have had many battles with the cockneys - none more so than with Chelsea one particular Friday night in May 1984. Both teams were going for promotion in the old second division and the game was live on TV.

I remember coming into town and walking into the Bulls Head opposite Piccadilly Station and being blown away by the sheer volume of City fans on view and I allowed myself a satisfied 'nod' of the head knowing that this was going to be good. Later, as we headed towards Maine Road, other lads were coming up to us saying that Chelsea were all over the place, in all the pubs in town and around the ground. I then spot a group of lads on the opposite side of the road and recognise one of them as a Spurs fan I had met on England trips. They were walking on ahead and then they stopped at a taxi rank and stood there laughing at us. A group of around forty City fans came running over to us, urging us to join them and we charged over the road and seconds later a cockney was laid out on the floor after being stabbed. His mates tried to make a stand, but they had no chance and they retreated. Unfortunately, they ran towards more Chelsea fans near Oxford Road station and suddenly we were heavily outnumbered. Now it was our turn to make a stand but we were backing off slowly towards The Ritz. The dibble arrived and we managed to break away in small numbers and make our own way to the ground.

As we have reached the Mancunian Way there was a huge mob of City fans so we joined up with them. Most of them were going on with themselves about what they are going to do if they see a Chelsea fan but I looked around and only recognised a few faces, which was a worry. 'We have to get this together or else we'll have problems and will get legged all over the place,' said Jimmy. He was right so we organised ourselves and made our way to the Clarence to meet up with the others. When we get there we can hear the singing and chanting booming out from the pub. But it wasn't City songs coming out, but Chelsea songs! The dibble had the place surrounded and quickly moved us on but contined to follow us, making sure we went towards the ground.

We saw a Chelsea firm walking down towards the ground, so we ran down the side streets and back alleys, picking up anything we could use - broken bricks, bottles and pieces of wood and ambushed them. They were backing off when sure enough the police appeared with their truncheons and either hit us or nicked us - or both in some cases! They held us against a wall and escorted the Chelsea mob to the ground. We then made our way to the forecourt outside the ground and fuck me, Chelsea were everywhere. The two groups stood there looking at each other waiting for the other to make a move. One of the lads with us grabbed me and said 'there's one of Tottenham's main boys there, I've been with him at England games', this confirmed the earlier sighting of another Spurs fan and proof that Spurs and Chelsea had teamed up together.

At that moment they ran at us, we tried to stand firm but there were simply too many of them and we ended up getting legged all over the place. One blue ended up getting his face slashed. Getting back to the ground we found the dibble had cornered off our section to allow the Chelsea in to the area. Fuck me, we were the home team and we were being surrounded by the cops for our protection! Inside the ground there must have been ten thousand cockneys, none wearing colours and all lads. Even for me it was a scary moment!

After the game (which we lost!) we tried to have a go but it was a waste of time - we were heavily outnumbered and the police were on hand to stop it. A good number of us met up at the Cypress Tavern on Princess Street - a well known City haunt - and we were able to have a pop at a small firm who were obviously lost.

That is the biggest mob I have ever witnessed at Maine Road and we had to make sure it was the first and last time they ever took the piss like that.

*　　　　　　*　　　　　　*

A couple of seasons later about fifteen of us chipped in and we hired a van and after a good Friday night's drinking in various city centre pubs we set off for London around 4am with Mick (sober) as the driver.

Normally at that time of day, you can get to London in four hours easily - but it took us much longer as we were stopping off at the service stations and robbing them blind! In one in particular, near Birmingham, we came out with a bag of cash! The old dear at the counter went into the back room for a few seconds - but that was enough, one of the lads noticed she'd left a cash bag under the counter and before she knew it - he grabbed it and we did one armed with Mars bars, crisps and drinks - is that why they call it self service?

In the van, the proud owner of the cash bag gave everyone a nice share of the proceeds and took care of the petrol money, keeping the rest to himself (rumoured to be a couple of hundred pounds) which was fair play to him.

Even at 7am some of the lads were still drinking away, others tried to get their heads down for a few minutes - which was just impossible with twelve lads in the back vying for space! It was going to be a long day in the smoke...

We headed for a pub not far from Stamford Bridge just on opening time. The landlord served us, clocked our accents and suggested we move on after this drink. Jimmy asked him why we would have to leave - knowing full well why - and he replies that 'this is a Chelsea pub, no away fans'. Jimmy looks around at the few Chelsea in there, looks back at the landlord and says 'it wont be a problem, they look harmless'.

So we all sit there, taking our time when two lads walk in - one was a right big twat, the other was slim, they looked like Laurel and Hardy! They stared at us and the big twat says (in his cockney accent) 'awwight?' We look back at him and then he said 'Man City?' and off he went to the bar to have a chat with the landlord, a few minutes later they left the pub. The landlord came over again and asked us to leave. Jimmy informed him we hadn't finished our pints yet and at that moment, the doors opened and in came a large number of boys. They ordered their drinks and just stared at us as more came in to join them. Three of them come over to us 'You know, you lot have got a right nerve coming in here', then adding 'my name is...' - as if we were bothered who he was. The next thing, one of our lads stands up and says 'yeah, and my name is...' it was just about to kick off, when in true Hollywood style, in come the London Bill to save the day (or the pub anyway!) who suggested we left in a stronger tone than the landlord. Chelsea were livid, we smiled at them, blowing kisses as we were escorted out and all they could do was call us varying names that always emphasised the word 'Northern'!

Outside, the Old Bill started laughing, telling us we had a lucky escape and that normally away fans caught out in that pub come out in body bags. Then they took our names and radioed them through to the station. Everyone's came out fine - until it came to mine.

'Oh, we have a right one here' he said to his colleagues, adding loudly, 'assault on police officers, football violence, fraud, shoplifting, stealing cars, smash and grabs', all the way to the ground, this copper kept winding me up. 'He loves us and the job we do,' he kept saying. He just wanted me to snap and do something so he could nick me, he was really taking the piss. To be honest, I would rather have got a whacking in the pub by Chelsea than to be having the piss taken out of me by a copper escorting us to the ground. At least I had a chance to fight back in the pub, here it was all one way. Then, he said 'this cunt is one of Fagin's gang' and thankfully at that point another copper said 'that'll do, leave it now.'

I must admit at that point I was about to lose it so the other officer's words were welcome. By now I just didn't want to be there, I didn't even fancy going to the game. I suppose unless it has happened to you, you cant truly understand the predicament I was in. All through the match I couldn't concentrate, I could just feel all of these eyes watching me, wanting me to do something, anything that they could use as an excuse to drag me out and give me a good hiding for assaulting a police officer elsewhere. I just wanted to get out of the ground without being arrested!

After the game we headed for the van and got as far as Kilburn in north west London, a traditional Irish area, and went into a pub for a few hours until one of the lads fell on the floor drunk! We carried him back to the van parked nearby while others went to the off license to stock up on the beers for the journey home.

We arrived back in town at around midnight and went into Brannigan's and it was full of United. Do we turn and walk out or do we walk up to the bar? Of course, we walk up to the bar - as we are getting served, someone calls out 'Fuck off you Blue bastards' and then two of our lads are getting smacked for fun. The next thing tables are being over-turned and we start picking up chairs to defend ourselves. We managed to get to the door where the bouncers were pushing us outside and at that point we gained the upper hand. The reds were trying to follow us out, but as the door was narrow, they couldn't all get out at once and charge us, so we were able to deal with them, forcing them back inside. Then we made a big mistake by backing off a little which allowed them all to get out and run at us, legging us all over the place. We managed to stay together and after running to the bottom of Market Street, we stopped, caught our breath and went at them.

There were just twenty of them now, most had gone back in to Brannigan's satisfied that they had chased us out and happy to get back to their pint. As we were half way up Market Street, they came at us again, there was a stand off, a lot of bouncing up and down giving it the 'come on'. Someone shouted, 'Come on City, lets have 'em' and forward we went as they went one step forward and three steps back. That was definitely a sign of weakness on their behalf and then one of the reds ran off, we just charged as another one or two reds fled, which for those left standing is the worst thing possible. We were at it for a good few minutes, running them, slapping them, getting slapped back - until we heard the sirens of the meat wagons and stopped, splitting into smaller numbers and disappearing into the night.

FULHAM

In 1984 we played Chelsea's West London rivals Fulham who

were then an unknown quantity, as we hadn't played them for years. We took two coaches down but we didn't bump into any Fulham fans that day – but that's not to say that the day was trouble free. Chelsea didn't have a game that day and with both west London grounds being less than a mile from each other, Chelsea's boys were looking for something to do on their 'free' Saturday. We were heading for the ground and reached the big park at the back of the away end when we saw a group of around 60 who we assumed were Fulham.

As we got nearer to them I recognised a couple of faces from England games, especially a Chelsea fan called Terry. We ran at them and it was a full on battle - three steps forward and two steps back - with regular fans diving out of the way as we fought. We had them backing off, which was fair enough, we did out number them, but they certainly were game for it and they came at us again until the dibble separated us. Even then, they waited for us after the match and we had another skirmish with them but the dibble kept things under control, herded us onto the coaches and escorted us away. Some of the lads said that they didn't realise Fulham had such a handy firm. I was the only one who recognised it was a Chelsea firm.

We stopped off at a pub on the outskirts of London, had a couple of pints before deciding it was time to get to work and pay Newport Pagnell service station a visit! Fortunately it was packed – just as we liked it. Me and Rob were walking through and spotted a door slightly ajar. Having looked around, I kept watch whilst he nipped in, emerging seconds later saying 'let's go'. We moved double quick, out of the shop and into the car park and to a quiet spot behind some lorries. He produced a bag from under his jacket and looked in it, then showing me the contents. 'Fuck me! pure fucking notes'. It was full of tenners and twenties. Rob pulled them out and started counting them, putting them into two piles. Having divided them up, he gave me my pile and we both put them in our pockets as Rob slung the bag into the bushes. We waited a few more moments before getting onto the coach. Once on, we stood out like a sore thumb. Everyone else had pockets bulging with drinks, crisps, chocolate bars and sandwiches. We walked on empty handed. We were getting jip from everyone, saying we must be going soft, losing our touch. All we could do was laugh back at them and joke about it – of course, had they known we had £400 in our pockets it would have been a different story.

After a while they felt sorry for us and shared their loot with us, offering us drinks and food. One or two still continued to give us grief for not pinching anything and eventually Rob stood up proudly and said 'Look, while you boys were stealing Mars bars, we were robbing pure cash'. Of course no one believed him – until Rob put his hand into his pocket and brought out the wad of notes, waving them about and singing 'Summer Holiday' and I soon joined him in a duet, whilst the others watched us - they weren't laughing now! At least the miserable twats cheered up when we bought the first few rounds.

WEST HAM

I mentioned the time that Chelsea bought a crew up to Maine Road like no other I had seen, well West Ham pushed them a close second!

I had a lot of respect for West Ham's firm, they were all genuine Eastenders - and some big fuckers too - and not from all over the capital like most London firms. We thought a good number of them had come up on the Friday and were staying at Sasha's Hotel, so we met up at the Millstone on nearby Church Street which we thought was somewhere the dibble wouldn't find us. Well, that was fine in theory but in no time a meat wagon pulled up outside and just sits there. We decided to move on and they followed, so we split into two groups as they could only follow one and not both. The good news was that they chose to follow the other group. The bad news is I ended up being with a number of lads who liked to talk a good fight but also liked to walk at the sight of a good fight! I'd been in this situation before, lads with new trainers and nice jackets that they didn't want to ruin and when you see them afterwards they're trying to impress their mates, making out they were right in the middle of it. Bullshit.

After a few minutes we came across a few blues who told us that the Hammers were down on Oxford Road station in the arches at The Salisbury. We set off, keeping to the back streets and as we got closer I estimated there was about forty of us. Making our way through what is now the Gay Village (then just derelict warehouses) we sent ahead a couple of spies to check it out and by the time we had made our way down Whitworth Street towards the Palace Theatre, they were making their way back.

They confirmed that the cockneys were in both The Salisbury, set back off the main road and Grand Central at the front on Oxford Rd. We were two minutes away now and as we turned onto Oxford Road, we crossed over and put a bit of a jog on, running down the side of Grand Central to charge at them, taking them by surprise as they were stood in the cobbled alley way between the two pubs. They immediately backed off as we came at them, then the next thing a cry went out 'NOW!' - and they charged us as more came out of both pubs, we were backing off now as they ran at us. We were being run all over the place, John fell to the floor and he was immediately surrounded and was on the receiving end of a fair few boots. Me and Jimmy and a few others grouped together and ran back at them, calling them all sorts of names (mostly Cockney Cunts!) and lashing out at them, we were at it for a good few minutes, each backing off slightly, regrouping and going off again. Eventually the police arrived and they attempted to push us into a corner whilst the Cockney wankers were left alone and they were stood there laughing at us, though when the dibble started turning their attentions to them they had a pop back which meant the cops dealing with us left us and waded into the West Ham - which made it easy for us to do one as fast as we could!

We made our way to Maine Road and came across another City gang. We told them what had happened and they described how they had been legged through Whitworth Park. We made our way to The Clarence and but it was empty. 'Where is everyone'? I asked. The landlord informed us that everyone was probably 'being chased or getting battered all round the ground!' We crossed over to The Albert and on to The Sherwood, but that was being guarded by dibble so we moved quickly down the alleyways coming onto Claremont Road via Kippax Street.

A tout I knew said that there was a large mob of cockneys on the forecourt by the ticket office, he described them as being 'suited and booted'.

They were there alright, surrounded by police. They were giving us the wanker signs... I got close up to this one big cunt and he looked at me and said 'where's your boys?' whilst another answered for him 'getting fucked all over shitty Moss Side by us' they laughed and took the piss more. I moved a little closer and said to him 'you're full of shit, you're just a tub of lard.' At this he started bouncing around coming out with all sorts and the police pushed him back but he kept on mouthing off and eventually he was nicked - stupid twat! More dibble arrived and we were moved on and 'helped' into The Kippax.

Once onto the terrace it was clear that the Hammer's had not gone into the away end terrace but descended into the Main Stand in the posh seats. There were over two hundred in there, booming out that fucking annoying 'Bubbles' song and also doing a bizarre version of 'The Hokey Cokey'.

After the game they came steaming out of the Main Stand, whacking everyone in sight making their way towards The Parkside. We had left the game early and were already waiting for them. It was mayhem - in every side street and alleyway it was kicking off. One bloke and his son got caught up in it and we helped him get to his car but as they got in the cockneys smashed the windscreen. We felt really sorry for the bloke but had to leave him or else we would have got battered ourselves. As the dibble gained control, they managed to get West Ham into one group and escort them down Lloyd Street. We ran through the estate ahead of them and came out facing them. As they approached us, you could see loads of them with their suits on giving out 'Come on, you're at home'. Then a voice shouts out 'Come on City, STAND!' and off we went. 'Let's give it these cunts, they've took the piss all day' shouted Jimmy and we steamed into them. I saw this one lad reach into his pocket as if he's got a blade on him. I've seen this ploy before - an act - to see if you are scared. However, this bastard was not acting and out comes a blade in his hand and he's looking at Mick. 'Watch out Mick' I called to him as the Cockney lashed out at him -

fortunately for Mick he only caught his coat sleeve.

Then a police dog ran in and bit Mick and one of the lads gave it an almighty kick and down it went. I looked around, the police horses were charging into us from all angles and the dibble were wading in with their truncheons. One blue fell to the floor and the dibble were whacking him all over, one copper lost his truncheon and he got a hiding with it as a result!

Police vans were being pelted with rocks and stones and the police were backing off. It remained this way for a good few hours, small fights breaking out around the top end of Hulme and around the universities and Piccadilly. As mentioned, Chelsea brought the best firm to Maine Road, but we knew other firms had teamed up with them, whereas West Ham came on their own and took the piss. Respect indeed.

*   *   *

We travelled to Upton Park in 1987 for the final game of the season and in typical City style we had to win or face relegation for the second time in four years.

We went down on the train - there was a football special organised and a fair few of the Mayne Line went on that and it was packed. I jibbed it with a large group on the service train. At Euston, we were met by the 'Old Bill' and made to walk in single or double file. Then they waded in and grabbed a lad and took him out - we were looking at what was going on and it turns out they are treating the whole thing like an identity parade, pointing at lads and either nodding or shaking their heads. If you got the nod you were out! It came to me and I got the nod. I tried to continue out of the station but was pinned against a wall. A few lads tried to help but that only meant they ended up in the back of a Black Mariah with me. They took us to a station and banged us up in cells - there were fifteen in my cell and over one hundred in total. And did they charge us for any offence? Did they fuck. They just kept us in there until about two hours after the game had finished (and yes we were relegated if you are interested!) and then let us go. Bastards.

We made our way towards Euston and went into a pub called The Lion and Lamb nearby. As we sat there with a pint, someone comes in and tells us that Spurs were arriving at Euston as they had been playing in the Midlands. Then, out of the blue a group of West Ham came in the pub asking us to join them in having a pop at Spurs, Arsenal AND Millwall! Fuck me! But we told him 'we're City and we don't join up with anyone' and we just stayed out of it.

Later we went into Euston, but the shithead Spurs fans wouldn't come off the platform! As we hung around the concourse, more City fans joined us from the game. They were telling tales of how, at full-time, West Ham fans had gone onto the pitch and walked towards the City fans applauding them, chanting 'Loyal Supporters' at the blues. Of course we had missed all of that, but it explains the attitude of the Hammers asking us to join up with them. It was a far cry from a few years previous through the back streets and alleyways of Moss Side!

TOTTENHAM

The week before the 1981 FA Cup final against Spurs was a nightmare, I couldn't sleep a wink I was too fucking excited... As far as I was concerned it didn't matter if I had a ticket or not, I was going to Wembley! We set off late on the Friday after the Bulls Head had closed, stocked the van up with beer and stopped off at a service stations along the M6 for petrol and a bit of 'shopping'. There were loads of people around, which was good, and I noticed a cash bag on a shelf under the counter where one woman was serving, so after a bit of persuasion I got Andy and Dave to distract the woman behind the counter and made a move.

They started arguing loudly over a bar of chocolate or something then went over to the checkout area but the other side to where the assistant was. She fell for it and as she helped them with their 'problem', I quickly reached under the counter, grabbed the bag and was off, giving the lads a wink as I passed them. As everyone came back to the van I urged them to get a move on, they all piled in and off we went for a short distance and then stopped. 'What the fuck have you stopped for?' I asked. 'I haven't paid for the petrol', Mick explained. 'You cant go back, no fucking way' I said, adding 'there's fifteen of us, we saw you pay, our word against one woman assistant, keep going!' Mick carried on, speeding off as quickly as the van would allow.

In the back of the van we counted the money, wraps of tenners and fivers. £220 in total plus £30 in change. I took £150 and the rest was divided up between the lads. Well this was to be a free weekend in London for us all! We stopped off again at Franklin services not far from London as daylight was breaking. Time for a top breakfast we thought! It was so easy to eat for free, just fill your plate up and then pile up to the counter to pay and whilst you surround the assistant, most of you just duck and walk around and find a table and enjoy. Worked every time!

We came off the M1 and headed for Wembley. We were looking for a B&B as we didn't fancy kipping in the van that night, not with fifteen of us, it just wouldn't work. We parked up and as we were walking around, we came across the 'Cider Gang' from Blackley, I knew them all, had done for years, they weren't hooligans or anything, just loved a drink – hence their name. They had been in London since Friday afternoon and were staying until Sunday. We came across a pub, had two pints in there and Pete said we had to make our way to Swiss Cottage as that was where all the blues were meeting.

As we got nearer we could hear the noise from the pub – it was full of blues! It was like a wedding or a funeral – all the old faces, like relatives that you see on special occasions! Here we used another one of our scams for free beer. The queue at the bar was five deep, so you would order more beers than what you wanted. When she went back to the pumps for the final time, you just slipped away into the back of the pub whilst the barmaid tried to remember who she was serving, the rest of the lads waiting to be served would make sure she didn't think too long about it by shouting 'come on love, over here' and they would do the same thing. You just had to make sure you didn't get served by the same member of staff if you repeated the trick a second time! In between, the cigarette machine and the durex machine in the toilets were relieved of their contents and into the pockets of appreciative City fans. So we were sorted for a smoke and a bit of action later on!

The time had come to make our way to Wembley. There were loads of us without tickets, but we all knew we were getting into the ground. As we got off the tube at Wembley, we were clocked by the dibble. They were London bill, but somehow they knew who we were. They tried to stop us going down Wembley Way but there were too many of us and we just walked past them. We met a few lads who said it had kicked off with Spurs in the car park, we walked over and could see a small firm of black lads and one white lad with a pony tail – I recognised him from England games, the pony tail being a dead giveaway! They came towards us and it was clear they were up for a ruck. Our problem wasn't the Yids, but the old bill who had followed us from the moment we got off the tube. One blue shouted 'let's 'ave 'em' and we went towards them. We hoped they would charge at us so this would mean the bill went for them not us, which would make life easier, but they pushed us back and that's when we had to be quick and seize the chance. We ran at them, we came at them from all angles, both firms were stood in front of each other, doing the usual posturing – one step forward and two back, offering each other out.

It was obvious we outnumbered them and eventually we charged, legging them all over the car park, in between coaches, minibuses and cars. This was our day. City fans coming off coaches were tripping them up and once they hit the deck they were whacked all over the place. It carried on for so long that by the time I got to the turnstiles the game had kicked off. I jumped the turnstile and was in. The old bill – who had followed us – didn't bother now, they just wanted us out of their way. Thankfully I was in the City end and got on with watching the game which ended in a 1-1 draw after the stuffy cockney twats scored with a free kick with ten minutes to go that deflected off Tommy Hutchison and past Joe Corrigan to set up a replay on the following Thursday.

We made our way to a pub after the game and I knew straight away I wasn't going home. Most of the other lads all had jobs so had no choice, whereas I was 'self employed' and had no one to answer to – apart from the dibble if I got caught, not that I ever thought about that! I bumped into a few of the Cider Gang again and one or two of them were also staying on until after the replay, so I knocked about with them, staying in their hotel.

On the Monday, I decided to 'go to work' and made my way into central London with my rucksack. I headed for Harrods in Knightsbridge, fuck me it was massive... City were playing at Wembley and I was grafting Harrods, what a dream! I didn't know where to start! I made my way to the men's department and clocked a load of Pringle jumpers and coats. I looked around to see if there were any store detectives, it was one thing putting gear in my bag, another dodging the detectives. I was on my own so there was no one to create a diversion. I went over to the jumpers, waited for a couple to move away from the area and put five straight into the bag. I then went to the coats and put one inside the other and did the same with a pair of Farah pants and headed for the changing room looking as if I only had a coat and a pair of trousers.

I looked at the price on the coat - £500! Anway, I rolled one up and placed it in the bag. I then put on a pair of trousers and went outside to look in the mirror, well, really to see who was out there. The coast was clear. Back in the changing room I slipped my cords over the Farah's and walked out. Soon I realised I didn't know the way out and butterflies set in as I realised I wasn't in control. I was paranoid, convinced I was being followed. I asked an assistant where the exit was and she gave me directions. Just as I saw the doors, two blokes moved towards me, 'bollocks, I've been rumbled', I thought, but then they bolted for another door – hotly pursued by two security guards! I laughed in relief, walked through the doors and out onto Knightsbridge Road with a bag full of clothes. 'Fuck me, I've just done Harrods!' I thought as I scurried off, I'd done plenty of department stores in Manchester but this was the big one - what a fucking buzz!

I made my way back to a pre-arranged pub and the City boys couldn't believe what I'd pilfered. They and the locals were more than happy to buy the stuff I'd nicked and it proved to be a fruitful day's work. I took quite a liking to London after that, thinking I might extend my stay after the replay - London seemed such easy pickings!

Eventually Thursday came around, the day of the replay. We'd been out on the piss the night before so we gave breakfast a miss and got up around 1pm and went straight to the pub.

Eventually it was time to get the tube to Wembley and at the station – not surprisingly – it was all Spurs. We just kept quiet as we got, changing a few stops further down. Here we were joined by a right Spurs mob. We looked at one another and I quietly said we should mingle with the other Spurs fans who were wearing scarves. If we were sussed we had no chance as we were heavily outnumbered. Finally the train arrived and it didn't look as if the firm were getting on it. The one good thing about the tube trains is the doors aren't open for long and it was a relief when they shut with the firm still on the platform.

Once off the tube at Wembley it became clear none of us had tickets for the game. Obviously there were less City fans there for the replay than had been for the first game and we saw a few touts who I knew with tickets, but they were for the Spurs end only. Everyone bought one except me – it doesn't matter how much I have in my pocket, I'll always try and jib in first.

We made our way towards the Spurs end and when we reached the turnstiles, I just squeezed in as the tickets were given to the operator, we made our way onto the terrace. I thought to myself it will be bad if they score and we don't respond accordingly. We spotted a few blues in with us (a small crew from Moston) and stood with them. There were around fifteen of us together by now and soon Spurs scored. The place went fucking mental and we became a bit obvious as all around us people were celebrating yet we were stood there motionless... a mob began to surround us.

Before they had a chance to do anything, City equalised with a belting twenty five yard volley from Steve McKenzie. We went ballistic! The next thing is we're being whacked by Yids with flag sticks from all angles. We'd fend off one attack from the right and they'd be coming at us from the left, then in front of us. It was wild with punches being thrown all over the place. Fortunately we were at the back of the terrace so the old bill could get to us easily and they took us to the front. We were being spat at and flag sticks were being hurled at us like javelins as we passed. More blues who were also in the Spurs end joined us for safety. There were around one hundred and fifty of us by now, holding firm, but when Ricky Bastard Villa scored THAT goal, the Yids were giving it us.

That was all we needed, we just wanted to fight - we pushed past the dibble and ran at them. After an initial rush from us and the Yids backing off, the old bill cornered us and took us out of the ground. I ended up in a small group of around twenty-five blues on Wembley Way, but soon began to regret being thrown out – we were surrounded by Yids and got kicked to fuck all down Wembley Way and through the car parks. My leather coat ended up getting slashed down the side, one lad had to have stitches on his face while another had his arm broken. But it didn't end there. Just as we reached the underground station, we faced another mob there and the dibble just stood there and watched as we were slapped all over the place again. Luckily a few more City were at the station and we were able to regroup and get the upper hand and have a proper go back – only now the police decide to get involved. Cockney wankers! I have to admit Spurs gave us a bit of a hiding that night but looking back, it was a Thursday night and we were outnumbered almost 3-1. Had this happened on the Saturday it would have been a different story.

Once on the tube I decide to return home. Having lost the cup final I wasn't in the mood to stay in London for a few more days, I just wanted to get home as quickly as possible, as did everyone else. The train was pretty quiet but after a few drinks a couple of lads started a sing song and after that the whole carriage was singing.

SPURS FA CUP QUARTER FINAL 1993

Twelve years later City were drawn to play Spurs in the last eight of the cup at Maine Road. TV showed endless repeats of Ricky Villa's goal and spoke of City's revenge on the pitch, many of us fans sought a different kind of revenge.

We met in the Clarence and soon the dibble were making their presence known by coming in and seeing who was around, there was a van outside filming fans going in and stopping and searching them. We'd had enough of this and decided to leave in dribs and drabs and head elsewhere. I went for the Denmark and others went for the Whitworth. As usual, we took the side streets and back alleys to avoid the dibble. All of a sudden – from out of nowhere – a van pulled up. A voice shouts out in a Cockney accent 'Are you Man City'?

'Yeah', we reply.

The next thing the back doors fly open and lads with baseball bats start on us. We tried to make a stand but when they are tooled up and you have fuck all to have a go back with, the odds are stacked against you – on top of that there were only seven of us and I only knew two of them. I had a split second to decide what to do – can I trust these people I barely know to stand their ground and fight or do we leg it? Well no disrespect to the other lads but I wasn't going to stay and be a hero and get battered to fuck by baseball bats, I was on my toes! We finally managed to lose them, though that was probably more to do with them not wanting to stray too far from the van than anything else.

We made it to the Denmark and as I was explaining to the lads there about how we'd just been been chased by a van full of tooled-up Yids, when one asks what colour the van was. 'What the fuck difference does it make?' I replied. 'Well there's a van that's just pulled up across the road into a side street and it looks like the driver's a bit lost".

Sure enough it was the same van. Unfortunately for them, they had driven into a dead end. There were a couple of younger fans sat on the wall outside and they ran in to tell us the van was turning round and coming out - we had them cornered as they had to pass us. We came out of the pub and hid behind a wall and then when the van passed us BANG – the windscreen went through as we pelted it with bricks, bottles, rocks, anything we could get our hands on. The van crash into a wall. We attacked them as they tried to get out of the van. One Yid was being dragged out of the front window, another was on the floor with his head half open. But credit due to some of them, they stood their ground despite getting fucked over – though whether they would have done so without their baseball bats is another matter. Soon the sound of the meat wagons came towards us and we just split, which was easy for us as we knew the side streets and alleyways very well.

Into the ground and on with the game. Despite being 1-0 up,

we were eventually 1-4 down. With not long to go Terry Phelan scored for City, it sparked a pitch invasion from the Platt Lane end which had opened that day after a year of re-development. The game was live on BBC so the nation watched hundreds of City fans running across the pitch to get at the Spurs fans. The police stood firm in front of the Yids and horses came onto the pitch to move blues back so nothing actually happened between the two sets of fans. Outside the ground after the game was a different story though. There were running battles in the side streets as we ran Spurs all over Moss Side. Police cars were trashed and there were two stabbings and twenty-five lads ended up in court. The police described it as the worst violence seen at Maine Road for a long, long time.

MILLWALL

After a double relegation in 1996 and 1998, City found themselves in the third tier of English football for the first time in their history. As embarrassing as this was for such a massive club, it had its compensations in that we were due to play Millwall! We hadn't met for over a decade when we took the piss out of them on their 'manor' (see 'End of Guvnors' chapter). We all knew they'd come up mob-handed and that season this game was definitely the big one. During the two week build up to this game it seemed that everyone was turning out, the old boys, new boys and those in between, once again it was great to see the old faces.

There were lots of phone calls and meetings between us, deciding where we were going to meet up and what the plan would be and the rendez-vous seemed to change everyday. On the day itself, we were in town when someone said that Millwall had got off at Stockport and had a bit of fisticuffs with United! Nothing at all was going off in the city centre so we made our way to Maine Road and waited for them outside the North Stand. They arrived but were heavily escorted, we tried to jump in at them but kept getting pushed back. Looking at them we soon realised we were not up against *just* Millwall, but London – even Reading were in there. I lost all respect for them that day. Millwall – tough boys from south east London? They only came mob-handed with the help of half a dozen firms from other clubs, the only London firm absent was West Ham. There were even a couple of Stockport County fans in there - a total embarrassment! This was even shown on *McIntyre Undercover* when he exposed the Chelsea Headhunters. They were all on the train travelling up together: Millwall, Chelsea, Spurs and Reading. What a bunch of cowards.

We were sat in the North Stand next to the stewards in the segregated area between the home and away fans. City scored the first goal in the second half and 'Millwall' erupted by smashing the seats and throwing them at us. They could have broken through the police line... but didn't. They made a lot of noise and there was the usual posturing but that was about it really. We were waiting for them to come out between the North Stand and the Kippax when all of a sudden we were being pelted with missiles: bottles, bin lids and bricks but it was City fans who were throwing them at us – one bottle just missed my head! They were younger lads who were trying to get at the dibble but instead were aiming too short and hitting us. 'We're City you stupid twats' we shouted at them, but it made no difference, we had to chase them off in the end but this just attracted police attention and then they followed us around the side streets.

We tried to regroup a number of times but when we did the dibble split us up and forced us in the direction of Rusholme and Wilmslow Road – away from Lloyd Street where Millwall were being escorted. We were that wound up we simply ended up trashing the Indian restaurants and takeaways along the Curry Mile. There were people sat in there having an enjoyable meal and chats with friends when all of a sudden the windows were put through. I'd seen this happen after relegation a few times, when people just got frustrated but I hadn't seen it after we'd won a game 3-0! Too many of us were too worked up and needed a release. A couple of Asian jewellery shops got smashed up too with a bit of looting taking place. I dare say the owners of the businesses on Curry Mile were glad to see the back of City fans when we moved out in 2003, at least I hope their insurance premiums went down!

We battled with the dibble all the way along Wilmslow Road

and Oxford Road and into the city centre. We had robbed fruit and veg from the shops on Wilmslow Road off the outside tables and were using them as ammunition! Millwall bought a mob of 1,000 yet they did fuck all and all we end up doing was having it with the police. A complete joke and I'd be ashamed if I was in a Millwall firm that day.

CHARLTON ATHLETIC

1985 and the last game of the season. City needed a victory to secure promotion to the 1st division and we were all buzzing. We met up in the Underground in the morning and then got the bus to the ground - the usual way of course, jumping on and not paying, thirty lads sharing a ticket or looking for a ticket! The driver refused to move until everyone had paid and he's getting a lot of grief. This increases when he threatens to get the police. Eventually a conductor gets on, assesses the situation and tells the driver to carry on to the ground. Everyone is laughing and chanting 'Nice one Blakey'.

Anyway Maine Road is hammered - more so than a derby day as it was all City fans, everywhere you looked. The last time it was like this was against Luton two years previously when we'd got relegated. That was a horrible day and I just hoped that today wouldn't end in similar disappointment. We met Donald outside the souvenir shop and he tells us that he is going to collect our tickets for the game (promised by manager Billy McNeill after the Notts County incident). Donald disappears inside the main entrance and emerges minutes later with a handful of tickets and dishes them out to us. He then says that he will meet us inside the ground, which was unusual as we normally went in together. I needed to have a piss, so I ducked down an alley to do the deed. The next thing, Roy comes up saying that he thinks Donald is up to something. As we walk out of the alley, we can see Donald some way off. Next thing, two blokes come up, hand him an envelope, he looks in, looks at the blokes, then legs it with the two blokes in pursuit. We run after him too, Roy was faster than me, but we still lost him and a bit later we see him emerge from the Beehive. Roy crept up behind him, put his hand on Donald's shoulder and said 'you're nicked!'

Donald's face was a sight, you could see he was ready to run again, before he clocked who it was.

'You stupid pair of twats'.

Roy then asked what the crack was with the two blokes he'd done over, but Donald denied everything. 'Fuck off', Roy said, and explains how we knew about his 'runner'. Donald asked if anyone else knew about it, to which we said no, just the two of us.

'Right' Donald said, 'well keep it that way, yeah? I can't go near the ground yet' he added, as he pulled out an envelope with about fifteen more tickets inside. We couldn't believe how many he had, but more surprised when he asked us to go and sell them outside the ground for him. We set off to sell them and arranged to meet him later on.

The tickets were very easy to sell given the game and we only had two left when were approached by two lads. We haggled over a price and agreed to sell them. As they were paying us, they started to tell us how they had come over from Belgium in a group of about ten. None of them had tickets but had been buying them outside from touts. They then described how one black guy had run off with their money as they were exchanging it for their tickets!

We tried to look sympathetic 'The bastard!' I said to the Belgians, adding, 'you just can't trust anyone around here, you know'. It wasn't easy to keep a straight face.

Having sold the tickets, we went into the ground and met up with Donald in the Main Stand, who was pleased and highly amused to hear we had sold the final two tickets to the Belgian guys he had ripped off. However, the laughter soon turned sour when City scored and everyone went mad. The people in the row in front of us turned round to celebrate and there they were - the two Belgians! Obviously all of the tickets were grouped together but Donald hadn't thought of that and he was soon jumping over the row of seats and was off down the gangway into the bar area. The Belgian's were going mad, reporting the incident to stewards but they weren't interested - they were too busy celebrating the goal! Me and Roy went after Donald and jibbed our way into the Platt Lane stand behind the goal. It was a great day all round as City routed Charlton 5-1 to secure promotion on the last day of the season. I even climbed over the fence when the third goal was scored, as did many of us and Billy McNeill came charging over, yelling at us to get off the pitch. At the final whistle, there was a great pitch invasion as fans from all corners ran on to celebrate. There were 48,000 blues there that day - including two Belgians who got ripped off by the leader of the Mayne Line! The only downer on the day is there was no trouble as Charlton had only brought a couple of hundred fans and none of them seemed up for a fight!

The Dark Side

Leeds United

If there is a set of fans with a feeling of superior self worth out of all proportion with their history it is Leeds United. Leeds rose to prominence on the pitch in the mid sixties and gained a reputation off it in the seventies - in the intervening years we've had many a battle with them, although we don't see too much of them anymore!

Leeds in the 1980's reminded me a lot of the 'Doc's Red`Army' in the 70's, they were very good at going around smashing places up in large mobs. They also had a reputation for going around and slapping lads who were wearing shirts and scarves which was definitely out of order. If one of us did that we would lay into whoever had done it, we only ever fought with lads who were up for it.

On one occasion we were all skint after Christmas and talked about jibbing our way there on the train but we soon discovered the trains didn't run on New Year's Day! Because of this Donald had only booked four coaches and tempers got a bit heated when some realised there wasn't going to be enough room for everyone. We were all up for this game, had been for weeks and no one wanted to miss out. Donald said he'd see if he could sort another coach at short notice. We stood around for a few minutes when some lads started getting back on a coach – that's when it kicked off, fists were flying as people got angry and we hadn't even left Manchester yet!

Donald broke it up – he was the only one who ever could do that. Whatever Donald said went. Fortunately – and much to Don's relief – the extra coach arrived after an hour, everyone had a seat and off we went but as soon as we crossed the Pennines the roadblocks started. We were pulled over and sat on the hard shoulder for thirty minutes. A few more coaches turned up and they escorted us right up to Elland Road. On arrival, we could see a mob of Leeds stood on the other side of the road. Everyone was trying to get out of the exit doors and get at them but the Yorkshire dibble had all the angles covered and escorted us to the ground. At this point Leeds were pelting us with all sorts: bottles, bricks, pieces of metal... the dibble just let them get on with it, concentrating on getting us into the ground. We were going mad, trying to break through the lines but the dibble wouldn't budge.

Leeds came round to the side of us and the police about turned and took us another way instead but they found another mob lying in wait for us there too. Again we came under fire from a hail of missiles, the police horses were being hit and one horse went up on it's back legs and threw a copper off. The police escorting us went to get him up and that crack in the line meant we could charge Leeds – there was no bouncing on our toes here - this was a pure charge at the Yorkshire twats. In front of us Leeds were backing off, 'Mayne Line, Mayne Line' we were chanting at them as they ran like fuck, 'stand and fight you Yorkshire twats, we thought you were big city boys', I heard someone shout as we chased them.

Leeds legged it all over the place, they were very brave bombarding us when we were in the escort and I suspect that their plan was pinned on the fact that the police line wouldn't break – and it probably wouldn't had they not thrown missiles at the horses - daft twats! The police tried to get it together again but we were now running the show. Finally they got us into the ground but the damage had already been done. Six police were taken to hospital, a couple of Panda cars were turned over, local buses were smashed and around thirty City fans arrested. After the game we were kept behind for ages and we were trying to charge a gate open but were being held back.

Finally they let us out and we tried to blag the dibble, saying we had come by train, but they knew it was New Year's Day and the trains didn't run so they pushed us around to the coaches. They started getting heavy handed and that was winding a few up. Donald went over and said to the dibble that if they carry on like that that would cause more trouble and they calmed down a bit. Besides Leeds were nowhere to be seen. We were on the coaches, sat there for ages and not moving, so a few lads decided to get off and stretch their legs but they were soon facing raised truncheons and were pushed back on. Once we had set off we were convinced that Leeds would be further up waiting to hit us, as we crawled past like sitting ducks but again they were nowhere to be seen. We were escorted onto the motorway and out of West Yorkshire. We pulled off once the dibble had left us and went to a small pub in Saddleworth before going home after a few pints. What a result, we'd run Leeds on their own turf, five coaches went and came back damage free – and City had won 1-0. A perfect, if belated, Christmas present!

*   *   *

A few seasons later Leeds came to Maine Road, or rather they were supposed to but by 2.45pm everyone was on the forecourt wondering where the Yorkshire twats were hiding, there was no sign of the fuckers. It was unusual for them not to show their faces so rumours spread about what they might be up to. Most had decided to go by this point as the game was starting but I waited and chatted to a tout – we agreed something wasn't quite right. The next thing I hear a whistle from one of our lads stood on the corner of Maine Road and Claremont Road, we look up and he's giving us hand signals. Leeds were here!

Unfortunately they were in an escort, there were sixty of us and we tried to break into it but were held back by the dibble. Leeds had some big twats in there and a few of the black City fans started laughing at them 'You turn up at five to three with a police escort, you must be shitting yourselves'. All the Leeds twats could do was respond with monkey chants. The police marched them into the Platt Lane end and we went into the Main Stand near the Platt Lane. We could see all their boys wearing Pringle tops trying to eyeball us, it was quite funny. City scored quite early on and the next thing is Leeds are ripping up the wooden seats and throwing them onto the pitch. We were going mad and trying to get into the Platt Lane but the dibble were wise to it and pushed us back into the Main Stand. This wound up a fair number of blues and with a few minutes to go we left the stand and get a mob together outside the ticket office. Soon five lads were spotted walking towards us on the opposite side of the road – all wearing Bennetton jumpers! They stood out like a sore thumb as no one in Manchester was wearing Bennetton at the time.

Once they realised they'd been sussed, they started giving it the 'come on then', which, when you think about it was the right thing to do. If you have been sussed, your one thought is 'how do we get out of this in one piece?' Yes you are shitting yourself but you need to attract the attention of the police to bail you out so creating a scene was their only option. These lads had obviously come by car and it's one thing to be followed and kicked to fuck and another to have your car smashed to fuck too. We jumped the lads and gave them a bit of a hiding before the dibble came to their rescue and led them to safety. To be honest, they were not Leeds 'boys' but they got whacked due to the fact that on many trips to Elland Road, plenty of City fans had come away with black eyes and bloody noses – not fans looking for trouble just lads watching the game. We only used to battle with lads looking for the same, we never got anything out of fighting someone or a kid who had no interest in fighting back.

Eventually the rest of them were escorted back to Victoria Station. The dibble made a big error in deciding to take them down the side streets. Both Leeds and the dibble got pelted with bricks, bottles and bits of wood. Some Leeds fans decided they were better off on their own and ran from the bombardment – again, a mistake. For away fans to be making their own way around the unfamiliar back streets of Moss Side was fatal. Around every corner there was a mob waiting for them, afterall it wasn't only the extreme element up for a scrap, regular fans were hyped up as well after they'd destroyed the Platt Lane benches. Leeds had turned up late, made monkey noises at black fans and smashed up the Platt Lane Stand and now they fancied their chances on the side streets of Moss Side? They had no chance! They got a hiding but what pissed me off were the papers the next day reporting 'Leeds fans causing trouble again' headlines, rather than 'Leeds fans kicked to fuck by City' which is what really happened.

The next day I received a phone call from a blue, asking me if I wanted to go to a wedding that afternoon in Halifax. Never one to turn down a decent day out, off I went and at the reception I was being introduced to other guests. We were chatting away when one lad came up and asked me where I was from. When I said 'Manchester', he said 'Oh, you'll have to meet my mate, he was there yesterday in Manchester watching Leeds at Man City – you'll recognise him when he comes in, his head is bandaged and he has a huge shiner – he was kicked to fuck after the game!'

After an hour, he came in and as his mate had said, he was easy to spot. He was with his wife and after a while my mate was talking to him and they kept pointing and looking over at me, stood at the bar. My mate then comes over and asks me to join them. We started talking about anything but football and buying each other a round and then he starts going on about yesterday's trouble at Maine Road. It turns out he was part of the group of five who got leathered outside the ticket office just before the end of the game! He said 'Once we were spotted we had no choice but to front it out. We knew we were fucked, all we could do was hope that police wouldn't be too far away. I got knocked to the floor and kicked in the head, one of the others had a broken arm and the others black eyes.' He went on to say he used to be in the Leeds Service Crew but got out of it when he got married. I asked him if he'd heard of The Mayne Line Crew telling him I used to be in that and he had 'it's a good crew that, a good reputation' he said, saying he knew of Donald. He left after a while and gave me his phone number, adding if I was in Leeds, to give him a ring and he'd take me for a pint before the game.

One of the strangest meetings I've had with the Leeds Service Crew happened in a night club, I can't say I particularly enjoyed it. The late 80's and early 90's saw the rise of Acid House, rave and ecstasy. A mate of mine invited me to a rave one night at Maxine's in Wigan. I hadn't been before so I thought it would be a laugh but told him I'd leave if I wasn't into it. We got there and there were reds from Salford, blues from Manchester – and a gang from Leeds. 'Great', I thought, 'a nice Friday night punch up with the dibble nowhere in sight!' But when I took a closer look, fuck me, I couldn't believe what I was seeing – everyone was shit faced and monged out of their skulls dancing their bollocks off. I recognised a few of the Leeds boys and ended up having a chat with them. They said the previous week they'd been to a rave near Derby and you had Derby and Forest fans dancing together. I laughed at them, saying it was bullshit, it would never happen, but they insisted it was true and that rave and ecstasy was 'chilling' everyone out. I wasn't having it and left. A few weeks later I went to the Hacienda and saw the same thing again with different firms all under one roof talking and dancing together. It was the last time I went to a rave! It just wasn't my scene...

BRADFORD CITY

Bradford's firm may not have been the biggest but they could certainly handle themselves as we found out one sunny afternoon in May 1989. City played them away, it was the last match of the season and the blues only needed a point to win promotion back to the First Division. The tickets for the City end sold very quickly and none of us got any. The Wednesday before the game I was sat at home when one of the lads rang me and said he had a contact in Bradford who could sort us out but we had to go down on the Friday night to get them. Rather than go on the train, I decided to drive, so we met up in Yates' Wine lodge at 7pm. We got a bit lost in Bradford but eventually found the pub. We were to meet a bloke called Jack and the landlord confirmed he would be in later on. Jack arrived an hour later with his wife. He had two tickets in the Bradford end but couldn't pick them up until the morning. He didn't realise there were three of us wanting tickets so he said he'd try and get another one. We were having a few drinks and then realised it was time to go home but Jack insisted we stayed at his house as long as we didn't mind sleeping on a camp bed! We got talking to a few Bradford boys and they were saying that Jack had a right reputation in the city for hooliganism – even though he wasn't a fan as such and rarely went to a game. Yet Jack himself seemed quite a private man and didn't go around boasting about it.

We stayed the night and in the morning his wife made us

breakfast and we went to the same pub again at lunchtime before getting a lift to the ground – I left my car in the pub car park. We didn't get the extra ticket and there was hundreds of blues there also without tickets – but as usual I still got in easily, jibbing my way into the home end behind the goal. It was packed in there and we just kept ourselves to ourselves as the game started. As I said, City only needed a draw to ensure promotion and we were soon a goal down despite playing well. In the second half we murdered them but couldn't get the equaliser until it came with four minutes remaining. Fuck me, all around City fans were going wild! There were small pockets of blues everywhere, who like us, had just kept quiet during the game. On the final whistle, we all scaled the fence and celebrated on the pitch, though in the process I ended up losing my mates which was a pain because I hadn't a clue where the pub or more importantly my car was parked!

Outside the ground I still couldn't find the lads so I headed towards the station and bumped into a handy lad called Russo. Bradford fans had made their way to the station looking for a bit of action and we certainly gave them some! They were heavily outnumbered and after a few slaps they realised they were onto a hiding to nothing and backed off. The dibble had arrived and were over keen to put everyone on the train and get them out of town, it didn't matter if you didn't have a ticket, you were put on the train regardless. I explained to the police that I had come in my car which was parked near the station which is why I was in the area and Russo said he was with me which was good as he could have got on the train and gone straight home.

As the train pulled off we made our way down the platform and out of the station, where the Bradford crew were gathered licking their wounds. It was a good job Russo had not got on that train! We had a quick look around and decided we would walk past them and as we did, another small crew appeared. It was obvious something was going to happen and soon we were surrounded. Someone shouted, 'lets give the bastards a good kickin' and we looked at each other and Russo said softly 'lets have 'em' and we steamed in. Unfortunately this was one of those occasions when we didn't quite think things through. After an initial burst of fists from us, we were soon up against a wall, trying to stay on our and feet and not go down, taking punches and kicks from all angles whilst covering our faces. Thankfully the dibble arrived on the scene and we were safe – well for the next ten minutes anyway. I tried to describe to the copper where the car was parked – behind a big church with a pub next to it - and he was able to give us the directions, so off we went. Now Bradford city centre is not very big and the mob knew all the back streets and short cuts.. It wasn't long before Russo said to me 'don't turn around but there are about twenty lads following us'. As we turned left, we could hear them hurrying to reach us. There were two cars parked on our side of the road and as we reached them Russo snapped off the car aerials and it was like a scene out of the film *The Warriors*!

I recognised the pub and said 'Russo, we're here', 'Aye, so are them cunts too'. I've seen Russo in action before, never one to run, he's stood in the middle of the road, 'offering' firms out on his own – basically he didn't give a fuck. We were within yards of the pub when they ran at us, Russo turned round and as he did, this small stocky cunt ran at him and Russo whacked him across the kipper with the aerial and he went down on his knees clutching his face screaming. 'Come on, who's next', Russo shouted. Even though we were greatly outnumbered, this seemed to stop them in their tracks as we moved towards them. They were bouncing around and gesturing at us and eventually we started to retreat as three lads came from the pub – it was the two lads I'd travelled with and Jack! Jack knew the Bradford boys and visa versa and he went over and spoke to them. It was clear that whatever Jack said went as far as the mob were concerned - they just turned and walked away. I bought a round of drinks for Russo and Jack and after a couple more, decided to go home. In the car park I had a flat tyre and a parking ticket! We made it home and straight to Albert Square where City fans were holding an unofficial 'Promotion Party', celebrating into the early hours under the ever watchful eye of the dibble!

*   *   *

The previous season had seen similar trouble, though I was able to do a bit of work that day too! It was a night match and around sixty of us caught the train around 3pm. We arrived at Bradford and immediately there was a big firm at the station. As we got off, one of their lads asked the usual 'got the time mate' question. A City fan called out, 'why don't you ask us who we are before you ask us the time?' Immediately there was all sorts of shit being thrown at us as we made good use of the bottles and cans we'd been drinking beer from on our journey. The lad who asked us the time probably regretted doing so as he was singled out and got a right crack on the head from one bottle. As ever, the dibble turned up and got the disturbance under control, separating both sides either side of a wall. Before long they put what we assumed to be Bradford fans on a train and kept us against the wall until it pulled out. It turns out they were not Bradford but Wolves' Subway Army who must have been playing at either Leeds or Halifax that night!

Once we were let go, we went into the city centre and I decided to do a bit of shopping as it didn't look as if anything was going to happen with Bradford. In one shop I stuffed a Spray Way jacket down my trousers and wore another as it should be. There were two shop assistants who were both busy serving as I slowly walked towards the door and straight outside and met up with the others who hadn't moved from when I left them. 'Right lads, who wants a Spray Way?'. One lad immediately said he'd have it as long as it wasn't at a silly price. '£60' I offered it at. He agreed, opened his wallet and pulled out loads of twenties and tenners. Fuck, I should have gone higher! Either way, I was £60 up and kept the other jacket for myself as I didn't have one anyway.

As we headed for the ground, we could see something was happening further up, the noise of lads bouncing around giving it the 'come ons' etc. We had to suss out who was who and realised that there was a group of local white lads and Asians. After more bouncing around, one City fan ran over and smacked a couple of them and within seconds we all joined in. The Asians legged it off and the Bradford fans remaining were kicked all over the place!

Sheffield Wednesday - 1984

Wednesday had a firm but they were not rated as highly as their neighbours Sheffield United. Yes, they had numbers but not much quality - or so we thought. As we pulled into the station, we made to get off when 'smash!' the windows went through one by one. There was bricks flying everywhere, we were trying to get off the train but we were kept back by the volley of shit being thrown at us. A few lads got cuts by flying glass or were hit by a brick, I put up my hood – I had a thick parker jacket with a padded hood – to protect myself. We then gathered the bricks they had thrown at us, opened the doors and ran at them. Once on the platform we were able to dodge the incoming bricks until they ran out of ammunition – and that's when we struck, running at them and chasing them out of the station.

As we charged them, a brick bounced off Billy's head, but he still carried on as if it had never happened – he hardly blinked! They managed to regroup in a car park outside and had a bit of a stand off but as more and more of us piled off the train they ended up on their toes. Anyway, we found our way to a pub near Hillsborough and there were that many of us that some had to go into another boozer further up the road, within sight of the first pub. A few moments later, a lad from the second pub came running back in saying it was kicking off in the other pub. When we got there we could see City fans struggling outside the pub as we got nearer, but the one thing Wednesday didn't know was that they were about to face twice the number of blues they thought they were taking on.

As soon as they saw us coming they legged it, but by then it was way too late. We smacked them all around Hillsborough, even chasing them into the Kop. We jumped the turnstiles and gathered in a group together as the game started. There were thirty of us and we were easy to spot as we were dressed differently. We were wearing semi-flared jeans or cords and not before long a group of Wednesday fancied their chances and attacked us from behind. Fortunately we cottoned on to them and let them get a bit nearer before turning and saying 'come on then'. This caught them off their guard as they were a bit slow.

They didn't seem sure of themselves, they were offering us out but backing off at the same time. It was clear nothing was going to happen.

Dave saw their firm in the stand next to us and we began gesturing to them to come and join us. The next thing they left their seats and went below the stand, we assumed they had just gone for a drink – but a few minutes later they appeared in the Kop behind us. They stood there looking at us and we thought, as this was their end and we were in it, it was up to them to come at us, but it was clear they didn't fancy their chances. Roy turned around and suggested that if we left it for a few moments and they still didn't make a move then we would take it to them. At half time, we moved down towards the bottom of the terrace towards the gates and waited for them to follow us down, which they did, but stopped well short of reaching us. Chalkie beckoned them to keep coming but they wouldn't have any of it. Then in frustration he said 'fuck it, lets get them' and off we walked up the terrace towards them. We could tell they were all on edge as we approached and they were all looking around at each other as if they didn't have a leader, someone to keep it all together. Roy then gave the command and we just went into them blazing like mad, there was one tall lad who looked like the singer out of 'Curiosity Killed The Cat' as he was wearing a stupid hat – he tried to run off but tripped on the terrace steps and got a right kicking.

We remained in their end for the second half and after the game waited for the rest of the blues to join us outside expecting Wednesday to regroup but they did they'd disappeared. We couldn't believe it, they had attacked us in the station and the pub when there was a hundred of us, but thirty of us in their end and they shit themselves! We went back to the pubs and they were empty. Making our way to the station, we recognised one of them from in the Kop and we chased him and cornered him - he was shitting himself. He tried to make out he was nothing to do with their firm and he was just on his way home. We just told him we weren't going to leather him (or we would have done it by now!) we just wanted to know where their firm was.

Eventually he admitted he was one of them and said that

the boys had all gone home. We just stood there laughing at him, humiliating him, before heading back to the station, pissed off that they had bottled it when it came to the crunch, yet felt brave enough when tooled up at the station and the pub. At the return game at Maine Road, we were outside the ground watching them being escorted in, when the lad who looked like the singer from 'Curiosity Killed The Cat' walked along in the escort. Everyone of us just pissed ourselves laughing at the posing cunt. We followed the escort just laughing at them as they were 'offering us out' behind the safety of the police escort. They were one firm that I just couldn't work out!

*　　　　　*　　　　　*

We didn't play Wednesday for a number of years, so when we met again in 1991, a good number of us travelled across the Pennines on the train at 9.30am. The train was packed and we didn't have a seat and there's no way I was standing all that way so three of us occupied the toilet, locked the door and drank a load of cans the whole way. We were pissing ourselves when every so often people would trying to come in, a queue had formed outside and they were banging on the door while we were sat there getting pissed up!

At Sheffield one of the lads said that Chesterfield were at home to Northampton and, as that was only twenty minutes away on the same train, thirty of us decided to have it. Arriving at Chesterfield, we went in search of a decent boozer near the station to wait for the 'Cobblers'. Whilst waiting I went to the bookies and put a few bets on the dogs and football games that day and whilst watching the dogs, a few more blues also came in and to be honest we forgot all about Northampton.

The next thing a bloke rushes in and locks the door behind him. We could hear a commotion going on outside but couldn't see anything. The bloke said 'don't go out there, it's kicking off with Chesterfield and Northampton fans!' We looked at each other and we knew we wanted out! 'Let us out!', we demanded. The bloke said 'you must be mad, it's chaos out there'. One lad said 'if you don't let us out, we'll knock you out the way. Either way we are going out there.' The bloke moved to one side, opened the door and the split second we were out, it slammed shut behind us.

Fuck me! We were right in the middle of the firing line as pure lads were at it without any dibble in sight. Andy was the first to be smacked as it was a case of just jumping at the nearest person to you. The next thing we were chasing a small group up a hill as they ran into a churchyard. Andy then stops and says 'we're chasing City fans!' Once those blues realised who we were, they turned round and joined us as we then charged back down the hill at Northampton. On seeing this, some of them backed off leaving those at the front totally exposed and on the end of a hiding. I managed to trip one of them up and just started whacking him all over. He managed to get up and I chased him again. When you are running down hill at full pelt it's hard to stop your self and I remember trying to throw a punch and missing but carrying on and running into these two lads and landing on top of them. I was trying to punch them when someone jumps on top of me and is thumping me on the head shouting 'fuck off you Northampton twats'. It was Tony. I shout back 'Fuck off Tony, it's me, Sully' and he stopped, laughing at the same time.

It was fucking crazy, like a Western with a pile up on the floor. I was just about to crack this lad when someone booted me right in the bollocks. Fuck that hurt! I was just about to go down on my knees when someone grabbed my arm, shouting, 'run, dibble'. Well, it's hard to run when you've just been twatted in the knackers but I had little choice as I limped along with Tony - I was in fucking agony! We dived into a pub and I'm bent double getting my breath back and counting my bollocks. I even went into the toilet and poured cold water on them. Eventually the pain eased and I returned to the bar. There was a drink waiting for me and of course everyone thought it was fucking hilarious. I have to admit that eventually I came to see the funny side, it's funny how everyone else thinks a kick in the bollocks is a laughing matter. I got my revenge, reminding the rest that me, Andy and Tony had legged the lot of them into the graveyard as they were that shit scared of us! That soon shut them up! The next thing is, one of our lads owns up to kicking me in the bollocks! He said he didn't look up, just lashed out. Everyone was killing themselves laughing. The whole episode had been confusing from start to finish as the bloke in the bookies had said it was Chesterfield v Northampton, when it was really City v Northampton!

By now it was gone 2pm so we made our way back to the station to get the next train to Sheffield. Somehow we ended up on the wrong train and didn't get to the ground until after half time so we went in a pub and waited until the gates opened and we could get in for free. On the final whistle, we ran on the pitch and picked up our goalkeeper Tony Coton and carried him off shoulder high. He couldn't believe it – at this point we didn't even know what the score was! Someone told us we'd won 1-0 and we just went wild on the pitch as we put Coton down and avoided the chasing stewards, taking the piss out of them.

On the way back to the station, someone suggested going back to Chesterfield and a handful of us did just that. We ended up going to the same pub but this time there were doormen at the front. We got talking to them and they told us there had been trouble for most of the day and they were laughing when we told them we knew that as it was us that had been involved! We ended up meeting a City fan from Chesterfield who knew a few of their lads and he introduced us to them. They said the cops had put Northampton on a train so they didn't think anything would kick off in the town that night. This proved to be right so after a few more drinks, we decided to get the rattler home. On the way to the station we passed a posh hotel and we could see everyone suited up and somehow we got invited in – it was a wedding – and we didn't even know anyone there! We walked around the tables, there was champagne and wine everywhere. Martin picked up a bottle of bubbly and we sat there drinking it. The next thing this girl comes over and asks me if I'd like to dance with her mate? She takes me over and before I know it I'm on the dance floor. A few minutes later, Andy comes over saying the others have gone and taken Martin as he had just puked up all over the table and floor! Me and Andy decide to stay till the end, we reckoned we were definitely on a promise later on.

The two of us left the hotel with the two girls and got a taxi back to one of their houses. Me and Andy kept on winking at each other, congratulating each other on what was about to happen. We got to the door, but we were then given the big brush off and to make matters worse, the taxi fucked off too! We had no idea where we were or in which direction to go. We began walking when Andy stops and says 'fuck this, I don't care if they have boyfriends or whatever, I'm going back'. We walked back and Andy's knocking on the door. This old bloke opens it and I nearly fell through it as I was just leaning against it and the next thing I remember is waking up in a police cell and not being able to remember what we'd done.

The copper told us what had happened and how we'd been abusive to the bloke and his wife. He added that Andy was in the next cell and he had also had a pop at the arresting officer. I asked if we were to apologise to the couple, would they forget it? He said they had already made a statement and we would be bailed in thirty minutes after being charged. I couldn't believe it! I just got back on my mat and went back to sleep. Then I was awoken by a copper telling me I had been charged and that I had to follow him. I went through to the desk where Andy was waiting. He read the charge to us, as two coppers in a side room were laughing at us. The officer asked if we had anything to say. We said 'no' and signed the papers. 'Right lads', he said, 'see you in court on Wednesday, Chesterfield Magistrates'.

We were outside the police station replacing our shoelaces when we tried to piece together what had happened. Andy recalled knocking on the door and then he thought we'd walked away. I don't remember anything other than getting out of the taxi and nearly falling through the door as it opened. We got the train home and arranged to meet the next day in town to see our brief. We tried to tell him all we could remember and gave him our brief sheets. He arranged to meet us at the court in Chesterfield on the Wednesday.

On the day itself, we were called through and the place was packed. The prosecution asked us how we pleaded and we both said guilty, then the details were relayed about the night's events by the clerk.

'The police received a phone call from a women saying that two young men were knocking on their door, asking her husband to see two girls, neither of whom lived at the address. The husband was trying to explain this when one of the young men said 'don't worry, we wont be long, you can have them back when we've shagged them.' The courtroom silence was broken by people struggling to contain their laughter - we looked at one another in embarrassment.

The clerk continued: 'When the women came down the stairs to support her husband, one of the young men said 'That's not one of them, but she'll do'.' Well, that was it - forget trying to laugh discretely, the whole room was in uproar. The judge adjourned the case for twenty minutes. We looked at each other and even our brief was smirking, even the judge seemed to be pissing himself as he headed for his chambers!

We went to get a drink from the café and these young women with their mums were laughing when they saw us. They came up and apologised but said they couldn't help it when the clerk read the charge sheet. One of them looked at Andy and said 'you're not bad looking, you can shag me anytime – I promise my mam won't report you to the police'. That was it, everyone in the café just cracked up laughing. Andy failed to see the humour 'look, it's not funny!' and everyone was apologetic but the more they tried not to laugh, the more they laughed. Even our brief said he couldn't wait to tell the girls back in his office, one of whom knew me. Back in court we ended up with a £150 fine and believe me, I've never moved so quickly out of court in my life!

I thought I'd be safe from this back home but a few nights later I was in the Lion & Lamb in Blackley when a group of girls walked up to me and very loudly told the whole pub what had happened and everyone started up again, taking the piss. Even in the Bull's Head in Piccadilly before the next game, the blue from Chesterfield came in and handed around photocopied news cuttings detailing the case – we just couldn't live it down, everyone was ripping into us.

In 1999 City played Chesterfield away in the league in what was the old Third division. Andy and I couldn't go – the memories of our previous visit was still too clear in our minds and one we wont ever forget!

MICKEYS

I've always had a soft spot for scousers. Maybe it's because I went to live in Liverpool with my auntie when I was a kid. Manchester and Liverpool have always been great rivals. The scousers never forgave Manchester for building the ship canal – bypassing the port of Liverpool and causing them to lay people off work. Today's rivalry isn't so much political but on the football field and in the music scene. It is well documented that Liverpool fans were the first abroad to go robbing as firms – mainly as they were always in Europe in the late 70's/early 80's where as City & United were not.

However, I knew Mancs who also went to Europe on the rob at the same time, going as individuals - they just didn't go around bragging about it. A few mates lived in North Manchester, blues and Reds, who used to travel to watch Liverpool in Europe – they never went to the games, nor were they hooligans, they were grafters and used the cover of Liverpool's support to rob as much as they could and brought back the fashionable clothes of the day. scousers like to believe that they were the first to wear Lacoste and their European adventures are usually used as evidence. They fail to mention the Mancs who also used to bring back gear from the continent - the scousers that travelled know the script, there were more than Scouse accents on those trips.

So much crap has been written by so called hooligans and most of it is pony. Take West Ham's ICF: they claimed to be wearing Stone Island jumpers and Burberry in 1979. Yet there are pictures of them all wearing fucking donkey jackets, V-necked jumpers and sporting long hair in pictures from that era. The cockneys were years behind the Mancs and scousers on the fashion front. This is fact.

However, one fashion item that all scousers seemed to carry – much to their shame – was the Stanley Knife. Fans today go on about Turkish fans carrying blades but the mickeys were doing it several decades ago. On their away trips legend has it that they would have a collection on the coach and whoever stabbed the most Mancs won the pot. In my eyes this is a shithouse trick. It is one thing kicking the shit out of an opposition fan but a completely different thing to scar someone for life. To me, football hooliganism meant fighting with your hands, head, fists and, if you were on the back foot, whatever there was around you to use. Purposely taking a knife was taking this to a different level and it is the option of a coward.

I've often been asked which firm I thought was the better of the scouse firms and I have to say Everton gets the nod. They were one mob we always looked out for as they were quite dangerous because of the reputations of their blade carrying members. They were called the 'Oxo Boys' – a sinister name implying if they caught you, they played noughts and crosses on your skin.

One evening game in 1983, Everton bought a big mob down. There was a lot of action outside the ground, running battles and brief skirmishes - as the dibble tried to break one fight up, another would start elsewhere, then Everton made a big mistake. Rather than go in the away end, they went into the Platt Lane stand behind the goal. This is the stand with wooden benches and usually where the older fans and Junior blues went as they were the cheapest seats. Normally we would have gone onto the Kippax Terrace but we saw where the mickeys went and sent a few scouts ahead to see where they had congregated. They had assumed we would go onto the Kippax but they couldn't have been more wrong. They went to the far corner of the Platt Lane stand and stayed at the front. We all went up the staircases at the back of the stand and sat at the back directly behind them.

During the first few minutes Everton scored and the daft twats jumped up and down, celebrating wildly - they may as well have got the tannoy to announce where they were in the ground! The next thing, Mikey led the charged from the back, down the aisles and over the bench seats and right into them. The stupid cunts were still looking at what was happening on the pitch rather than what was coming up behind and we just whacked them - the poor bastards got leathered. They were trying to climb up the fencing to escape onto the pitch but we kept pulling them down off the fence. They also got a taste of their own medicine as a few blues carried knives that night and were slashing at them indiscriminately. Normally I wouldn't condone that but against the mickeys you had to fight fire with fire – they would cut you up at their place regardless... The police were on the other side of the fence and took a while to get into the stand, which meant we could completely spank the Toffee twats.

Personally I thought Everton were on their own that night, by that I mean it wasn't uncommon for both Liverpool and Everton to join together for the big games, especially those in Manchester. That's the difference between the two cities and again emphasises their 'scousers against the world' mentality. The thought of City and United joining together on regular occasions is unthinkable.

Another score was supposed to be settled that night as two rival factions of City fans – National Front and black fans from Moss Side were due to clash. This put me in a predicament as a large number of the NF firm came from Blackley and I had grown up with them while I hung around with many of the black lads from Moss Side. I wanted nothing to do with it. Fortunately, the fight never took place although the animosity between the two groups continued for a long time afterwards.

*   *   *

One Scouse trick was to arrive quite early in the morning so they could do a bit of 'shopping', return home with the loot and come back for the game! On one occasion we were in the Arndale double early as we were expecting them to arrive that morning. There were about twenty of us there when a mob of about the same number walked past us with sports bags. We looked at them but they just carried on past us. 'They're mickeys,' I said, 'check their feet, they're wearing Kickers,' our trademark footwear was Adidas Samba. Then, two other lads wearing Kickers appeared behind them but I knew them – a lad from Moston and another from Blackley. They gave a signal to keep our distance, I clocked it and followed loosely behind.

Well, what happened next I had not seen before nor since. It was like watching a film. They stopped outside this jewellers and threw these little magnets at the window that cracked the glass, then they waded in, grabbing whatever they could, they didn't give a fuck - they emptied the window display and stuffed the goods in the bags. I could see the two lads from Moston and Blackley joining in as if they were one of the gang. There was no noise, other than the windows going in - it was a precision job and then they were off running straight towards us! One or two tried to put up a fight but we just went for the lads with the bags and eventually they realised that too and simply dropped the bags and legged it – thanks very much, we'll collect the loot!

On another occasion, a big mob from Everton rampaged down the fashionable shops on King Street. They bricked the windows and made off with the clothes. You had people running to get away with the loot and others running to get away from the looters, even shop assistants wanted to get out of the way! Of course, there is always one hero – one shop worker tried to put up a fight, the next thing he was running into the street with blood gushing from his arm. These kind of stunts were pulled up and down the country by Mancs and scousers, including one on a Friday morning in Liverpool. We were playing Everton the next day but decided to catch them out and go a day early. We travelled down in cars and pulled up outside the shops - four lads ran straight into the shops and straight back into the cars and off again. There were four cars in total and we did both sides of two streets within a matter of minutes and then back down the M62 with a carful of goodies.

*   *   *

The games at Anfield and Goodison were dodgy as fuck to go to and you needed eyes in the back of your head to survive. You knew that they would be waiting for you and you also knew that their dibble didn't give a fuck either - they hated us as much as Liverpool and Everton's fans did! One time in 1982 we got off the train at Lime Street and the police said, 'you're on your own, Goodison is that way lads, start walking!' Fuck me, it was like having a death warrant signed! You'd make your way to the ground and the scousers were crossing over the road and trying to mingle with you, waiting to greet you with their 'Uncle Stanley'.

We came out of Lime Street to receive a charming welcome of bricks, bottles and coins. There were about one hundred of us and we ended up getting back into the station near one of the platforms. We managed to regroup but we knew we were heavily out-numbered. One lad said that if we stayed where we were we were dead so we may as well just go for them. Within seconds it was mad, they came at us from all angles. Then one lad spots a load of trolleys next to the platform and we charged at them down the platform and they all jumped out of the way. This gave us a few seconds to get out of the station – but we still had to get to the ground! It was scary as fuck. We stuck together and carried on walking, some lads still had the trolleys to protect them and keep enough distance between them and the mickeys to avoid getting stabbed.

The next thing is the dibble had had enough and rounded us up and put us up against a wall. They gave us two choices – we either got on a bus or we walked on our own to the ground - it was Hobson's fucking choice. There was absolutely no way we were going to make it on our own to Goodison without getting carved up – again it would be like a scene from The Warriors only we would never have made it to the end! We had been there before when there were a load of us and we still shat ourselves. So we took the bus and the dibble made sure that Everton didn't join us for the ride. The bus was driving slowly through the traffic and the mickeys just followed it. We went upstairs, and ripped the seats out in preparation for what was to come next. We could hear the dibble telling the driver not to stop or let anyone on regardless. Just in case they did, we blocked up the stairs with the seats. We looked at each other, trying to gear each other up, knowing it would be a miracle if we came out of this unscathed. There were hundreds of scousers following the bus, looking at us and running a finger across their throats but somehow we made it to Stanley Park without the bus getting bricked.

Just as we thought we'd made it, we heard a smash of a downstairs window, as we turned the corner towards the ground and the bus crashed into a wall – the doors opened and the bus was surrounded by mickeys piling onto the bus. The top windows were put in and everyone was on the floor covering from the shower of glass. We got up and threw seats out of the open windows onto the mickeys below and then flung more seats down the stairwell, blocking their way up. A good number of us had cuts to the head from flying glass and bricks as more and more mickeys tried to get upstairs but the bricks they had used to smash our windows were now used against them as they tried to climb up - it was pretty desperate as we held them back. At one point a scaffolding pole was thrown like a javelin at us and went through a window – but again we were able to use that to keep the scousers at bay. We were all high on adrenalin – thirty of us had got on the train that morning knowing we were likely to be up against it, but no one had backed down and here we were fighting for our lives.

It seemed like ages before the dibble got things under control. Even as they took us off the bus and walked us to the ground the mickeys were seething that they couldn't get at us as much as they tried. We walked through the turnstile with a great sense of pride and relief! Even now, over twenty years later, my hand is shaking writing this as I remember the events of that day which was definitely one of the scariest I've faced.

*   *   *

On another occasion, we were playing at Anfield and I bumped into a lad I recognised from years back with the Cool Cats, he'd been grafting in Austria with a few other lads and he invited me to go over with him on his next trip - but that's a different story for a different book! We all caught the train at Victoria and before long we were at Lime Street. We had caught a later train than the main mob but the dibble were still waiting for us and wanting to put us all on a bus. We carried on walking past them and out of the station - it was quite a surprise that nothing of any note happened on the way to the ground – but as I said, Everton had a much more rated crew than their red rivals. After the game we were again pushed onto buses but again we were up for walking. The dibble tried their best to get us on the buses and started to get a bit heavy-handed and a battle ensued. One uniform was smacked against a bus cracking his head in the process which then gave the other dibble an excuse to wade in. They chased us away from the ground and I was at the front with Colin. We turned a corner and there were a few Liverpool fans who fancied their chances but soon regretted it as we leathered them all over the street - fists and boots laying into them. They managed to back off as the dibble caught up with us and they were trying to nick lads and drag them away.

The City buses were now passing by and a good handful of blues managed to get off and give us a helping hand. At one point we split into two – one lot chasing and slapping the mickeys through Stanley Park and the other lot dealing with the dibble. The mickeys thought we'd back off but we just went for them as they pelted us with what ever they could find. They hid behind trees and walls but we just continued to steam into them. They were lost in their own backyard! Finally we regrouped and made our way back to the station, laughing all the way! It was a piss poor show from Liverpool – Everton would never have let us do that to them on their own patch. In a way, Everton were like City – shite football team living in the shadows of more illustrious neighbours but what they lacked on the pitch, their fans more than made up for on the streets.

The cockneys go on about the ICF and the Head Hunters, but I don't give a fuck about them or what they think, to me, Everton were one of the top firms in the country. It was strange how we never rated Liverpool, yet talk to United fans and they say the opposite – they always had a rougher time of it at Anfield than at Goodison. Why was it that they couldn't be arsed bothering with us to the same degree?

UNITED V LIVERPOOL - MAINE ROAD - 1985

The 1984-85 season was perhaps the worst ever for full-on football violence. When United played Liverpool in the FA Cup semi-final at Goodison there had been a nice welcoming party for the United fans. The replay was a chance for revenge and also for City to defend their own patch. There were rumours of a joint City – United firm and leaflets were being distributed around certain pubs on the nights leading up to the game. This was then reported in the *Manchester Evening News*, which if anything, just advertised it even more! I got a phone call on the afternoon of the game telling me to meet in the Spinners in Moss Side. Just before I walked in, I bumped into two other blues and we walked in together. Fuck me, it was like the out of town bandit walking into a saloon bar in a Western. The atmosphere was cut dead at that moment, then someone said 'well, well, it's the bluenoses – where's the rest of you?'.

I managed to clock a few faces I recognised John, Clinton, Benny and Sam – who all lived near me and whom I knew. They told us not to worry as we were with them now. We didn't want to stay but we also didn't want to walk out and lose face either. Of course, there is always one clever dick who makes a snide comment about us being there but one of the reds we were with jumped in and told them to cut it out. When another comment was made, I said 'look, there's three of us, if anyone wants to have a go, come on, lets have it, if not, shut the fuck up'. Then, amazingly, the four reds stuck up for us again, saying if anyone wanted to have a pop at us, they had to have a pop at them too. That shut any other reds up from saying anything.

As we left the pub, it felt like we were leading their crew – we knew the side streets and alleyways better than them for a start and eventually we came across a large mob being escorted towards the ground. John said 'right, it's now or never' and we steamed into them, scattering them from the larger group and chasing them down the alleyways. They were on the receiving end of it good and proper, falling down like flies, getting kicked and smacked. One lad was cracked on the head with a bottle – blood came pouring out of his head. I had blood on my jeans and Clint had it all over his shoes. The reds went into the ground just before the game started while we waited outside for the mickeys to come out at the end. We were soon joined by a young City firm who were also looking for some after game action. There were only about fifteen of them but they were game as fuck. It wasn't long after the final whistle when we were chasing the mickeys again through the back streets of Moss Side and battering them. The young blues were certainly earning their spurs that night. I then bumped into John, Benny and Sam. 'Where's Clinton?' I asked. Apparently he'd been nicked before the game at the back of the Kippax. He'd queued up with the scousers to get in their end and then just went wild, lashing out in the queue. Ignoring the fact that they were reds, I can tell you now, if I wanted a few handy lads to fight with knowing they would stand and not run, then I'd have those four with me every time. There was definitely a mutual respect for each other's firms at that time.

The year before Liverpool and Everton had played at Maine Road in the League Cup final replay after drawing at Wembley. Over fifty thousand mickeys in Moss Side – an opportunity not to be missed! There was about twenty of us walking towards the ground and we were just picking them off as we went along. We came across a group of around thirty Everton and legged them down the road, which turned out to be a big mistake! As we turned the corner, there was a huge mob there and within seconds the cry had gone out 'Mancs'. It didn't need a committee meeting between us to work out our next step as we just fucking legged it.

Fuck me, they legged us everywhere. This was basically a home game for both Everton and Liverpool seeing as they had been given over 25,000 tickets each. Just when you thought you'd escaped them, we bumped into another mob and off we'd go again on our toes. Eventually we had enough and rather than run around Moss Side we ended up in the Union pub in Ardwick, near the Apollo Theatre. Some lads wanted to carry on, saying the mickeys were taking the piss on our patch. I argued back that they weren't taking the piss out of us – it wasn't a City game but a Scouse derby and we had no chance against 50,000 of the cunts!

Munichs

'In all the time I was going to football, not once did they [City] call it on with us before the game. They never said 'We are meeting here, where are you meeting, we'll come and get you'. They always kept schtum. We'd end up running around Fallowfield or wherever, trying to find them, and they'd be hiding. Everyone knows where we meet but City never come to attack us there. They want to pick people off on their own.'

RED ARMY GENERAL

What a load of bollocks... As you would expect, I've had many a battle with the munichs down the years. In pubs, inside and near the grounds, in fields – you name it, we've had it with them! I actually have a fair bit of respect for their firm even though I hate them with a passion. As already mentioned, I knew a good number of them, especially those from the north Manchester area. However, I couldn't understand the so called 'Red Army General' that wrote the above, claiming we were hiding from them. When I recall battles with the reds, they always say 'you remember that fight in the Sawyers Arms' or such and such a place. The thing that annoys me is every hooligan knows he is talking bullshit but those fans not into fighting will read it and, as it is in print, will take it as the gospel truth. Next he'll be telling us that during the 5-1 game at Maine Road in 1989, it was United fans who smacked their own in the North Stand at the beginning of the game? Those reds getting tangoed had to climb over the fencing to prevent getting a further hiding, resulting in the game being temporarily suspended. Well it couldn't have been City fans leathering them could it? After all, according to him, we were still hiding in the toilets in a pub in Fallowfield! The fact is United were well and truly fucked that day – both on and off the pitch!

The first fight I ever had with the munichs was in the late 70s. I was about fifteen and couldn't sleep the night before. In the morning when I woke up, I was punching the fuck out of my pillow to psyche myself up. I made my way to the Brunswick pub just down from Piccadilly station Approach. I felt ten feet tall, invincible, nothing could stop me that day. I was the youngest there and the others had been geeing me up all week, gearing me up for the battle ahead. I was buzzing like never before. Once in the Brunswick, the crew were split as to what the plan of action should be. Then Donald came in and demanded the arguing stop and we would all go down to the ground together, he asked for people to lead from the front and everyone would follow them. One lad said he had heard that United were meeting up in Hulme but that would have been just one firm. There were quite a few different firms – one from Miles Platting known as The Grey Mare and a couple of out of town crews including the Cockney Reds. Even though the game was at Old Trafford, we headed for the Clarence on Wilmslow Road, going through the back streets to avoid the dibble as we knew they'd be out looking for us. We were met at the Clarence by a much bigger mob and decided to go in search of the bastards in the direction of Hulme. We then heard they were in the Henry Royce pub – named after one of the blokes who made the Rolls-Royce car as their first factory was in Hulme – and made our way there as quickly and as inconspicuously as possible, we split into two groups going in different directions. I went with Donald and as we got nearer to the pub I saw his face change, like a wild animal about to go in for the kill. His face was focused and eyes alert as he stalked his prey.

Donald sent a scout in first. It was the usual trick, send one lad in to check out the situation and report back with all the info we needed. He came back and confirmed the place was full of munichs. As the other crew arrived, we surrounded the pub and ambushed it, putting the windows in with bricks, some of us even got inside via the back exit – the reds had no chance and they no idea what had hit them, they were cowering under the tables and those that didn't either got hit by flying glass or flying fists! At one point we backed off to let them come out but they wouldn't leave the sanctuary of the pub, so we headed back to the Claremont and then the Beehive both on Claremont Road. We went there as we thought they would assume we were heading off towards Old Trafford, rather than back towards Maine Road. This one lad told me they had done this many a time, to confuse the reds and the dibble who would both be looking for us nearer the ground. We were just about to set off when it was decided to leave it a bit longer so we had another thirty minutes in the pub and then made our way to OT.

Donald kept psyching us up, telling us we could do them today as long as we stuck together. I looked around, it seemed like hundreds of us walking together, it was a hell of a sight for a fifteen year old to be a part of. You could hear Donald telling everyone 'We've got to do these bastards today' and you could see the hate in his eyes. Pretty much everyone was there that day, we all went together and the older lot were all saying 'this is the one boys, this is the one.' They were telling us how in the past the munichs had the upper hand on us, but 'that was going to change today'.

As we got closer to the ground, Donald told us that if we got split up, to meet at the Grove pub on the Hulme/Old Trafford border about fifteen minutes from the ground. We made our way round to the back of the cricket ground and up along Warwick Road as we figured they'd be around the Trafford. We decided to split up but to keep in touching distance with each other. As we carried on walking, someone said 'everyone quiet, what's that?' We all turned around and there was a mob of around sixty coming towards us - we stood there and then realised they were City fans! They were a firm that we knew and they would never join up with us as they had leanings towards the NF and as we had lots of Black lads running with us - they didn't want to know.

There was nothing happening on Chester Road so we carried on and they were waiting for us on the bridge just by the forecourt. They crossed over towards us, bouncing like fuck gesturing for us to have a pop. We were well up for it and we were about to strike when from behind us, the other firm came out in front of us and steamed in, whacking them all over the place. The munichs were running away and even tried to regroup but it wasn't happening for them. It was like this before and after the game, they were out-fought and out-thought in all they tried to do. Wherever they went, they got smacked. Later we were in the city centre and couldn't find one munich, the Cockney Reds were nowhere to be seen. Then we heard that the Cockney Reds had been fighting in a pub against the Salford reds! We celebrated in Brannigans – City took a point on the pitch and we got a great result off it – our name and reputation was well known around Old Trafford now!

The following day Donald got a phone call from Sam, the leader of the Cockney Reds and he was telling Donald how he was amazed that we had got such a good firm together and that we had gone to OT and run them all over the place. He confirmed that they had been in a battle with Salford after the game and it had not gone well and a few of them received a good hiding. Donald tried to offer his sympathies but the reality was he couldn't give a fuck about the Cockney wanker and was just gutted it wasn't us that had leathered the bastards!

*   *   *

A few years later, at the 1984 home game, with the Mayne Line, we knew they would try and have a pop on the forecourt after the game but we were well prepared, leaving just before the end but they never showed. We decided to spread ourselves around the back of the Kippax, waiting for them to leave the ground but again, there was a no-show. Fuck knows how they got out of the ground and Moss Side that day without being spotted but the bastards did. We sent scouts to all the pubs in the area and they all came back with nothing to report. We headed into town and by 10pm some of the lads were ready to go when all of a sudden we spotted a mob walking across Piccadilly gardens. We ran over, chanting 'MCFC Mayne Line' As they turned around to see us, some of them came forward but then when they realised that half of their firm had done one, they legged it pretty quickly. We followed them but they managed to lose us, so we made our way back towards the Brunswick – where who should we bump into but the Cockney Reds making their way to get the last train home!

I remember Donald fronting Sam, 'come on, just me and you, no one else, lets have it now'. The offer was declined. They also had an Asian lad with them who used to carry an umbrella with a sharpened end. He was always immaculately dressed in Farrah pants, a V-neck jumper with a Polo neck and shoes – never trainers. They simply didn't want any bother so we chased them up the station approach road and onto the platform and slapped them around until the dibble came and got to grips with it, they couldn't get away from us as punches and kicks were raining down on them on the platforms. I remember saying to one lad about the number of times we played United and only ever ended up fighting the Cockney Reds. This was supposed to be about City v United, Mancs v Salford/Stretford or other local areas. The Cockney Reds were a joke. All them clubs to support in London and they go and chose to support a team 200 miles north!

*   *   *

THE GREY MARE REDS

I moved from Blackley to Collyhurst in 1991 and it was definitely a red area, though thankfully quite a few more blues live there now. At that time, over the other side of Oldham Road on Varley Street in Miles Platting, was a pub that was very much a red stronghold - The Grey Mare. It was only a small pub and everyone in there knew each other. A bit of a firm developed from there and they were very tight. They always showed their faces at derby day and headed for the forecourt outside Maine Road looking for action.

They were a strange lot, appearing to act on their own. They also became notorious for their 'Monday Club' drinking sessions. On a regular basis they would all take a Monday off work (those who were working anyway!) and make their way into the city centre, usually the pubs along Oldham Street, where they spent the day drinking. It began with a handful of them but soon grew to large numbers, sometimes over forty. It didn't take long before trouble occurred and they were banned from all city centre pubs. They then moved onto drinking at all the pubs along Moston Lane in Moston before being banned there too. The *Manchester Evening News* gave them a full page feature, interviewing the main players in a sympathetic article. A few of them were amongst the original gang to go abroad on the rob in the late 70's.

There was one lad in Collyhurst among the Monday Club who I got to know called Paul - who told me that they had a few run ins with the Cockney Reds. Apparently the Cockney Reds had turned on them a couple of times at away games in London and as a result there was bad blood between them. The Grey Mare is long gone now, one of many pubs in north Manchester to disappear over the last decade, though the memory of the Monday Club and their firm remains firmly in my mind.

*   *   *

Another time we clashed with the munichs when we were all out on a Saturday night in town and after we'd had a few, we decided to have a final drink in Brannigan's and call it a night. There were around thirty of us and we thought we'd never get in together so we went along in smaller numbers. They must have had new bouncers on the door as we all got in no problem. As we entered, straight away we could see it was full of munichs. Fuck me it was heaving with the cunts, but we carried on towards the bar. Next thing the whole pub is looking at us and Roy turns and says 'Fuck me, them over there... Cockney Reds'. He wasn't wrong either and big bastards they were too. These flash bastards weren't drinking pints but champagne and shorts.

Roy and Chalkie continued to the bar and we followed right behind them. Roy turned around to say something but as he did a pint glass came flying over, missing us but hitting a girl in the face. That was it - we just ran at them, grabbing whatever was on the tables as we went – glasses, bottles, ash-trays – and bombarded them. Of course, they were doing the same to us. We were now both at the bar just throwing shit at each other but we got the upper hand when we got behind the bar first and this gave us much more ammunition. The bar staff legged it and locked themselves in a side room. One red tried to get over the bar and was whacked on the face with a beer tray. I looked across at Chalkie who was on the receiving end of about six pairs of trainers. One of the attackers had picked up a bar stool and was about to hit Chalkie with it when Roy appeared with a bottle in each hand and smashed one in the face of the lad with the stool and cracked another lad over the head with the other one. That was my cue to join in and help Chalkie, so I jumped the bar and from out of nowhere I was hit on the head by a bottle. Despite the agony I kept on going, they were backing off and making for the door. As I got outside I came over all dizzy, I recall seeing the dibble arrive in a van but the next thing I knew I was in a hospital bed with Chalkie two beds up from me. I didn't even know what day it was!

The dibble came and questioned us but it was the usual 'I was in there for a quiet drink officer, I don't remember anything else'. They were snapping at me and Chalkie, telling us there was a lad in another ward on a life support machine in a bad way. We overheard the police say the lad was from London – Chalkie just looked at me, smiled and put his thumbs up. I tried to do the same but as I moved my head, it was pounding. The nurse came, got the needle out and told me it wouldn't hurt. Fuck me, she stuck it right up my arse and fuck me it hurt - you should have seen the size of it! I ended up fainting! When I woke up, the nurse said I'd been asleep all day and night. It was now 11am, Chalkie said that the lads had been round to see us but they left me alone as I was out of it. They were also questioned when they turned up but they said nothing other than we were enjoying a drink together when we were attacked.

The doctor came round and after examining us both he said we had to stay in for another day. When we finally got to leave we were stopped by the boys in blue, they wanted to question us. 'Cant this wait a day or two', we asked, 'we're not really up to it at the moment'. 'No it can't wait' we were told and we were taken to a police station and put in separate cells for a couple of hours.

Eventually they came for me and took me to an interview room.

Police: 'OK Mr Sullivan, we've interviewed a few of your

mates and they told us what happened'.

Me: 'Well you don't need to interview me now then do you?'

Plod: 'All right Sullivan you cocky twat'

Me: 'I'm not being called a cocky twat, you were the ones that came out with that statement.'

That hit them and they backed off.

Officer Dibble: 'We've looked at your record, you have previous for football hooliganism, theft and assaults on police officers. You've been up to quite a lot haven't you?'

Me: 'Behave yourselves, you're taking the piss'

Officer: 'No Mr Sullivan we're not, now look you stupid twat'

Me: 'Oh I'm a stupid twat now? That'll sound good on the tape'

Police: 'Actually it won't – we've not started the tape yet. Look, all we want to know is what happened that night, there are two lads still in hospital in a bad way.'

They then switched the recording on and began in the usual way of introducing everyone present in the room and then with the following statement:

We received a call at 10.30pm saying the there was a disturbance inside Brannigans and as we arrived it had spilled outside onto the street and we made a number of arrests. What is your story of the nights events?

I looked at them and shrugged my shoulders.

'I cant remember too much, I was in there having a drink, then I was hit on the head by a bottle and I wake up in hospital with a nurse sticking a great big needle up my arse!'

They kept repeating the question over and over again and eventually stopped the tape. I demanded that if they were to continue then I wanted to see my brief. They took me back to the cell and called the brief – obviously not doing so in any great rush. He arrived at midnight. I asked him if Chalkie was still being held and he said that he was. I made sure the brief went to see him as well. They kept bringing us back into the room to ask the same questions throughout the early hours but we still gave them the same reply. Finally at 8am we were released and bailed to appear in two week's time with a couple of other lads they had nabbed on the night. It went on for ages, we kept going back, being asked the same questions and giving the same replies, until after about two months they dropped the investigation.

Did it put me off continuing to fight at matches? Did it fuck. It was all I knew what to do other than graft. My life was robbing Monday to Friday and fighting on a Saturday. Sunday – as the good Lord has decreed - is a day of rest! Of course, nowadays, football on Sky TV and Sunday shopping has put paid to that day of rest but that's progress for you!

*   *   *

On another occasion, again in the 80s, we were outside the Cypress Tavern on Princess Street. They were inside and we were on our way in. We then made a big mistake in letting them out. This is fine if you know there are more of you than them, otherwise you end up being chased around town. When you are the firm having a go from the outside, you always look larger than you really are because they don't know how many more are behind you. Why give them the opportunity to gain the upper hand? We had a toe-to-toe on the street and one United fan was stabbed and I ended up with a black eye. I was kicking this one red whilst he was on his knees when a mate of his cracked me in the face from the side. The dibble came and separated us. One red had been stabbed and a blue wrongly ended up in Strangeways as a result.

Anyway, a couple of years later we played the red bastards again and after the game we were in the Bowling Green pub with no sign of any reds. We kept hearing the same shit that they were on their way or were nearby but nothing happened. People were getting angry and started arguing among each other, getting on each other's nerves. One of the older lads smacked a younger lad, which was out of order. There was no leadership or direction - lads were just doing their own thing which is a recipe for disaster. Some had had enough and started to drift off – you knew who they were, the same usual suspects every time who talked the talk but failed to walk the walk. If you are going to turn up then you have to stick it out and stay together and don't drop your guard or turn on your own. I grew up alongside many of these lads and you could trust them with your life, they were like family and whatever happened we stuck together. A few lads felt let down by what went on that night.

The City anthem, *The Boys In Blue* contains the lines 'Even if we're playing down at Maine Road, or if we play a million miles away, we'll always have our loyal fans behind us, to cheer us on our way.' That is followed by 'Even in another generation, when other lads have come to take our place, we'll carry on the glory of the City…' That is exactly how many of us feel. We are the loyal fans behind the club and within a few years another generation of fans will come through the ranks and take our place and fight the Blue cause against United and everyone else, so to see blues fighting among themselves was a disappointment to say the least.

Eventually the munichs turned up. One blue had been discretely following them, overtaken them via the side streets and told us what was going on. What followed next was a fucking joke. Three lads from Blackley and one from Levenshulme ran out, urging the others to follow. Some came, some didn't. We should have demanded that everyone come out and stand together waiting to fight but it never happened. I saw an army of reds run to the traffic lights towards us and I shouted 'they're over here', but as I turned I saw blues fighting amongst themselves to get back into the pub as fast as possible. At that point I couldn't even be bothered with them so I chased this lad down the road and turned a corner right into the middle of the munichs. As I went into them I soon ended up on the deck with feet kicking into me from every possible angle. Then a car came screeching round the corner and driving towards the mob. They moved out of the way and I tried to as well but I couldn't move after the kicking. The car continued right into the middle of them. One ended up flying over the bonnet and onto the road. That's all I recall from the night as the continued kicking I received knocked me unconscious and then once again I woke up in a hospital bed all wired up to a machine.

The lads visited me and we decided that next time we play United we would hand pick a firm of around 60 who we knew we could trust to stand and fight and not run back into the pub!

That night was a turning point, a shock to my system - and I had two weeks in hospital to think about what had happened. We had turned on ourselves, run from the reds and been overrun by them on our own turf. Things had to change, so we planned our revenge at the game at Old Trafford later that season. I could have been killed that night or seriously injured, but all I could focus on was making sure the red bastards paid for that night and I wasn't alone in wanting that to happen.

*   *   *

One of the times we came off worse was one morning, when we were well and truly caught by surprise and believe me, it was a fucking wake up call for us all – I've never seen a mob like that at 10am before, fuck me the munichs must have had good alarm clocks! I arrived at the Whalley pub at around 9.30am - back door job – and we were arriving in dribs and drabs. I was still knackered from the night before as were most of us, numbering around sixty. All of a sudden one of the lads who had been sat outside came in saying 'United are here'. We told him to 'fuck off' telling him to stop winding us up, it was way too early for them to be here. One lad looked out of the window and his jaw dropped to the floor. He picked a bottle up and said 'we're dead'. Fuck me, it was like a military operation, hundreds of them had surrounded the pub and more were coming from across the road as the pub is on a four-way junction.

The next thing we just heard the windows going through. Some blues tried to get out and one lad who did ended up with a broken arm. We tried to pick up a fruit machine and throw it at them through the window but it wouldn't fit through. Thankfully, as it was kicking off, a large number of blues turned up and joined with us so after a short period we were able to stand the red twats off and eventually we legged them back towards Old Trafford. There were running battles here and there and we eventually got the upper hand. It was frightening thinking of what they could have done to us at the Whalley had help not arrived in time.

Of course there has been some myth making surrounding this particular tale. United tend to tell the first half of this story but conveniently forget to tell the second half of what went on that day, when City got the upper hand and spanked the reds all over Old Trafford. What really gets me though, is how they managed to get that far without being spotted in the morning - we could never walk anywhere in groups of twenty or more without being picked up and separated, yet they managed to meet up and make their way to the Whalley in large numbers without the dibble noticing.

For a long time, the munichs thought they were the dogs bollocks around town. We still had a firm, but it was a younger generation coming through and forging their own identity. Sure there were still some of us older lot around – I was knocking around with a group called 'The Beer Monsters', but these younger lads were fair game and made a name for themselves. At one derby game we were in the Millstone on Thomas Street and heard the munichs were nearby in Yates's on High Street, opposite the Arndale. We made our way round there and the young un's were having it out with them on Shudehill, there were red bastards being kicked down Shudehill literally rolling over on the road as cars dodged past – naturally we joined in and gave them a further hiding and for the next few weeks, these new kids on the block were the talk of the town.

A few weeks later we went to Chelsea and they were on the train carrying family saver tickets! Some of them looked as if they were still at junior school but they certainly knew how to cause some damage and before long opposition crews knew there was more to City than the Beer Monsters! At one derby game, we were battling with the Cockney Reds on Piccadilly Approach. We'd had the dibble on our arses all day and finally got a bit of action when the young un's appeared and told us to get out of there as we'd be nicked as the dibble were around the corner. I simply couldn't leave at that point, so I cracked this lad and promptly got arrested. The lad I smacked turned out to be an undercover cop!

That'll do nicely…. 'One year in jail', the judge said and off I went to Kirkham via a short stint in Strangeways and it so happened that my release coincided with another derby at Maine Road - perfect timing!

We met in the Clarence and soon heard that the red bastards

were on their way. We waited and as they approached I went out via the back door to be greeted by a handful of reds who were about to make their way in. There were a good number of us and soon they backed off – all except one who stood his ground and was battered on the spot! We ran around to the front onto Wilmslow Road and United were standing there across the road. We steamed into them lashing out with our fists, feet, slapping and kicking them all over the place, when – as usual – the dibble came to their rescue. We walked away from the area. There was me, Andy and Bren, keeping our heads down walking towards the ground when the dibble ran after us and grabbed us. We managed to break away and leg it but more dibble arrived and they caught the three of us again. Whilst putting us into the back of the meat wagon the bastards cracked my head on the roof of the van and the next thing there is blood everywhere and I'm holding my head in agony. Ben was going mental about it but it did no good, he only ended up with a black eye for his efforts. The usual happened, they kept us in a cell at the station until after the game and let us go without charge which was a relief as I assumed I'd be in the shit having just been released. Perhaps the dibble knew that the injuries we'd received would look bad in court had they pressed charges - let's just say we certainly didn't argue with their decision.

After that we played Chelsea at home, but I just kept a low profile which wasn't a problem as they brought nothing up worth bothering with but this was the day when the young un's really came to the fore. They ran Chelsea all over Moss Side and Rusholme and after that they were the dogs bollocks of City firms. I didn't attend another City game after that for a while... I was nicked again - but not for football violence this time. I was in a pub in Blackley one night and someone sussed out there was plain clothes police in there too. Someone announced this via the DJ's microphone and the next thing all hell let loose. I smacked one copper and made my getaway. The next thing that happened was pretty comical and I certainly never saw it coming. As we bolted for the exit, the dibble had driven a van right up to the doors so we just stumbled into the back of a police van... I turned around to see the doors locked behind us! I was later charged and sent down again for six months - welcome back to Kirkham via Strangeways once more!

I was itching to get out as friends visiting me would tell me how the 'young un's' had now become known as The Guvnors and were really running the show. Apparently United's boys wouldn't even drink in the city centre they were that afraid and tended to drink on the outskirts. I never knew if this was true or just bullshit whilst inside, so on my release I ventured into town one Friday to find out for myself. I ended up in one club where all the Guvnors were and looked around – all I could see were City boys, young and old and not a Munich in sight. More people came into the club and I recognised everyone – again, all blues! Still not convinced, I repeated the same thing the following weekend and the same thing happened. Manchester was a red-free zone come the weekend evenings.

*   *   *

After the Guvnors had ended, there was still battles with the munichs to come. By the early nineties I'd kept my head down and was living in Southampton, but more of that later. I started to knock around with the lads again, as I'd been coming up for home games and meeting up but I was going straight back down to the south coast afterwards. That's the one thing I missed about not being in Manchester – not having a drink with the lads. I guess that was one of the main reasons I returned as I just missed the regular buzz. However, it was clear that things were nowhere near the same. A lot of lads were missing, either on remand or keeping a low profile. The Guvnors and Beer Monsters were no more but there were still a few more lads out there trying to forge a name for themselves, carrying on the City fans tradition of having a credible firm.

By way of an example, after one home game we were in the city centre drinking. Someone mentioned that the munichs were at Arsenal and would be due back in town later on and word was out that they wanted some action. Having been away for so long I was well up for it, to make up for lost time! We all stayed together in the one pub, having a laugh as usual, when two blokes came in to the pub and immediately the atmosphere changed. Everyone clocked them and they came over with a beer each, trying to talk to one or two of us. Someone whispered, 'they're dibble' – everyone was already on edge following Operation Omega so we really didn't need this. We just agreed to say nothing, drink up and move on. But whatever pub we went into, they followed us. Fuck me, how were we supposed to get to Piccadilly and have a rumble with these two clowns on our tails?

In the final pub, John called them both over and had a chat with them about football. Apparently they were City daft and had been following the blues for years. Then the questions began.

'Who scored the winner in the 1976 League Cup final?'

'Don't know'

'What was the score the last time we beat the munichs?' The term munichs really confused them. They didn't know and tried to switch the conversation, but John wouldn't let up.

'Name the current City team?' The idiots couldn't answer that one either. John just looked at them. 'So you claim to be mad City fans and you can't answer three questions, one of which is to name the current team?' Their arses dropped and Brian 'suggested' that they would be better leaving the pub quick style. This they did but what they didn't know at that time is a few of the lads went out the back door and jumped them, giving them a good hiding in the process.

So back to business - we sent a few scouts up to the station and they came back saying the train was delayed by thirty minutes so we went to another pub a bit nearer, had one more drink and made our way to Piccadilly via the back streets. At the station we went up the car park road behind the main approach road and waited for the train to arrive. As it pulled in we were ready, about forty of us and as they came onto the platform, we waited until they got closer and then 'one, two, three, GO!' We ran at them and they ran back onto the platform – some back on to the train, probably to hide in the toilet! They wouldn't budge and eventually the dibble came and tried to get us off the platform and out of the station. In the end we gave up and left – or so they thought! We were hanging around by Dale Street and as they left the station we walked down the approach road and waited for them. BANG! One lad pulled out a hammer and cracked a copper over the head.

Monday's papers were full of it, detailing how City had attacked United and one officer had been hospitalised whilst others were treated for injuries. After that it was a bit of tit for tat as both sets of fans tried to catch each other off guard. It was amazing how all of a sudden, with City's main players out of the equation, the red twats found the bottle to show their faces around the city centre. Before Omega, it had been two years of the blues 'owning' the city centre without any sign of a red!

Eventually the Cypress Tavern closed down so we started going to 'Rosie's Bar' on Fountain Street and, like the Cypress, they played all the Manchester stuff we loved, Stone Roses, Happy Mondays, The Smiths, New Order, James etc. It soon became known as a City pub and I remember Stockport County coming in once and leaving faster than they came in, being chased back to Piccadilly in the process. There was another occasion when Huddersfield played at Bury. We had heard a few of them fancied a Saturday night out in Manchester, so we wanted to give them one they would never forget! We were in a bar near Piccadilly Gardens with a few scouts by the Metrolink stop in the gardens. We thought they might be arriving around 7.30pm but by then they hadn't showed so we assumed it was a false alarm. The next tram was due in in about twenty minutes so we gave it one last chance and sure enough, as it came in we could see the cocky Tyke twats giving it large, singing on the tram. We hid behind the bushes in the gardens and watched them walk right towards us and as they reached 'WALLOP' we just ambushed them. It was the last thing they were expecting and they were caught off guard. We laid into them, and they ran their arses right back to Piccadilly station whilst getting whacked all over. Afterwards we headed back to Rosie's bar to celebrate.

By now more and more City fans came into the pub as word spread around over the following weeks, though some were right fucking nuggets who just thought that by being in there they were the dogs bollocks when all they were was mouthy twats, lots of talk but no walk. On one occasion we thought we'd pile down Deansgate and have it with the munichs who were in

The Moon Under Water pub. We got to Shambles Square where we were met by the friendly neighbourhood dibble, who split us up. I hated that as once you were split up you'd look around and realise you were with lads you either didn't know or who ran at the first sight of trouble! We walked past a pub and a big mob came out and saw us. As per usual, because there were only ten of us and around forty of them, they fancied their chances – had it been ten a piece you wouldn't have seen them for dust.

They came across the road towards us, expecting us to leg it. For once we stood our ground and faced them. As they got closer you could hear them shouting 'come on you blue bastards', so we ran at them which clearly stunned them. We knew the dibble were around the corner but we also knew they would happily stand by and watch us get leathered. We had caused them far more problems down the years than the reds so this was their way of seeking revenge on us. I ended up toe-to-toe with one game fucker. It was like a Rocky movie, exchanging punches with each other but no one going down. There was no kicking – just punching. We started off near the McDonalds and carried on to the cathedral - there was no one else with us, somehow we had been so engrossed in what we were doing we had moved away from everyone else. In the end we were both that fucked and exhausted, we stopped, looked at each other covered in blood – and started laughing together. Then we made our way back separately to our respective pubs. I got a loud cheer when I entered Rosie's bar looking like I'd gone seven rounds with Sylvester Stallone!

On another occasion United had played at Leeds and a few of us had been to a concert in town. We were walking around and I was my usual self, talking loudly about City and the next thing one of the lads says 'Sully, shut the fuck up about City, you're going to get us killed if you carry on like that'. I was so busy going on with myself that I hadn't realised what was going on around us and we were walking towards a mob of about 120 red twats. Thankfully they carried on past us – but where were they heading? 'Rosie's bar', I told the lads we had to get there first to get everyone ready. Some of the others tried to stop me but I had to do it, no way were those cunts going to take the piss out of us. I went around the back streets and as they came towards the bar I ran out and smacked one of them, causing a diversion – the next thing I shouted 'Come on munichs' but I was promptly grabbed by the dibble and put into the back of a van! The van didn't move and I watched out of the window for the next ten minutes as the dibble charged the munichs and finally got rid of them. Then they opened the door to the van and let me go with no charge! A few weeks later Rosie's bar was closed down – again, its licence was revoked after it was claimed that City fans had been causing too much trouble in there.

We moved around to a few other pubs after that, not wanting to draw too much attention and on one occasion a firm from Bolton became easily the most embarrassing I've ever had the displeasure of fighting against! Bolton had been playing at City and we were sat in a pub on the Saturday night. Someone said 'Bolton are outside' and there were a few of them giving it the usual 'come on' and beckoning us out so myself and a couple of lads walked over towards them. They had already started backing off yet continued with the 'come on's'. We looked at each other and continued forward and again they continued to retreat. I said to Karl, 'this is a fucking joke' and we finally ran at them and they did a fast one down the road. Some of the younger lads continued to chase them all the way down to Victoria – I couldn't even be bothered doing that, maybe a few years ago, of course! A bit later, three other Bolton fans came in who I recognised from England games. A few lads were going to start on them but I told them they were OK and to leave them alone. They said they had only come in there because they saw me walking in a few minutes before. I told the what had happened and told them that their firm were an embarrassment!

FAREWELL MAINE ROAD

After years of watching City at Maine Road it was the end of an era in May 2003. I remember walking around the area before the last match with Billy and Leon, recalling all the pubs we'd drunk in, side streets we'd fought in, memorable games we'd watched. I first met Leon in the Whitworth pub on a derby day in 2000 and, as we were being introduced, the dibble appeared from nowhere and started filming us all - only their camera batteries ran out and we stood there taking the piss out of the thick dibble twats embarrassed to fuck and unable to do a thing about it.

A few minutes later, someone called out 'munichs' and off we ran over the road to where about thirty red fuckers were running away around a corner towards a grey van parking up down the road with the engine running. Billy and Leon were leading from the front and just steaming in as we caught the slow runners. At one point I tripped over whilst smacking a munich and got a good kick in the stomach from a blue until he sussed out who I was and helped me back up, apologising to fuck. The red twats now realised that their best chance was getting back in the van and driving off - no chance. Billy & Leon caught the last two trying to get in and they were slapped all over the place, I was trying to drag a third one out of the van and one or two windows were put through but then the dibble came along and saved their skins. They completely got it wrong that day, they should have checked us out before getting out of the van, they would have seen immediately that they were heavily outnumbered and should have left it as that and not shown their faces when they did.

The other thing to mention, is that we actually didn't take liberties with the reds that day, just let them know we were there and not to fuck around with us. Had it been the other way round at Old Trafford, they would have given us their all. Either way, it was some introduction to Billy and Leon! Leon was a tall lad, a genuine Rusholme Ruffian and one you definitely wanted on your side and was a bit of a handy boxer too, well built with a skin head. Billy was a smaller lad but game as fuck from a large and well known family in Burnage.

You may be surprised to see I included memorable games in my memories of the old ground. The usual cliché every time football violence is mentioned is to claim that 'these are not real football fans'. I can tell you now, we are real football fans and we love our football club as much as the fans who don't go along to fight. I have travelled all over the country spending thousands of pounds over the years, standing on freezing cold and wet terraces supporting my team and when City have been stuffed and the home fans are singing 'You're shit, and you know you are', that hurts me as much as anyone else connected with the club. So spare me the platitudes and don't tell me I'm not a real football fan - that's just bollocks.

Anyway with Maine Road on the verge of demolition, there were just a few chances left to make sure the old ground was given a grand send off.

In that final season there had been a strong build up to what was the 'Last Ever Derby Game At Maine Road' in November 2002. A few weeks before, before the Liverpool game, we had met in the Salutation, a small red brick pub set back on the edge of the University campus at the top end of Hulme. It was the first time I'd been in there and after a few minutes a lad came in saying a minibus of scousers had just pulled up outside. Great stuff – this pub was way off limits for the dibble based around the ground. Out we ran, but we were disappointed to see a group of dads and lads get out and ask us for directions. We told them they'd be safe here and walk to the ground, it was about a mile away, but they didn't fancy that so we gave them directions to the ground and told them to ask a policeman where the official parking for away fans was. Who said we didn't have a caring attitude towards away fans! At that point we decided to go down to the ground so we went to my car parked outside the pub. As I was letting the others in, a meat wagon came around the corner and a copper gets out.

'Mr Sullivan do you mind please showing me what you have in your boot?'

'Do you have a warrant?' I asked. He repeated the question, so I told him to 'fuck off unless you have a warrant'. I got out of the car. 'Look there are two other cars parked here along with mine, why are you not asking them to open their boots?'

'You are standing too close to me, do you mind moving away?' the officer replied. So I moved a couple of steps away when his colleague then takes two steps nearer to me. I looked at the second colleague and said 'he's just told me to move away from him, so I did and what do you go and do – move nearer to me, I don't get it'.

'Shut the fuck up or I'll nick you!' he responded.

I was close to snapping now 'You're taking the piss, just coz you're in a kid's outfit that your mam bought you doesn't mean to say you can go around treating people like shit'. One of the lads pulled me away urging me to calm down, but I continued as this copper kept looking at me. 'Do you think I'm scared of you? I've had bigger shits than you'.

The dibble cut in, 'you should listen to your mate before giving it large, he knows we are not joking and that my colleague is doing a PNC on you right now'. We stood there in silence until a voice came over on the radio 'Yes, Mr Sullivan has got a number of convictions for police assaults'. You should have seen his face! In the end he let me go without any further action or demands on looking in my boot and off they went. I looked at my mates who were gob smacked whilst looking back at me. 'Fuck me, I never knew you'd be done for smacking dibble' one of them said. I modestly replied that they were like skittles – knock one down and you can knock them all down!

After the game we were walking back down Wilmslow Road past the student bars and someone came up to us saying there was a group of munichs in The Grafton, City were in The Phoenix. We debated this for a while as United were at Leeds, but we had forgotten their game was a lunchtime kick-off, so off we set for the Phoenix. As we arrived, we could see a load of lads in black coats running towards us. As we got in the dibble were right behind us - fuck me, where did they come from? I made for the side door but they had that blocked off too. Then they grabbed the lads who were outside and pushed them inside, whilst the lads in black coats carried on running past the pub and down the road.

Eventually they let us out in small groups, we didn't know why at first but it soon became clear. They were filming us and were asking us to stand in front of the camera and speak. When it came to me, the copper said 'OK Mr Sullivan, are you still living in Collyhurst?' before I could answer he asked me to tell him my name and where I lived for the camera! I never understood why they did that?

Later that evening I was at someone's house and this twat was going on about the munichs 'doing City over this afternoon'.

'Do you mean outside the Phoenix?' I said.

'Yes!' he replied ecstatically.

I laughed. 'If you think a group of idiots wearing black coats running past a pub while the dibble are barricading the exit doors is 'doing us over', then you need to go to the doctors.' I never understood why they came out with all this shit, I mean it wasn't as if it was our main crew either, it was a 'D squad' that they didn't even lay a finger on! After that I was well wound up and couldn't wait for the forthcoming derby.

On the day of the game I was outside the Parkside with a handy firm, but there was not a red in sight. Someone said they were in the Denmark having a drink. Time was getting nearer to kick off and as we were about to go in the ground the red bastards appeared from around the corner - they were stood next to railings put up outside the Main Stand (to protect the Sky vans), they came round it trying to charge at us. There were around one hundred of them, maybe more, but I noticed one blue sneak through the railings to go behind them and I followed with a few more. We were just about to crack the bastards when – as usual – the dibble appeared and pushed us back through the railings, whilst the munichs looked on. A few of us were hanging around, waiting to see what they were going to do when they caught us off guard – we didn't see them sneaking through the railings to get behind us, we just heard the roar of 'Come on' and they came towards us – two steps forward and three back. As we got closer, bottles were aimed right at us – one just flew over my head – that set me off, straight into them with two other lads, I was punching this one lad in the head whilst the other two were whacking them with planks of wood. The three of us were right next to each other so they couldn't get any punches in on us but then the dibble came in and forced us back.

We saw another City fan holding off a few reds at the turnstiles so we ran over to help him out and fucked them off as the dibble again went for us, telling us to go the other way and into the ground. The dibble were getting wound up and heavy handed, they grabbed one lad telling him to take the scarf from around his face – obviously the whole thing was being filmed and they wanted to identify him. I told the lad to keep it on and to tell the copper to fuck off. I looked over and there was a group of munichs laughing, calling out my name, saying 'Nick him, nick Sully' and pointing at me. Some of them knew me and knew I was due in court on the Monday. Some of the dibble knew this too and one warned me, 'If I see you again this afternoon you are nicked'. I just laughed and walked away.

We got in the ground and missed the first fifteen minutes of the game. What we couldn't understand was how come there were only ten or thirteen of us and the dibble were on our cases, yet a mob of around one hundred were allowed to walk around as they wished. Even in the city centre the dibble were following us, splitting us up. The bastards. As mentioned before, our reputation always worked against us where the police were concerned.

In any event, the game was a great success for City – the last ever Maine Road derby ended City 3 United 1 with The Goat being the hero of the day along with that red twat Gary Neville having a nightmare allowing Anelka to score a memorable goal that went into City folklore and Maine Road history. Sweet.

I went home straight after the game – as mentioned I was in court on the Monday and didn't want to add to my woes. I later heard that City smacked the munichs outside the Denmark when they made the mistake of returning there after the game. I always seemed to miss out on occasions like that when the dibble *didn't* turn up! But I was already on a probation order so couldn't risk adding to the charge I faced. I had broken my Community Order by missing two days as I couldn't be arsed attending and was given a final warning to finish the order or face being sent down.

END OF THE GUVNORS

For two years we ran the city centre until the dibble finally took action against us. This followed a game at Millwall in an FA Cup replay in January 1990. There was a big build up for this – City hadn't played Millwall for decades and although we'd had many a battle with Chelsea, Spurs and West Ham in the capital, Millwall fans had a fearsome reputation. Like Cardiff City, they had rioted their way through the lower divisions for years without getting the opportunity to have it out with the big boys. We met in the Brunswick the Friday night before the game and decided to go down by train rather than coach as we would have more freedom to travel around the capital rather than be stuck on a coach leaving ourselves to be either attacked by Millwall or escorted in by the old bill.

On the day of the game I woke up knackered – I couldn't sleep all night in anticipation for the big day. Once up, I changed my clothes over and over again, unable to decide what to wear. In the end I opted for a bubble coat rather than a thin jacket – in case I got slashed. At Piccadilly, the place was buzzing and the train was packed with City fans – all of them up for a ruck. On the way down we were chatting about Millwall. They were an unknown quantity, all we could do was wait and see what happened when we got there. After what seemed like ages we arrived at the station near the Den, the old ground not the new one. I don't mind admitting that I had butterflies and I suspect everyone else did as well. It really was the fear of the unknown and being on unfamiliar territory, we knew all the places to go to around Stamford Bridge, White Hart Lane and Upton Park. When you first went to these grounds in the company of lads who had fought there before, they passed on the information to you -- but no one had ever been to Cold Blow Lane, so as much as we fancied ourselves, we were also aware that we hadn't a clue as to what to expect.

The one thing everyone insisted on was that we all stuck together no matter what happened. We were walking along the platform when all of a sudden we heard a very quiet chant that grew louder as we continued walking – 'Millwall, Millwall, Millwall'. The chanting got louder and louder and all of a sudden they were right in front of us. They assumed we would run but they couldn't have been more wrong – we stood firm like never before and as they came at us we launched into them – we just ran at them, everyone together and the cockneys scattered, running out of the station. We knew then, once we'd done that, that we had won the psychological battle. We were on top.

Eventually the police cornered us and escorted us to the ground. Millwall followed us and tried to have a go but kept retreating as we tried to retaliate. Again, I admit, it was scary as fuck but as long as we stuck together we were in no trouble. Between the station and the ground there are a few blocks of high rise flats which we had to pass and this proved troublesome. There was one elderly woman on a balcony above us – she had no fucking teeth for fucks sake - throwing what we assumed was water from a pan at us but we soon realised was piss. 'Fack off you Northern twats' she shouted, hurling the contents of her bedpan at us. Others joined her from other balconies, throwing buckets of shit and eggs down on us, we'd never witnessed anything like this before, it was one thing looking over your shoulder keeping an eye on Millwall without having to look up and dodging the stuff from above!

There was a slight scuffle outside the ground but with lots of police in the area nothing really happened. Once inside all Millwall did was sing that song about no one liking them. Was that meant to intimidate us? Well if it was, it didn't work! After the game we were kept behind as usual, knowing that this was giving Millwall time to get into good positions to have a go when we returned to the station. A few lads were nervous but I think this was more to do with just wanting to get out and get on with it rather than being kept behind and not able to see what was happening on the other side of the wall. I bumped into a few lads who came down on a coach and they told me how Millwall had ambushed the coaches and bricked the windows on a number of them. I told them that this was why we'd come down on the train, we didn't want to be sitting targets.

Eventually we were let out and we were off and soon passing the infamous block of flats, this time the police were outside it and nothing was being hurled at us. We could see ahead of us that the younger lads were in front and to be honest, as game as they were, they were getting licked. We were trying to join them and those in between were happy to retreat! We made our way back to the station and believed that a big mob would be waiting for us on the bridge over the railway lines and sure enough, they were there. As we reached the bridge we sprinted towards them and steamed in, we all stood our ground as we clashed with them. The police didn't get involved at first but once we had the upper hand and started chasing them around the bridge area, they stepped in and forced us down on to the platform.

It was a great result for us that night, we all stood together. For once there were no heroes going off with their own little mob, that night we were one and we gave it to Millwall on their own 'manor'. Apart from the odd cut and black eye, the vast majority of us came home unscathed and we were certainly in good voice on the train home! Yet there was something else on that journey home that niggled at the back of my mind. Something wasn't quite right. Why did the police just stand back and let us fight? And looking around at all the faces, there were two blokes I didn't recognise, just sat there watching us all sing our heads off. Yes they had City badges on their jackets, but they stood out a mile. Were they plain clothes cops mingling in with us, trying to infiltrate us? Either way, they sensed I was onto them and they looked quite relieved when we got back to Piccadilly and we all went our separate ways...

*   *   *

Two days later I packed my bags and headed for Jersey. This had been planned for a few weeks – a mate from Blackley had been over and I was staying with his brother. I hadn't told too many people I was going, I thought I'd be away for a fortnight. I made my way to Piccadilly station. The plan was to take the train to Knutsford, walk to the services on the M6 and hitch all the way to Portsmouth and catch the ferry from there to Jersey. On the short journey to Knutsford I sat in the toilet hiding from the guard. I was buzzing. I loved travelling – especially when I didn't have to pay for the privilege! Walking to the services was a complete eye opener. The houses certainly didn't look like the houses I'd grown up in around north Manchester. They had big driveways with two, three or four cars parked up. It was like being on the set of Dallas! After a short walk I was on the edge of the exit slip road at the services, thumb out and hoping for a lift to the south coast. Within ten minutes a lorry pulled up, he was going to London and I jumped in. Over the next two hours we shared stories – my hitch-hiking stories all around Europe and his tales of picking up hitch-hikers!

He dropped me at Watford Gap, saying that this would be the best place to catch a lift to the south coast as here drivers from the M1 and M6 merged together. As he pulled away a lorry took his parking spot. I simply asked the driver if he was heading anywhere near Portsmouth. 'Southampton', he replied. 'Any chance of a lift?' I enquired and he agreed. Again we had a good chat, he was originally from Warrington but had been living and working from Southampton for a few years. Eventually I nodded off and when I woke up we were near Eastleigh, just outside Southampton. The driver then made a very kind gesture and offered to take me all the way to Portsmouth – well I could hardly refuse could I?! I couldn't thank him enough as he pulled away.

I was a bit hungry and thirsty by then so I found a café and was sat there having a snack and I soon got talking to a couple sat on the next table, they were going to Guernsey to visit family relations. They then told me that there were no further ferries that day leaving Portsmouth and that they were just setting off to drive to Plymouth to catch a ferry and I could join them if I wanted to. So off we set for Plymouth, with me fast asleep for most of the journey. We arrived at 3am and there was a ferry leaving in 15 minutes. I left the car, thanking the couple again and watched what was going on, in order to jib my way onto the ferry. After a few minutes I realised it would be a piece of piss! The bloke who was supposed to be collecting tickets and checking passports was only checking passports – and he wasn't even doing that properly! So I got in the queue and with passport in hand he was calling out for people to hurry up. The ferry was due to leave and he just wanted everyone on board.

Then a women two in front of me, showed him his passport and he just waved her through. 'But you haven't even seen the picture,' she stood there telling him. 'you stupid cow, you're going to fuck this up for me', I thought. The man just gave it a quick glance and waved her through again but she wasn't having it 'do your job properly' she demanded. I'd seen enough and walked over to her. 'Look love', I said, 'I'm sorry, I'm not being rude but there's all these people behind you who want to get on this ferry, I've got family waiting for me in Jersey so I cant afford to miss it.' She apologised and moved forward towards the ferry. I showed the man my passport, he seemed more interested in thanking me for getting rid of the women than he was in checking it and I was on board. The relief was huge and the fact I'd travelled all the way down on a train, two lorries and a car from Manchester to Plymouth via Portsmouth free of charge was also very satisfying. A good buzz indeed!

I was outside on deck when a young woman came out too and after a while we struck up a conversation. She was also heading for Jersey, visiting a friend. It was obvious from her accent that she was from Liverpool. Of course, with me living in Liverpool for a while I knew the city quite well, so asked her what area she came from. She (Karen) insisted I would never have heard of the area, telling me it was Netherley. 'No way' I said, but she thought I was blagging. 'You've never heard of it', she insisted. I told her that I had relatives near there, in Gateacre and started to name a few and the next thing she is saying 'no way'! Turns out she went to school with my cousin George!

We were hungry so we decided to go to the café. Trying to impress her, not to mention trying to kop off with her, I offered to 'pay' for the meal. The meal was quite expensive and I only had £80 in total for my trip. She told me what she wanted and I suggested she go over and save us a table. As she did that I had the plates and drinks on a tray and looked over at the till which was quite busy, as was the serving area, so I made my way back through the entrance, picked up the cutlery and walked around to the table. She was looking out of the window so didn't see which direction I had come from. 'There you go, enjoy that', I said proudly as I put the tray on the table. After the meal, we chatted for a while longer and by 7am we were both knackered and with seven more hours to go, she suggested getting a cheap cabin. Bingo! So we went over to the desk and she enquired about the cabin. As Karen was paying and filling in the forms, the assistant placed the cash on the side next to a money box at one end of the desk – where I was. Karen called her back to question her over something and as quick as I could I grabbed the box and took a few tenners out. Better still, when I placed it back, I could see a money bag on the floor. My leg was able to get underneath the desk and I slowly dragged the bag back with my foot and was just about to bend down and pick it up when a couple came along and joined the queue. I had my foot on the bag but just hoped that the assistant wouldn't see it. The couple stood there for about 4 – 5 minutes until they'd had enough so I bent down, picked the bag up and put it up my jacket. 'Just nipping to the toilet', I told Karen, 'back in a few minutes'. I went into one of the cubicles and opened the bag – it was full of fivers, tenners and twenties. At first I just put it all in my pocket and opened a window and threw the bag into the sea. I also threw away £60 just to be on the safe side as a few notes had been marked with '£100' on them. I then took the money from my pocket and began to count the lot. In total there was just short of a grand! I was buzzing to fuck – one minute I'm leaving Manchester with £80 in my pocket, the next day I'm on a ferry to Jersey with a grand in my pocket – and I hadn't even hit the duty free shop yet... I returned to Karen who by now had finished booking the cabin and was waiting for me. As we made our way to our room, I was already excited about what might happen - but it never did. As hard as I tried I couldn't get into her knickers, she wasn't having any of it and soon she fell fast asleep. I was still awake so decided to pay a little visit to the duty free shop.

The place was busy, both tills had queues and there was no

one watching the exit. I picked up a couple of items, Lacoste and Ralph t-shirts, went into the changing room and stuffed them into my bag and walked over to the perfume section. I picked up a few bottles and put them in my pocket and a couple of boxes of cigarettes in my bag with the t-shirts and then walked out and headed back to the cabin. Karen was still asleep as I put everything into my big bag, which was now full. I went back to the duty free shop and to the section where they had bags. Picking one up, I ripped the price label off and went over to the aftershave and threw a number of bottles into it, then going over to the cigarettes again, I picked up a basket and put a box of 200 in there. Going over to the counter I joined the busy queue but as I got to the front I said to the bloke on the till, 'oh wait, I forgot something, I'll be back in a few minutes'. I left the basket there as he began to serve other customers. Returning to the cigarettes I simply opened the bag and filled it up and with a quick glance at the bloke at the till, still busily serving, I was out of the exit door and heading toward the cabin again. Karen was still fast asleep, I put the bag under the bed and lay on my bed and fell asleep myself.

The next thing is the tannoy announces that 'we will be docking at Jersey in the next twenty minutes'. We woke up, got our things together and I suggested we'd best be grabbing a quick coffee before the ferry docked – and I offered to pay again! Once off the ship, Karen's friend was waiting for her, waving as she spotted her walking off. Jersey was only a small island, so I said to Karen that I hoped we'd bump into each other one night. I went into my bag, looked at Karen and said 'I bought this for you' and gave her a bottle of perfume – she was made up. I then looked at her friend and gave her a bottle too, which was also well received. Karen gave me her friend's phone number and address, asking me to give her a call one night and they'd meet up. We parted and then, as I was walking away from the ferry towards the town, a car pulled up alongside – it was Karen and her friend. They offered to give me a lift to their place so I knew where they lived if I wanted to pop round. Again, I was not about to turn her down!

It was a small, cosy flat, nice and warm. The TV was on

when we walked in and whilst her friend was making a drink I walked over to the window to admire the view. The next thing that happened shook me to the core! I heard the newsreader on the TV say 'Several arrests have been made this morning in dawn raids in Manchester as part of Operation Omega'. I turned around to watch the news, the words of the presenter catching my attention - and the next thing is they are showing scenes of football hooliganism and using the name 'The Guvnors' a few times. I turned it up - the screen was flashing up scenes filmed at Millwall just a few days ago, including a shot of City fans sat in their seats inside the ground.

As we watched Karen shouted 'THAT'S YOU!!!' I just didn't know what to say or do! They both quizzed me – 'are you a hooligan?' Of course I denied it, saying that all they had shown was City fans sitting in the seats and I just happened to be there. I asked Karen's friend if I could borrow a phone for a few minutes. I called one of the few people I had told I was coming to Jersey just to say I had arrived safely. His mum answered and straight away asked if I'd heard what was happening, she agreed that it was best if no one knew where I was. With no ferry ticket in my name I could not be traced to the island so the less people knowing where I was, the better. After that I made no contact with anyone in Manchester to ensure I was safe.

I got a lift to the Sussex pub, which was where I was supposed to meet my friend. I asked the bar man if he knew my friend and reckoned he was in there every evening. I left a message with the barman and left the pub and, as it was a scorching hot day, we made for the beach. I was lying down on the sand half asleep when I heard Julie and Karen talking about me, suggesting they thought I was on the run. I rolled over and laughed at them 'I'm not on the run, I'm just here for my holidays but can't find my mates until the evening.' We got talking and in the end I admitted I'd been involved in a few fights. I told them 'look, it's just a buzz, a scary one, but I can't explain it, I've been beaten up and put in hospital and come straight out and started fighting again.' I didn't tell them I had been nicked before but did tell them I was scared of getting nicked. We carried on talking, it was strange, I'd only met Karen a few hours before yet it felt like I'd known her for years and I told her that. Karen replied that she had thought the same about me on the ferry and we ended up laughing. Julie then said if I wanted to stay at her flat I was welcome – again another offer that was far too good to turn down.

It was about four days later when I finally met my friends, bumping into them one night in a pub. I walked in with Karen and Wayne saw us. 'Fuck me' he said, apologising for swearing on seeing Karen. He went off on one saying he was worried sick as I had rang to say I was coming, left messages in the pub saying I was here and then vanished for days! Honestly, I didn't know he cared! Of course once he'd realised where I'd been staying he understood fully and didn't blame me at all! Wayne began to joke around, asking Karen if I'd tried it on with her or had been on the rob. She laughed, telling him yes I had tried it on but no he hadn't been successful, but that I hadn't been on the rob. She delighted in telling Wayne that I had bought her a meal on the ferry. Wayne was in stitches 'yes, but did you see him buy the meal?' he asked. 'No I was sat down when he bought it,' she replied. Wayne jumped in, 'but did you actually see him at the till?' he continued, 'he doesn't even know what a till is love!'. Karen leapt to my defence, 'he bought me some really nice perfume from the duty free shop too'. Wayne cracked up, looking at me, telling me to let her know how I had got the perfume in the first place.

Then Paul came in, gave me a hug, changing the conversation only shortly before asking if I managed to do a job on the ferry. Wayne told Paul he was trying to convince Karen of my 'hobby' but she wouldn't believe him. Paul began to tell me how I'd love it in Jersey and how it was a piece of piss to rob the shops, they were years behind in security and how the shops had all the top labels. It was time for me to bail out, I made my excuses, saying I was knackered and agreed to meet up another time and me and Karen left the pub. Karen was straight on my case asking if it was true or were they just winding me up. She wouldn't let up and eventually I told her the truth! I reassured her I'd never robbed a household and wouldn't rob her or Julie, I only robbed shops and I did it for a living. She was in stitches. 'Great', she said, 'I've met a shoplifter *and* a football hooligan all in one!'

I thought that might ruin it between us as far as romance went, but we actually got closer. Finally on my birthday Karen gave me the best present ever – and it was well worth the wait! It felt like Big Ben was ringing its bells for two hours solid! I continued to graft in the shops, even having a close shave one time when a jacket I had wrapped around my waste hidden under another jacket was showing the price tag. The assistant stopped me, but fortunately I had robbed that jacket from another shop, so I was able to explain I had bought it from another shop but didn't notice the price tag was still on – she helped me take it off!

The robbing became more frequent and easier, yet a few days later I was in trouble – but not for thieving. I went out with Paul one night and on the way back he bet that I couldn't climb up this tree. No problem I thought and up I went. After a few minutes this voice kept calling me to come down. 'Fuck off', I shouted back down, 'I haven't got to the top yet'. I heard it again and shouted down 'piss off, you owe me a fiver'. I got to the top and looked down – there were three police officers ordering me down. Unless you have been to Jersey, you may not be aware that they don't tolerate things as much as they do in England. Dropping litter, begging and being drunk are unacceptable and they clamp down hard on you.

The two of us and Karen attended the court hearing, we assumed I'd get a fine but were shocked when I was given a two week 'cooling off period'. This was totally different to English prisons. It was more open than an open prison, I even managed to have a drink inside as well as play volleyball and other activities. I met a lad from Wythenshawe in there, he was telling me how easy it was to rob but they wouldn't put up with it if you got caught. Apparently they were not keen on lads coming over from the main land. If you were found sleeping rough they charged you with destitution and put you on the next ferry home. On my release, Karen and Paul couldn't believe how tanned I was – I'd been sun bathing for two weeks solid!

On another day we walked over the sands to a castle but when the tide came in you had to catch a small boat back. On our return, I wasn't watching where I was walking and bumped into a man with a big TV camera. I apologised and walked off. After a few seconds he called me back, we began talking and he asked me if I was free to be an extra on 'Bergerac'! He offered me £60 a day but I talked him up to £80. I turned up early on the beach the next day and sat around waiting for my big part, which wasn't until after lunch. I got talking to a women who turned to be Lisa Goddard and I was introduced to John Nettles, Bergerac himself. Then it was my turn to be filmed. The original 'walk on, walk off' role they had for me had been changed and now they had a bigger role in mind. I was instructed to run up the stairs on the beach and grab this women's bag and run off with it. I would be chased and then caught by the police and put in the police car. The irony of my role had me laughing to myself. The director began 'Tape to action, camera roll' and off I went. And again. And again. I couldn't believe how many times we had to do the scene! After that we had to go to the 'police station' to film me being taken there. I was involved in the filming for a full week, getting to know Lisa Goddard and John Nettles quite well. They told me how sometimes a scene can take two days, adding that the work was hard work but enjoyable.

After the filming it didn't take long before I was caught by the police again – but this time they were not actors! There was an annual football game between Jersey and Guernsey and myself, Wayne and Paul went along to cheer Jersey on. At half time it was 0-0, but Guernsey scored straight after the second half started. The visiting fans started getting a bit cocky, giving out a bit of abuse. I said to the others that there might be a bit of trouble here. I started giving a bit of shit back to the Guernsey boys and within minutes I was fighting them. The other two joined in and it soon became a free-for-all with many more joining in and with no dibble in sight it lasted nearly an hour, stopping and starting all the time until the police finally turned up. Even then it was comical. Their police had no experience of riots and hooliganism so they didn't have the equipment needed, so they just let us carry on until we had either finished or were too fucked to continue and then they just went in and snatched us one at a time! I was up in court again and was given six weeks.

On release I was sleeping rough – Karen had had enough by now – and was caught sleeping on a park bench and given a further three weeks and then deported. They put me on a plane, I asked the stewardess where it was heading for as I didn't want to go home. She told me it was heading for Eastleigh airport, outside Southampton. My two week stay in Jersey had lasted almost three months.

I decided to stay in Southampton and found a small flat near to the Saints old ground at The Dell. It took a while to get to know people, they were not as welcoming as northerners but each night I'd go in a pub called The Winston which was opposite the ground and the best pub in the area. Eventually I got to know a scouser (there's always a scouser!) who supported Everton and a local mate of his. They worked on the newspapers and within a month I had moved into their bigger flat, which helped with the finances.

Within a few weeks they had introduced me to their circle of friends, two of whom were from Stretford and things got easier – though only with the lads, the girls in Southampton were a hard nut to crack if they didn't know you! One night we went out clubbing when someone suggested we go to a club situated on the other side of the water from Southampton. We were able to get a bus going there but coming back was a different story. We were walking along the waterfront wondering how to get home – there wasn't a taxi in sight – when one of the lads spotted a rowing boat. Well that was it, no hesitation, everyone in and take shifts rowing. There was quite a stretch of water to cross, it wasn't a canal or small river and it was fast flowing too as the estuary lead out into the sea.

Anyway, off we set and before long we were roughly in the middle of the water when we were joined alongside by a motor boat, the driver of which threw out a rope and told us to tie it onto the front of the rowing boat and he'd take us in. 'Fantastic', we thought, congratulating each other on a great journey home – until we reached the other bank and where the dibble waited for us to land. Despite our drunken pleas that we meant no harm and that we just wanted to get back home, we ended up being arrested and taken to the police station and charged. In court we all gave a sob story on how we were not local, new to the area, got lost, a little prank that backfired and how sorry we were and there was no damage to the boat and the judge must have fallen for it. We all got a conditional discharge. He knew I'd been in trouble before but as it was not for a football or violence related offence, he put it down as just being drunk. We walked into the pub that evening to loud cheers and a few free beers. The locals then started showing us that day's local evening newspaper and how the article described 'Three Manchester men taking a rowing boat and attempting to cross the water'. They even pinned the article on the wall. At least one good thing came of this episode – it broke the ice with some of the girls and all of a sudden they were keen to speak to us and wanted to get to know us better!

While I was down there I attended a couple of Southampton games and at one game in particular I was thrown out for giving a gentle slap to this Saints fan who insisted on referring to me as a scouser – something I wasn't prepared to accept! It kicked off a little bit and the two of us were ejected. Outside, I looked around at the perimeter wall, it wasn't very high, so I climbed up and jumped back in, landing right next to the players' entrance - only when I landed, I almost fell onto Danny Wallace, one of the three Wallace brothers at the club at that time. He was recovering from an injury so he was making his way to his seat rather than on to the pitch. I apologised and he just laughed, asking me where I was from. I told him and we struck up a conversation. I told him I was staying near the Winston pub which he knew about. We ended up sitting next to each other and after the game he invited me into the Players Lounge – fuck me, there I was being introduced to the other two Wallace brothers, Matt Le Tissier and Lawrie McMenemy, the Saints manager! It was completely different to City, a much smaller club with crowds of around 15,000 but so much friendlier, everyone knew everybody else's name.

When I eventually left the ground and returned to the Winston, the woman behind the bar calls out 'I heard you were thrown out ages ago, where have you been?' So I began to tell them my tale and of course no one believed me. I then said,

'Well, Danny has invited me to come to the pub, The Two Birds, on Friday as they always have a meal there on that day'. One of the lads admitted that the players did go there each week. 'See, how would I have known that?' I asked them.

The following week we were in The Two Birds pub and who should come walking in? Danny Wallace! To the amazement and shock of my friends, he comes straight up to me and shakes my hand, greeting me by name. I asked him to explain to everyone how we met and he backed my story up before heading off home. Everyone was gobsmacked. 'Fuck me, you've only been here a few weeks and you are on first name terms with half of Southampton's players', said one. Anyway, as with the rowing boat incident, it caught the attention of the girls and landed me a date with the barmaid Joanne. The landlady said I was a bit of a dark horse and within a month I'd moved in with her! On one occasion I told her I was going back to Manchester for a few days. She wanted to come with me but I said 'next time' because the next morning I caught a ferry to France and went on a little shopping spree. I ended up being away for almost two and a half weeks and Joanne went mad when I returned, reminding me that I had said 'just a couple of days'. I tried to make it up to her and told her I'd actually been to France, Germany and Switzerland.

She couldn't believe where I'd been – nor with the 'goodies' I'd brought back (I told her I had bought them on the cheap). She then commented on how when she and her friends first saw me they were all impressed with how I had dressed, always smarter than the locals, with good labels on, she added that I stuck out a mile and all the girls said the same in a complimentary way (though I was still a bit miffed that it took me ages to get to chat with them!). I told her that what the locals were wearing in Southampton, I had been wearing a few years ago and my idea was always to change style, keeping one step ahead of the pack, letting others follow my lead. Back in the pub and there was no shortage of takers for the gear. Some people cottoned on to what I was doing – even Joanne herself eventually – but she stood by me, though thinking about it, she did quite well out of it too, I was bringing in good money and treating her well with the proceeds. Eventually, eight months after leaving Manchester for Jersey for what was supposed to be a two week getaway, I decided to say goodbye to Joanne and Southampton and return home.

A few months later, I was in Cheers Bar in Prestwich and a rumour was going round that a few footballers were due in that night. A few moments later, the doors open and in walks Ryan Giggs with United's new signing – Danny Wallace! I looked over at him and he walked over to greet me. My mates were completely gobsmacked at this, but although I knew he was now a red, I couldn't ignore him. We reminisced about the time we met and the fact that he hardly knew anyone from Manchester other than the players and all of a sudden he bumps into me in this bar! He got a round of drinks in and asked me to join his party in the VIP area upstairs. At this point Paul Ince came in. I asked Danny not to bring Ince over to us, explaining that I wasn't being funny but it would be like a Saints fan talking to a Pompey player and although he was now a red I never saw him as one but still as a Saints player. He was really cool about that and understood where I was coming from. Danny said he had to go upstairs or his party would think he was ignoring them. We exchanged phone numbers and kept in touch over the coming months. He was at United for a few years until he was sold to Birmingham and that's when I lost touch with him. He's had a rough time over the last few years having been diagnosed with multiple sclerosis and I hope he is able to live as full a life as is possible under the circumstances.

West Midlands

Fans of Birmingham, West Brom and Wolves may have appalling accents but they also have had some decent firms down the years, although they also seem to attract the biggest bunch of wankers (masquerading as police officers) in the country.

Wolves

On one visit to Wolves in the early eighties we went on the train. They had a strong firm called 'The Subway Army' – anyone who has been there and had to walk under the flyover using the subway will know why they had that name! It was a night game and we set off around late afternoon. There were a good number of us and we were really up for it as we knew the odds were in favour of it going off at some point during the evening. Out of the station we made our way to the ground free of an escort and approached the subway. Everyone was very close together so no one could penetrate the group and split us up – then it just went mad, a few Wolves ended up being stabbed as we were going at them. One little black lad I'd not seen before had a small penknife and he was just jibbing at them as we went through the subway. We moved quickly, lashing out with fists and feet, the twats couldn't get out of the way and received slaps from a good number of us as we went through the subway.

Even in the ground it was kicking off, we jumped the turnstiles of what we thought was the away fan's terrace but turned out to be the home end – the terrace was split down the middle into two sections one for each set of fans – we received a warm welcome and there were running battles up and down the terrace. We got completely spanked, there was around thirty of us against half a terrace! You could do this at smaller grounds and smaller clubs but not at a place like Wolves, it was asking for a good kicking and we got it. The police came to our rescue and turfed us into the away end and to safety. Throughout the game the Wolves fans were hurling bottles, bricks and other items at us. There were lads getting on the train going home with their heads bandaged up. I was never into that, just generally lobbing shit into crowded sections full of fans of all ages and sexes and then bragging to their mates about 'what they'd done to the other team's fans'. They are cowards, they should be hard enough to stand and fight with fans who want to do likewise, then we'll see how brave they are. On the train home we couldn't see Roy or Chalkie. We later found out they had been nicked and released the next day.

We met up again in the Underground and talked about what had happened the night before. The little black lad came in and got a great cheer. He was only thirteen but no one gave a fuck and from that day onwards he was in. It turned out he was also a dab hand at shoplifting – he was in good company - full of role models!

BIRMINGHAM

In 1983, following relegation, we'd come to terms with the fact we were no longer going to be playing the two Merseyside teams, West Ham and Spurs in London, Leeds and, of course, the munichs, instead we examined the 2nd division and realised it wasn't the end of the world. There was Chelsea, Birmingham, Wolves, Newcastle, Sheffield Wednesday and others to battle with as well as places such as Grimsby, Carlisle, Charlton and Portsmouth that we hadn't visited before.

One of the first away games of the season was a night match at Birmingham and this was one ground where we definitely needed good numbers as they were well known for providing a nice Brummie welcome. They had a lot of black lads in their firm and were known as 'The Zulu's' - they were as game as they come. We arrived around 4pm and parked the van up around halfway between the ground and the Bull Ring – which is Birmingham's equivalent of Manchester's Arndale with the train station below it - and we headed off to meet those blues coming down on the train. As we entered the shopping area, there were lads all over the show watching us, we just stayed tight together and carried on walking – we thought 'We're City and we don't give a fuck and if you want it then you can have it'.

Unfortunately it was the wrong move to make – as we carried on through it seemed all eyes were on us and by the second more and more lads were coming behind us and following at a distance. Jimmy turned round, had a quick look and said 'We're going to get a fucking good hiding here'. Within seconds we heard the chant 'Zulu's, Zulu's' over and over again as they started walking faster towards us, catching us up. Then they just charged at us, fists flying all over the place. We had nowhere to go and just had to stand there and have it with them. There were blokes out with their wives or girlfriends joining in. One bloke came at me swinging a bag full of shopping, the bag split and tins went rolling all over the floor, some of our lads picked them up and used them against the brummies as I went over and twatted the bloke, decking him onto the floor. The next thing there is someone on my back trying to scratch my face – it was the bloke's girlfriend! I was also hit on the head with a shoe while lads were trying to punch me, I just had to get her off my back! I ran backwards into a shop front, smacking her against the wall and she let go but I still had two or three lads in front of me and I was getting it from all angles. Dave and Jimmy were next to me battling like fuck – it was a massive pile up, bodies on the floor still fighting, twisting around trying to get the upper hand, everywhere you looked it was mayhem, no weapons were used, just a good old-fashioned punch up. The police came and tried to get us against the wall but the Zulus kept jumping in and getting at us. Eventually they managed to get us out of there and marched us straight to the ground and into the away end. None of us had a ticket but they weren't interested in that, they just wanted us in the ground, the exit gate was opened and we were let in.

After the game we were kept in for the obligatory hour (despite it being a night game) and once we were let out we knew there was a burger van down the road where their mob would wait for you. The police were trying to organise an escort for the station but about twenty of us managed to slip out and make our own way back to our van. We turned left before the burger van but hadn't a clue where we were going. We ended up on a housing estate that became a dead end. We could see a street behind the houses so we had the choice of jumping through back gardens or going back to the top of the estate - we chose to go fence hopping across gardens! We made our way down the side of one house and crept through the garden and one at a time scaled the fence, going through the garden on the other side and down the side of the house and onto the road. About half of us were over the fence when a women came out to empty her bin. She took one look at us and called out to her husband in the thickest Brummie accent 'Here Stan. There's a load of lads in our garden jumping the fence'. By the time he came out to see, the last of us were smiling at him as he jumped over to the other side.

Once we walked down the road, we were feeling so pleased with ourselves having found the short cut that none of us had noticed that there was still plenty of brummies about. We followed the road down and came to a roundabout where the Zulu's were stood around. We carried on walking, heads down but we stood out a mile in our semi flared jeans and white Dunlop trainers and jackets. 'Just keep on going' we said to each other and as we passed them they were giving us the eye when one of the lads said something stupid to them – and that was it, they were all over us like a rash. They were right up next to us and one of the Zulus recognised us from before and said 'It's those Manc cunts from the Bull Ring'. Dave then said 'fuck this' and whacked the nearest Brummie to him and that was it - all hell let loose. We were fighting them up against a wall, fists and boots flying in left, right and centre. we were heavily outnumbered – there must have been around a hundred of them – and we were being leathered all over the place, lads were on the floor getting kicked to fuck. The next thing was one of their black lads, who was well over six foot, called everyone back, 'leave it now, they've had enough'. He must have been the leader as they obeyed his order and I'll give them credit for that, most other firms would have carried on fighting and not given a fuck. They went off as we licked our wounds, we had cut eyes, bleeding noses, broken noses, split lips and sore heads with blood all over our clothes. The icing on the cake was discovering the minibus (eventually, after walking around for ages) – minus all of its windows. It was one of the longest journeys we ever took, driving up the M6 for eighty miles without any windows, covered in blood and aching all over.

*   *   *

The following season we played them again at St Andrews – this time the plan was to go down on coaches, only they didn't turn up, so half of us walked to Piccadilly station and the other half got the bus there. At the station there were three to four firms altogether and in terms of numbers about three hundred of us – a far cry from the twenty the previous season. The train was due in fifteen minutes, so we had a quick pint in the station. Whilst drinking, one of the jibbers came over and said that everyone was together on this one.

A lad from another firm, Ricky, overheard this and asked what was going on. We explained to him that once down there, everyone of us was going to stick together and no one firm was going to go this way or that way. Ricky looked at us and said 'Yeah, right'. Dave jumped in, 'OK, you do what you want to do, but if you go your own way then good luck to you – you'll need it'. Ricky asked him what he meant and Dave told him about last season and that we could expect similar treatment tonight. One of Ricky's mates joined in 'you lot really think you're something special don't ya'.

'No, I'm just telling you the score, if you don't want to listen then do it your way,' said Dave 'just don't come running to us for help.' There was a bit of arguing and pushing and Dave lost his rag 'Who the fuck are you lot anyway? You show face when there's enough of us going down, but if there ain't enough then you are never around.' That seemed to rattle them and it looked like it was going to go off until Jimmy jumped in and cooled things down, saying we could sort this out back in Manchester later that evening.

By now it was time to get the train and we all got on, the atmosphere was tense amongst ourselves and you could see lads giving each other evils. As we left Wolverhampton with New

Street just one stop away, lads were getting itchy, the jibbers were walking up and down the train, there were around thirty of them. Ricky's mob stood up near the doors and as we came into the station, we decided to let them lead, to see what they were made of. Normally we would lead and the jibbers would get in amongst them and do their business, knowing that we were there with them one hundred percent.

So we all walk out of the station, up through the Bull Ring and out onto the street, following Ricky and his boys. As soon as we came round the corner there was a big welcoming committee outside the pub waiting for us – and once the word was relayed into the pub that committee got a hell of a lot bigger! They came out of the pub in huge numbers and once they started chanting 'Zulus, Zulus' then you knew that they were about to charge – and they did! The first bottle came flying over and before the second one hit the floor it was all systems go. Well Ricky's firm, who were supposed to be leading from the front, were all backing off into us and all you could hear was 'stand City, stand'! They ran across the road and piled into us, we had no option but to back off into the shopping area – all we could see were bodies coming at us and at this point Chalkie stopped and turned and shouted at us 'come on, we'll lead now'. We all moved forward, with the jibbers ready to do what they do best. We didn't run at them, but just moved forward as they came running at us, one lad shouted 'Come on the Mayne Line' and we knew we didn't have to worry about looking over our shoulder to see where the next man was, we knew we would could rely on one another.

We started to back them off, it was if running at us made them run out of steam, now it was their turn to be on their toes – the golden rule that Birmingham broke was once you have a firm on their toes, then keep them on their toes, don't back off or allow them to regroup. Now we were battling with them outside the Bull Ring and there was a hell of a lot more of us than last year and they never expected that. We had them backing off, though a couple of heroes tried to take us on and received a hiding for their efforts. The dibble separated us and marched us to the ground. Once there, we passed the away coaches and they were all smashed up with glass everywhere. Inside the ground the chant of 'Zulus, Zulus' was regularly coming out from the stand nearest to us, the game was pretty boring so we decided to leave with about twenty minutes to go, in small groups so as not to raise suspicion with the dibble.

We tried two pubs near the ground but they wouldn't serve us. At the second pub, one lad was picking a chair up that he was going to throw through a window but he was stopped by another lad who told him we didn't want to invite the dibble here and be escorted to the station. Eventually we found a pub down a back street that would serve us and we stayed there for an hour and a half until we hoped things would have cooled down a bit outside. We had done well to keep such large numbers together, Brian's firm and the jibbers were still with us – the only absentees was Ricky's mob, who proved to be all mouth and no action. We had decided to have one more drink and then go and look for the Zulus but we didn't have to wait very long as one of our scouts outside came running in shouting 'they're here, they're here'. We grabbed our pint pots and bottles and anything else we could throw and ran out of the pub towards them. There was only about forty of them but it was strange as there was no 'Zulu' chant coming from them. All became clearer as we got close to them and it turned out they were an older, NF City firm from Blackley! They told us City had just been legged all over the place by the brummies, outside a pub about five minutes away. We decided to all go together to this pub and front them and as we got there we could see that there was no one outside keeping watch, so we sent a lad ahead to have a peek through a window. He gave us the signal to confirm that they were inside and we got ourselves ready and then just ran straight in.

They had to fight us as there was no place to run, the bottles and glasses we had brought with us were being thrown at them from close range, one lad was sent through the pub window with blood pouring out of his head as a piece of glass stuck in it. They were kicked to fuck and the pub was trashed, table and chairs overturned and thrown around. The dibble turned up and escorted us to the station but it was battles all the way there as they came out from the estates to have it with us. At one point a mob came at us from a side street and we were trying to break the escort and have a pop at us when we realised they were a City firm! We were well pissed off at them, I mean we were in a fucking police escort so why did they think we were brummies? They had been throwing bottles and a few of our lot were walking around with gashed heads as a result of being attacked by our own. Looking back, I suppose it was the football hooligan equivalent of being hit by 'friendly fire'!

Once at the station, our anger and frustration boiled over as City fought City on the platform. The dibble hadn't got a clue how to deal with it and it was fellow blues who separated the different factions. In the end one group got on one train and we waited a while longer for the next train. However, once on this train, we hadn't got as far as Wolverhampton when it kicked off again. Two lads were arguing as to who had stabbed this Brummie. Fuck me, the pair of them just squared up to each other and were going at it toe-to-toe. We broke it up but it was a waste of time as they soon started up again and as we were trying to sort that out again, a few lads further down the carriage started at each other's throats and then mates joined in as other lads were being smacked. It was fucking crazy. By the time we got to Stoke everyone had had enough and was just sat slumped in their seats, trying to get a bit of a kip. The dibble came on board but nothing was happening, they just went all the way to Manchester with us to make sure nothing else went off.

At Piccadilly we all got off and went walking down the platform and out of the blue there is a firm waiting for us. Was it United? The Cockney Reds? Was it fuck, it was Ricky's firm, those mouthy fuckers who shat themselves earlier on in the day and were waiting for Mayne Line to come back! However, as soon as he saw Brian and the lads from Blackley, he wanted it with them as they had a reputation for being in the National Front and most of Ricky's firm were black. It went off for a bit, but it was mostly verbals and pushing rather than fists and feet and the dibble who had been on the train with us broke it up. After that a lot of lads were pissed off with each other, pitting firm against firm. It was never the same after that, as much as we tried to patch things up over the months, it never really happened and firms just went their own way and did their own thing.

*   *   *

The next time we played Birmingham, a few years later, it was on a Tuesday night. We went down by coach and five of us were playing cards. Donald wasn't involved but he came up and said 'Lets play a game where the loser has to come in the home end with me'. We all looked at each other thinking 'you're fucking mad' – but the thing with Donald, as ever, is you could never say that to him and of course, you knew he meant it! So on with the game and whoever was left with the ace had to go in with Donald. Towards the end, Billy, Roy and Dave were out so it was just me and Jimmy. Fortunately for me, Jimmy took the wrong card and he lost, not that I was scared of going in their end, I just didn't fancy another stay in hospital! Jimmy actually wanted to lose as he was well up for the idea anyway! The next thing Donald said 'didn't I say three of us were going in their end?' We looked at each other not knowing whether to laugh or cry and the cards were dealt again.

At one point I thought I was out of the game but it was called void for some reason and whilst Billy was shuffling the cards again Donald turned and said 'don't bother dealing, Sully, you're the third man!' I began to wonder how long we'd last in the ground, before being taken to hospital - five minutes? Would we even get as far as the turnstiles? Then Chalkie starts taking bets on whether we will get in their end and this turns into bets on how long we will stay in there. There were some mad bets going on and the one thing about the Mayne Line is you had to follow it through or you were out. At some point you had to do something to prove yourself, like an initiation test - and this was my test!

As the coach parked up, we were escorted to the away end. The three of us went over to the dibble who at first tried to stop us leaving but then Donald has a word and convinced them to let us through the police line and away from the City fans. As we walked towards their main stand, I was sure we had been clocked – not so much me and Jimmy, but Donald's face was well known from the days of The Cool Cats. Donald said, 'right, we're going in here' and as he went to the turnstile and paid, I jumped over and Jimmy slid underneath. All we had to do now was to find a seat, keep our mouths shut and not get sussed out. Easy!

The game was about to start when Donald took a quick look around and back again, saying to us that the Zulus were about three rows behind us. We were sat in the corner of the Main Stand next to where the their fans were standing. What made the situation worse for us was that their fans had spotted us in there and were pointing us out to their mates. This alerted the Zulus that something was going on in front of them. I just kept thinking of being in hospital again - in terms of hospital trips I was top of the Mayne Line league! Finally the Zulus sussed out what was in before them and thankfully the dibble cottoned on that something wasn't right and they stepped in - Donald turned around and smiled at them as he left. We were taken out to shouts of 'you fookin' Manc bastards' and other derogatory farewells and although we received one or two slaps, it seemed to be mission accomplished and we looked forward to collecting our winnings from the lads! We were hoping to get taken straight into the City end but they just slung us out and as much as we tried we couldn't blag our way into being in the away end. I then looked around and Donald had disappeared, so it was just me and Jimmy. A few minutes later we were joined by another Donald, Donald Farrer - known to all City fans as 'Daft Donald' - who had been thrown out of the City end.

The three of us decided to wait outside the gate and when they opened it to let people out early we would go in. There wasn't long left in the game when a gate was half opened and a few blues came out – that was all we needed. We pushed past the steward, knocking him over as he lost his balance, calling us all names under the sun at the same time and we were in! We walked around the terrace until we came across the rest of the lads at the front. We were there for a few minutes when along came the dibble and the steward, pointing us out. The dibble have hold of us and the steward says 'yes, that's definitely them' as we were arguing back. 'What you on about? We've been stood here all game', the steward was having none of it. 'You know what you did, you just ran in here without paying'. This got Daft Donald's back up. 'Without paying?' he said, adding, 'there's like ten minutes left and you want us to pay?' It was all in vain as once again we were turfed out of the ground! I don't know what it was about the West Midlands police, it was like it was in Liverpool, it's like they actually wanted you to get a good hiding.

So once more we were outside the gate waiting for the lads to come out and as the final whistle went, the brummies came out, City fans were kept behind for ages. Jimmy said 'fuck it, lets go back to the coach' and off we went – the place was crawling with small mobs here and there, gangs of twenty and thirty on each corner all waiting for City. We just thought it was only a matter of time before we were clocked, in fact we were amazed at how far we walked without being challenged. One lad asked Jimmy the time and he looked at his watch and told him. What we didn't know was there was a small firm following behind us and one of their lads caught up with Jimmy and asked him the time. Jimmy didn't say anything, so the lad asked him again a bit sterner. Jimmy looked at him and just decked him right there on the spot. That set the place alight, within seconds we were fucked, getting hit from all angles – Jimmy was on the floor and Daft Donald and me were trying to fight around him so he could get up, the next thing I was kicked in the bollocks and went down under a hail of fists and feet. Daft Donald was now down too, holding his chest in pure agony but at that moment they all stopped and ran up the road leaving us to pick ourselves up. The dibble had let City out and the mob were after richer pickings. I was covered in blood whilst Jimmy lay motionless on the floor. The problem we had was what to do next as we could hardly walk. Every time Daft Donald moved he was in great pain which made it harder for us both to try and pick Jimmy up. We didn't notice that a group of around nine lads had come up to us – we knew they were Zulus as the main man was the black lad we had come across before.

They recognised we were helpless so helped us up, in particular Jimmy. They asked us how we got here and we told them on the coach. They said that all the coaches had left a few minutes ago, escorted out by the police and that they would take us to the station to make sure we got there safely. Whilst we were walking, one of them asked if it was us that was in their Main Stand before the game, we told them that it was me, Jimmy and the other Donald and that we'd done for a bet with the rest of the lads on the coach. They laughed and said we had some balls and that we were also lucky not to have got kicked to fuck to which we agreed. We stopped off at a pub so we could freshen up a bit and clean our faces up in the toilet. We then got talking about the previous two battles we had in Birmingham, the one by the roundabout when again they let us go after we had been leathered and last year at the Bull Ring. Jimmy was going on about the fight when the bloke with the shopping bag lashed out and the bag split sending cans flying everywhere and when his woman jumped on my back and started scratching my face to fuck. They remembered each incident as we did and we discussed each other's tactics and chatted about battles with other firms and rating the best Cockney firm.

They said the pub across the road from the Bull Ring was where they always met up and just sat in their drinking and waiting for the away team to come straight out and into them. We told them it was the same with us and The Brunswick. After a laugh and a joke, we had to make our way to New Street to catch the last train home. We told them that next time we play in Manchester, after a battle we would meet up and have a drink with them.

WEST BROMWICH ALBION

The first few games of the season are always a buzz. You get to see new players, you have high hopes for the team - and you get back out across the country looking for action after the summer break. On one such trip we were away at West Bromwich Albion and we all met up outside the Brunswick pub and made the short walk to Piccadilly to catch the train to Birmingham. The there was an announcement that the train would be an hour late so we went off to get something to eat. Whilst doing this we recognised a couple of lads who had come off a train from Crewe. They were telling us that the Cockney Reds were on their train and coming this way. We thought they were winding us up but then out from the platform they came towards us. Everyone just abandoned their food and drinks and raced towards the end of the platform. There were about seventy of them altogether including one tall black lad who we instantly recognised as Cockney Sam. Donald told us all to leave him alone – he was Donald's for the taking. We all waited a few more seconds and Donald was just itching to pounce and then he did 'crack!' on the side of his head. We all waded in and it was running battles the platform. It was pretty even for a while but we started to get the upper hand. Donald was having his private ding dong with Sam which was crazy, it just carried on and on. A fair few of the cockneys were covered in blood from their noses or cuts to mouths or above the eyes – some were on the deck getting kicked to fuck. The police turned up and eventually broke it up, they managed to get the Cockney Reds lined up against a wall as our train came in. We made our way towards the train and we then saw Donald and Sam still at it! By the look of it Sam was the much worse off of the two, his nose was bleeding like mad and his glasses were smashed. Donald came over to get on the train, he turned to Sam and said 'We'll be back after 7pm – make sure you are waiting for us!'

On the train down Donald was seething, he kept saying 'I'm having him, I'm having that cunt'. Donald was definitely one to bear grudges - he never forgot a thing! We arrived at New Street and were greeted by the West Midlands dibble complete with barking dogs. We were kept on the station for ages and Donald asked a plod why. He was told Wolves and Birmingham were having a pop at each other which was weird as Wolves were away at Newcastle that day but had come into Birmingham to change rather than go direct from Wolverhampton. Eventually after Wolves had left the station we made our way out to a pub outside New Street but the police were not letting us in there 'we've just spent twenty-five minutes keeping Birmingham in and the Wolves out of there so there's no way you lot are going in!' one said. They tried to put us on buses to Smethwick but we weren't having it and began to walk with the dogs at our side barking like mad. When someone told us how long it was to walk we jumped on the bus offered.

On the bus Donald suggested we took it easy and didn't do anything to get arrested, he wasn't bothered about the brummie twats – his mind was back in Piccadilly station later that evening. We went into a pub across the road from the Hawthorns but didn't stay long as it was just full of regular blokes having a drink. We ended up going in the home end behind the goal. Cyril Regis scored for the Albion after a few minutes and then we equalised straight away and naturally we celebrated in style, going mad. The next thing it was going off – we didn't think Albion had a decent crew but we underestimated them and they certainly had a go at us, outnumbering us obviously and I wasn't the only one who got smacked and soon we were being rounded up and marched out of the home end and into the away end.

After the game there were a few scuffles but nothing notable. We made our way back to New Street by bus and had a drink in a near by boozer before getting the train back home. We knew that the Cockney Reds always stayed in town for a drink and caught the last train home around 10pm so when we arrived we left scouts around the station (the under 18's) and had a few drinks in the Brunswick.

Well time was getting on and surprise surprise there was no sign of the Cockney twats. However, good news did come our way when the scouts came running down to tell us Spurs had turned up to catch the train! Fuck knows where they were playing but we didn't really care! Off we ran, going up the back way via the car park road behind the station approach, sending the scouts in to see where they were. They were in the bar and the train wasn't due to leave for another twenty minutes. We crept onto the platform and actually onto their train and sat there waiting for them to turn up. Eventually they did and we moved further along the carriages until we knew they were on the train and in their seats. Then we went back down the carriages and ambushed them, they were totally unprepared. They didn't know what hit them and they were getting it from all angles, everyone got punches in with very few of us getting one back, we certainly gave them a bruise or two to nurse on the way home. The announcement that the train was due to leave and the fact that the dibble were coming into the station had us all exiting the train and going off in different directions to avoid being nicked. Three of the lads were nicked but they 'only' ended up in the back of a meat wagon and being given a few slaps and then let go. Not within the law by any means, but a much preferred alternative to ending up in court on the Monday!

FURTHER ADVENTURES

We came across other firms - some pathetic - here are a few examples:

BURNLEY

City were playing Blackburn Rovers at home during one of our frequent seasons in the Second Division. We all met in the Brunswick and had scouts down at Piccadilly and Victoria stations – remember this was years before the luxury of mobile phones, so if anything was happening the scouts had to run back to the pub to inform us. It was a frustrating afternoon as Blackburn were nowhere to be seen in the town centre and around Maine Road – before or after the game. United didn't have a game that day so we knew they wouldn't be around either so we resigned ourselves to a day of drinking when one lad ran in to tell us that Burnley had arrived and were drinking in the Bull's Head. Burnley had a decent firm called 'The Suicide Squad' so we thought this would an ideal time to introduce ourselves. We made our way down there, sending scouts out ahead and they confirmed that they were still in there but we didn't want to have it with them in the Bull's Head, we knew the landlord and he was a decent bloke, so we went into the Waldorf nearby leaving the scouts outside watching Burnley.

They had had been playing at Stockport and fancied a pint or two in Manchester before heading back home after changing trains - there were about a hundred of them. A lot of us were impatient and wanted to have them there and then, but Donald said 'no' and when Donald said 'no', he meant 'NO'! Eventually, the scouts came into the Waldorf and said that they were drifting out in ones and twos. We went outside and followed them walking along London Road – but we were walking along the side streets discretely. They then stopped and looked around as if they were lost. They turned back around and headed back towards the Bulls Head, went past it and crossed over, heading towards Piccadilly Approach. We were able to sneak right round and as they reached the approach we just ran at them. They scarpered like fuck, the attack was a total surprise to them, they were tripping over each other as we were giving it to them. A couple of heroes decided to stand and face us and they were quickly wasted. One lad was on the receiving end of a right kicking but even we knew when to stop - there is no glory in just kicking someone senseless, ten lads onto one.

We bumped into Burnley a few years later having played at Bradford. Getting home from West Yorkshire by van or coach always saw us taking a wrong turn and we'd end up in somewhere like Skipton. So a few pints and a bag of chips later, we were heading towards Burnley and pulled into the town centre for a few beers. Being in a large group we were easily clocked by some locals (who thought we were scousers!) and continued walking into a pub. Here we were met by a large mob and one of them kindly suggested that we leave before 'we got killed'. Well as soon as he said that, we gave each other the nod and ran at the fuckers! Jimmy picked up a pint glass and smashed it in this lad's face, we ran out of the pub, collecting bottles and glasses on the way and waited for them to follow. We were right outside the door and as they came out, we greeted them with bottles, glasses and fists. We were well on top when from a side street came another mob. It was like Rawtenstall all over again with the Lancashire Hillbillies!

We moved back to regroup but by now we were getting whacked from all angles, there was only 25 of us. Then a strange thing happened as we were backing off – we heard a shout 'come on, lets give them a hand' and we were joined by a small group of lads. One of them was quite small and he just waded into them for fun, knocking them flying in the process. Another one was very tall and the others had quite large builds – we had no idea who they were or where they came from but we appreciated their help nonetheless! After that I don't recall a thing – I was cracked on the head (again!) and woke up in hospital! I came round as a nurse was checking on me and then the doctor came and said they were keeping me in overnight as a precaution. The nurse told me another lad from Manchester was two beds up and also in for the night. I looked over and there was Dave looking at me, we smiled to each other and then laughed as quietly as we could, though this hurt a little as my face was bruised. Dave said that he saw me hit the deck and he went in to get me up and that's when he got smacked on the head - the next thing he remembers is waking up in hospital!

In the morning we were discharged and made our way to the train station. On the train, it wasn't too long before the guard came along asking for our tickets. We told him that we had just been released from hospital having been attacked and robbed the night before in Burnley and therefore had no money. It was obvious from our wounds that we had been in hospital and the guard told us not to worry about the tickets. He then began to tell us of a similar incident that happened to him and by the time we had got to Manchester we knew his whole life story! As we got off at Victoria, Dave said to me 'Fuck me, my head was sore from last night, he's just made it ten times worse!'

IPSWICH TOWN

We played away at Ipswich one Saturday in the mid 90's and met up on the Friday night and it was freezing. We were in the Brunswick and lads were dropping out left, right and centre. Most just couldn't be bothered as it was too far away or Ipswich just had little or nothing to offer. In the end there were about twenty-five of us left. Donald couldn't be bothered going and there wasn't enough for a coach so we decided to get an early morning train to London and change there for the train to Ipswich. At least we could get our heads down on the way – or so we thought!

We were all playing cards and drinking the beer we brought with us when two girls appeared on the train. Naturally we were all trying to impress them and trying to chat them up. We took the piss out of them when they said they supported United. One of them was a red head and you could tell she was up for a shag! She was leaning over Dave when talking to him and enjoying the fact that he was fondling her tits whilst she leant over him. Dave and the red head eventually sneaked off to another compartment thinking we hadn't noticed, but we gave them a little bit of quality time together before tracking them down. The daft twats hadn't even locked the compartment door! Soon the door burst open and we were spraying their bare arses with beer. That didn't stop them so we took their clothes and one of the lads was running around the carriage with this bird's knickers on his head. Jimmy shouted to the lad that he could see a skid mark on the knickers and he ran into the toilet washing his head and hair! We ended up burning them and throwing them of out the window.

Eventually, after a long journey via London, we got to Ipswich and decided to blag a hotel room for a few hours so we could get ready for the match. We found a small hotel and a few of us went inside and asked for three rooms for the night. Clearly the bloke on reception was more used to things being a lot slower - and dare I say a bit more honest - as he failed to see so many of us creep past him as we made a barrier in front of him as the rest went upstairs. Not only that but he seemed more than happy when we offered to pay him later after we had caught up on some sleep and we all piled into the three rooms, bodies all over the place as we got our heads down until early afternoon. At 2pm someone came around waking us all up and we got ourselves together and made our way out. The hotel manager even told us the way to the ground, wished us good luck and said we could settle the bill after the game...

We made our way in the direction he gave us and came across a bus stop with a few blues waiting as well as a few Ipswich too. As the bus turned up, those in front got on and then as we got on, a few spoke to the driver, causing a distraction, whilst the rest of us jibbed it. One of the few Ipswich fans started grumbling about the length of time we were at the bus stop. Jay turned around and said in a strong voice 'Why don't you just shut the fuck up?' They just looked at Jay as if to say 'and who do you think you are?' By now we were sat all around them and Jay said to them 'lads, sit down, shut up and we'll be on our way'. They looked around and on recognising they were both outnumbered and surrounded, decided to do as they were told! After that we started talking to them, winding them up and after a while we could see they were crapping it so we told them we weren't going to do anything to them. After that, we had a laugh with them and they were OK.

Once off the bus we headed for the away end and as usual, we were doubling up with lads who were paying to get in. Others didn't bother waiting until someone paying came along and simply vaulted the turnstile! Just as Dave and I were about to vault through, the door on the turnstile slammed shut – Dave was almost in mid-air and he came to a halt, before falling on the floor. He was about to get up when I told him to stay down on the ground. Jimmy and I legged it to the next turnstile to explain to the operator there that Dave was just about to pay to go in when the operator slammed the door on him and now he is hurt on the ground. We told him that we wanted to see the operator from the next turnstile or we would get the police. The man came and we explained what happened and that if he didn't let us in for free we would call the police and he'd probably lose his job. Well he didn't need too long to think about what to do, so we 'carefully' helped Dave up and onto his feet and we all got in buckshee!

By this time the game had kicked off and we decided to get a quick beer and take it on to the terrace. As we were being served, Ipswich scored. As we were waiting for everyone to get their beer, one of the lads spotted a door slightly ajar, so a few of us kept watch whilst he nipped inside. Within seconds he was out saying quietly 'come on, fuck the drink, let's go'. We moved into the toilet area and a cash bag was produced and we counted out £200 in notes and £30 in 50p coins, ditched the bag and went to watch the game. As the second half started, so did the snow and after a while we were fed up with the boring game and decided to leave the ground and head for a pub. On our way out, Tommy – who had the money in his pocket – received a tap on the shoulder. He shit himself whilst a women told him he had dropped some money on the floor on his way out. Embarrassed, he took it off her and thanked her. Just as we left the ground, we heard a mini roar and soon sussed out that City had equalised. Even then, it was too cold as the snow fell heavier and we couldn't be arsed going back in and headed for the pub instead.

We tried to get in the supporters club but they wouldn't have it – even as we blagged and blagged, they wouldn't budge and let us in. We were told there was a boozer two minutes away. When we got there there were a few lads in the corner giving us the evils from the start. The landlord had a small radio on the bar that was relaying commentary from the game and with minutes to go City scored their second goal to go 2-1 up. We cheered and, as the lads in the corner looked on, we exaggerated our celebrations even more. The next thing a glass went flying in our direction, just missing Jimmy's head. That was it – Jimmy grabbed a chair and ran at them, with the rest of us picking up stools and chairs, smashing them up and using the wood as weapons and battling with them. They were heading for the door but we cut them off, whacking them with the chair legs and one was cracked on the head with a bottle.

Eventually they got outside but so did we - charging after them, chasing them down the road. There must have been seventy of them and only twenty-five of us but we didn't give a fuck, we knew we could take them. Once we stopped chasing, they disappeared around a corner and we knew they would regroup and come back at us. So we carried on forward, but instead of following them around the corner, we carried straight on ahead, pretending we hadn't noticed them turn the corner. Then, as we had gone ahead of them, Jimmy said 'next right lads' and as we did, Dave told us to keep going and he and two others would drop back and wait to see if they followed us. The three of them jumped into a garden and hid whilst we carried on. Sure enough the twats followed us so we carried on and turned the next corner and then waited for them to catch us up. Just as they were about to reach us, we turned back around the corner and fronted them – just as Dave and the other two are steaming in from behind them. We charged them and they legged it, Jimmy just waded in - the Tractor Boys ran like fuck and that was the last we saw of them!

OLDHAM ATHLETIC - GOOD FRIDAY 1984

This game became infamous. City hadn't played outside the top flight for nearly twenty years so this visit to our near neighbours was always going to attract a large 'away' following - in the end it turned into a City home game.

Donald arranged for everyone to meet in the city centre to catch the bus to Oldham, but as it was easier for me to catch a bus from Middleton, I arranged to meet the lads in Yonner land. I caught the bus around 10am and there was quite a few blues from Blackley on it. We all got off near Yates's Wine Lodge and there was already a queue of blues waiting for it to open. They were already drinking and were armed with a load of cans from an off licence around the corner. The next train wasn't due for 25 minutes so while I waited I took in the assorted faces in the crowd. At the time City had four firms in action. Donald and Co arrived and they were with a blue from Chadderton who knew the area and took us to a quieter pub away from the city centre and dibble. As kick-off approached we made our way to the ground and Oldham were no where to be seen blues were everywhere.

Once inside it didn't take long for it to kick-off. City fans to the right of the away end had somehow obtained a ladder and they climbed up from the terrace into the seats above them, beating off stewards and Oldham fans in the process. Once the stewards and Oldham fans abandoned the seats, City fans in their dozens climbed up the ladder from the terrace and took the seated area! Across the other side of the ground in the Chaddy End, there was a big fight too. Lads were being kicked down the terrace steps. From the opposite end we assumed it was Oldham v City – I later found out it was City v City as gangs from neighbouring Blackley and Moston decided to settle local issues inside Boundary Park.

In my early days I was involved in a fair few fights between the two areas, with me coming from Blackley, but through football and the Mayne Line I got to know a few Moston lads and never got involved in local battles after that. The dibble were overwhelmed as it was going off on all three sides of the ground, the only exception being the away end, the end where we were! After the game we were let out and went on a looting spree of local shops and off licences, gathering the night's beer and food for when we were back home. Again, the dibble just couldn't be everywhere at the same time and it ended up as a free-for-all. The game was on Good Friday. The *Manchester Evening News* christened the day 'Black Friday', showing pictures of City fans going wild. It was featured on Granada reports and BBC North West too.

The following season we heard they were bringing a firm down to Maine Road, looking for revenge. We have never pissed ourselves so much. They turned up on one coach, receiving a full escort in and out of the ground rather than come alone on the train and have a go. For the reverse fixture back at Boundary Park we arrived early again and we heard they didn't even go to the game! If they did, they certainly didn't show their faces. A few years later (following a promotion and another relegation) we played them again and we went to look for them in Yates. The stupid twats wouldn't come out, so we smashed the place up, the windows went through, table and chairs flying everywhere. The barman grabbed the till and ran through the fire escape! The dibble were nowhere to be seen for a while and when the scouts left outside the pub gave the call that they were on their way, we just ran out in all directions. Both the pub and Oldham were turned over good style that day.

Years later, in 2005, we lost to Oldham in the cup. I was staggered when a lad from a young City firm told me that they had a bit of a set to with Oldham in Failsworth – he said groups from Carlisle United and Hibernian came down to help Oldham out!

LUTON - 1983

The scene was set – it was the last match of the season and City were fourth from bottom and playing Luton who were third from bottom, occupying the final relegation spot. City were a point ahead of the Hatters and only needed a draw at Maine Road to stay in the 1st Division. Luton had been in and around the bottom three all season – City had been in the top six at

Christmas and had slowly slipped down the table with John Bond resigning as manager along the way, to be replaced by his assistant John Benson.

All week it was very tense. The last time City had been relegated was in 1962 and since then we'd won all the domestic trophies and the European Cup Winners' Cup under Joe Mercer in the late 60's/early 70's. A whole generation of blues had grown up with a reasonably successful side and it was only two years before that we'd been a few minutes away from winning the FA Cup against Spurs in 1981.

On the day of the game we were all in the pub, people were drinking but it remained tense, we were singing, trying not to think about the nightmare of going down. I walked past the Kippax, round the North Stand and jibbed my way into the Main Stand. I was stood up at the back, with a load of other lads, the stand seemed full and people were complaining about lads being sat in their seats – hundreds must have jibbed their way in that day! Apart from the away end, the ground was packed. Luton fans were housed in the top corner of the Kippax and barely filled up their pen. It was a very tense game but you just couldn't see City losing. Time went on and it was still 0-0 so we were still safe - as long as we didn't concede...

With four minutes to go a Luton player crossed the ball into the City box, Alex Williams – City's keeper – punched the ball out straight to Raddy Antic, the Luton sub who had only been on the pitch a few minutes. Antic smashed he ball home and Luton were winning 1-0. The crowd went quiet, the Kippax was heaving yet seemed paralysed, silenced and motionless. As the seconds ticked away, the police and stewards were arranging themselves around the pitch and at the final whistle, a stunned home crowd watched in horror as David Pleat, Luton's manager, did his infamous run onto the pitch to greet his players who had run to the corner of the Kippax where the away fans were housed. That was the cue for City fans to invade the pitch. Stewards and dibble were brushed aside as fans from all four sides of the ground took their anger and frustration out on the Luton players, who went from celebrating to running for their lives. Pleat was punched in the face as he retreated and one or two of the players, Ricky Hill in particular, were surrounded by mobs, holding his fists up and constantly turning around as lads got nearer and nearer to them.

They were rescued by mounted police who charged onto the pitch having come in through the tunnel under the open Kippax corner – and escorted off the pitch safely. I came out of the Main Stand and onto Maine Road, outside the entrance to the ground there was an angry mob chanting 'Swales Out' (it was the first time I had heard the chant – and it certainly wasn't going to be the last time it was vented over the next decade!). City fans then began to fight amongst themselves as anti and pro-Swales factions squared up to each other. I remember trying to break up one fight but as I did that two other fights were starting up around me. I shouted out 'fuck me, we're supposed to be after Luton, not each other!'

I met up with a few lads and we made our way around the ground to the back of the Kippax where the away fans were, but the police wouldn't let us down the alleyway behind the Platt Lane stand as it was kicking off with them and City in the Kippax car park. The police were under fire from all sorts of missiles, as were the Luton fans as bottles and bricks were thrown over the high wall protecting them. We finally managed to make our way down the back alley and could see all the missiles being thrown and for a minute they thought we were Luton and started throwing all sorts of shit at us. 'Fuck off you daft twats, we're City' we shouted and finally they stopped and we joined the mob waiting for Luton to come out.

The dibble had no chance. Normally they would be dealing with a few hundred hooligans – there were over a thousand on the car park venting their frustration so it didn't matter how many times they charged us or how many they nicked, there was just too many of us for them to do anything about it. Nothing was going to stop us. Police vans were overturned, officers were injured, City fans cars were caught in the hail of bricks and bottles and windows were smashed, it was like Beirut. The Luton fans coaches were parked over by Hough End Fields and lads made their way over there to smash them up. Luton fans were walking towards the coaches in small numbers, wearing their distinctive orange colours as they had no jackets to hide them and were getting chased, caught and kicked to fuck. A coach came towards us on Princess Parkway and we stood there with bricks in our hands and luckily (for them) we saw two blokes at the front of the coach frantically waving City scarves at us to indicate they were blues. It was the Leicester & Rugby branch of the City Supporters Club who followed the blues everywhere - they looked pretty relieved as we acknowledged them and allowed them by. I knew one of their members and he told me when I next saw him that all the Luton coaches that they passed on the motorway had most of their windows put through, with Luton fans hanging out of the windows celebrating their win.

That night was a real night of violence in the city centre - anyone who wasn't a blue was getting smacked. What was worse is it eventually became City v City as it ended up with no one to fight. Certainly Luton fans were not going to show their faces and United had the brains to stay away too, so blues took their anger out on each other for whatever reason, maybe district v district having ago at each other over long-running territorial battles, I don't know, but the police sirens were going off all night long. The next day in the papers and on the news, it was all about the match – both on and off the pitch – and they even showed Pleat getting smacked and we all recognised the lad who did it, he was one of Mayne Line, yet he was never caught and charged for it, we just couldn't believe it!

SUNDERLAND

One Saturday in the early 80s we played Sunderland at home and we assumed they would come to Maine Road with a firm. We met up early and it was a good job too. The train came in at 11am at Piccadilly and as we stood around sussing them out, there was plenty of lads with red and white striped shirts on, who we let go past as behind them was around 50 lads wearing no colours. We waited for them behind Piccadilly Approach and as they came out we hit them. We chased them down the approach road and they turned the wrong corner and ended up being trapped. It was show-time as there was no way out other than behind us. They had one really big lad trying to keep it together but to no avail. We targeted him and as much as we admired him for standing there and taking it, soon he was on the deck getting a good kicking, covered in blood. He got up and wanted more, but we knew when to stop and he had definitely had enough. We left them to lick their wounds and went in search of more Mackems. We found a group of around three hundred being escorted to the ground and followed them, hoping for a way in, to split the escort and cause confusion and to steam in. There were little gangs of City fans on most street corners trying to do the same as us but the dibble had it sorted and they managed to get them into the away end without trouble.

After the match it was a different story – as they were being taken towards the Sherwood pub, we ambushed them. The plan was to get kids to bombard them with whatever they could lay their hands on, bricks, bottles etc. This caused the confusion needed and split them up and we just picked them off as they ran. There were too many of us for the dibble to deal with. I remember one City lad running along with a brick in his hand and just smashing it into a Mackem's face as he passed him. I was on a right buzz and caught up with one lad and was just hitting him and hitting him until he went down. All the way back to the station it was running battles all over the place. They were totally spanked that day.

Strangeways Here I Come

Sheffield United

As mentioned in the Sheffield Wednesday piece, Sheffield United had a good firm with some game lads. They were also a bit like Everton in carrying blades – quite appropriate given their nickname! On one occasion in 1984 we got there quite early and they were already there with a welcoming committee. We were on our way from the station into the city centre and they jumped us from behind some bus shelters. We stood our ground and battled with them, they were pulling out knives and lashing out at us. By now a few stragglers from the station had caught up and joined us, some of them had small rounders bats and one had a meat cleaver! One Sheffield lad was in front of us brandishing his blade as one of us just ran at him, rounders bat in hand and cracked him across the head, yet with blood pouring from his wound he never went down, he still stood there waving his knife around. We eventually got them backing off – all except the lad with the head wound, he was well over six foot tall and standing his ground. We all left him alone, telling him to go home and get cleaned up but he wasn't having it and wanted to carry on.

We walked away and headed for the ground. There were little battles all the way there as we walked past pubs and side streets. A few of us managed to get into their end and were fighting sporadically throughout the game. I tried to jib my way into their end but got slung out by stewards as quickly as I had got in. I then tried to get in a few other turnstiles but they were on to me. After the game I was on my own and their firm had got together and were standing at the end of the road. I mingled in among their fans and walked along with them. The firm were on their tip-toes, clocking everyone who went past, my heart was pounding like fuck. I did get clocked, but it was by a United fan wearing a shirt and scarf. I thought he was going to point me out as he tapped me on the shoulder, but he didn't, instead he said 'Here, put this on' as he handed me a scarf to put around my neck. I was very grateful but still shitting it as I got near to them - I hadn't got a clue which direction I was going, where the station was or where the other lads were. As I'm walking past them, one of them must have sensed my nervousness and again my new found friend helped me out by talking to me as if we were together. I made it worse by looking at this lad looking at me. He was sure I was a City fan but thankfully confused by the scarf and my 'friend' wearing a United shirt.

We got round the corner – with a huge sigh of relief – and within seconds a taxi appeared. My 'friends' flagged it down and they told me to join them inside. They asked the driver to go to the town centre and we drove very slowly through the crowds. In fact it would have been quicker to walk. Within a few minutes I looked behind and could see a mob walking the same way we were going – and catching us up. I thought they were City at first and was going to make a move but decided to wait as I didn't want to get out and find out they were Blades. As they walked past I recognised a few faces and said to the lads in the taxi that I would get out here. I offered them some taxi fare but they wouldn't have it. I said to them that if it wasn't for them I'd have been killed back there, I asked the driver to borrow a pen and bit of paper and gave them my phone number and said if they wanted to come to Maine Road I'd make sure they had a good time. They gave me their number and we shook hands.

I was just about to get out when there was a big 'BANG' on the side of the taxi. I looked around and it was Dave laughing his head off at me. 'You daft twat' I shouted 'you shit me up' I added, before reassuring the lads in the taxi and the driver that everything was OK. The taxi went off and I told the lads what had happened to me and Dave was saying that they hadn't seen any Blades since leaving the ground. Both sides of the road leading back into the city centre was pure City. Dave told me that everyone was heading home - Chelsea were playing at Bolton and there had been a few phone calls between City and

Chelsea and a meet had been arranged. This definitely sounded better than hanging around Sheffield so we walked a bit quicker to make sure we didn't miss the train.

As we got to the station, we heard a big roar as women, kids and men came running out off the platform and into the main station concourse. We ran through onto the platform and City were backing the Blades off – unfortunately we were on the end of the platform where United were. We tried to make our way through them to get to the City end and join the boys – but I ended up getting whacked by none other than Jimmy! He was bouncing around all over the place until he saw it was me he had hit! The next thing to happen was my arm was twisted up my back and two coppers knocked me to the floor. I was struggling a bit and ended up getting my head knocked against the concrete floor. At the station, some fucking Blade idiot spat in my face whilst I was stood there with my hands behind my back, I went over and was lashing out at him, kicking him with my feet. The dibble came over and threw me in a cell.

In court, I was given a suspended sentence and a £50 fine. Then two weeks later (1st December 1984) against Oldham, I was nicked again and sent down. After the game we had gone looking for Oldham in the town centre and found them in Yates's. There were around twenty five of us but we were soon sussed out by the dibble who told us all to move along and get back to Manchester. I refused and was promptly taken away in the back of a van. The judge was this weedy little twat with small specs on that he kept pushing up his nose every time they slipped down. He was giving me a lecture for about twenty minutes, saying 'people like you never learn, do you Sullivan?' I just kept looking at him as if to say 'shut the fuck up, you stupid twat'. After he finished going on with himself, he said, 'I sentence you to twelve months imprisonment, take him down'.

I spent the night in the court cells next to some smack head doing cold turkey. I had one blanket, the place was fucking freezing and dark as the windows were blackened. I pressed the buzzer and asked a screw for an extra blanket and eventually he came with one. The junkie in the next cell kept shouting out 'Boss, Boss, I want to see a doctor'. I shouted back at him 'shut the fuck up and go to sleep'. He called back at me 'look, you don't understand...' I interrupted him and said 'I don't understand what you silly twat? You took the fucking drugs so now do your cold turkey and shut up.' This seemed to get through to him and it was quiet for the rest of the night, not that I got much sleep in that freezing cell.

In the morning I was taken to Strangeways and a mate of mine, Alex (from Blackley), was in the same van! We convinced a screw that we were cousins and they put us in a cell together. Our cell had four beds and it turns out that Alex knew one of them who was from Langley, whilst the other lad was from Moston – we had many funny discussions of gang fights between Blackley and both Middleton and Moston lads when we were younger! After a week at Strangeways, we were individually called out to see the allocation officer. I was told I was going to Kirkham – halfway between Preston and Blackpool, an open prison, some of the lads said it really was like a holiday camp! The lad from Langley was also being sent there but we were gutted when Alex told us he was being shipped out to Risley.

On our final night in Strangeways we couldn't sleep so we just stayed awake chatting. In the morning we were stood in the yard waiting for the transport and they read all the names out for Kirkham. There weren't many names read out, but the last one shocked us – it was Alex, who by now was laughing at us both. He had been allocated to Kirkham all along but had wanted to wind us up - I couldn't believe he had been able to keep it up for so long! We were all chuffed as fuck to be in there together. Again they put us in together and once again Alex knew a few faces in there which is always a help so you don't get mither from lads trying it on thinking you don't know anyone inside. Compared to Strangeways, Kirkham was a different world – a holiday.

The time seemed to fly by once you had a routine. I decided to do a full-time education course because there was no way I was going to work full-time for £8 a week, earning them twats a load of money. On release it felt strange going through the gates, as one of the lads picked me up and drove me home I fell asleep in the car. The first night at home I couldn't sleep and it took a week or two to adjust to my own bed, but once I found a new routine to follow, I got back to normality. And of course, 'normal' for me involved meeting up with the lads and going to Maine Road!

One night, Don and Geoff invited me out with them to 'Rotters', what could be termed a notorious Manchester nightspot. Don started going on with himself about how great Mayne Line were and how the younger lads had kept it going. Geoff told Don to leave it out but he just kept going on and on. I snapped 'If it wasn't for us lot at the Arndale, there wouldn't be a Mayne Line, we were there at the start and we got you the fucking reputation you and the younger ones have now, when you've needed to show face the young un's aren't even there and it's us that have stood and fought.' Donald started laughing, 'Calm down. I'm just having a laugh with you, I was just trying to see if the passion and fight was still in you or if that bird had softened you up, I'm pleased to see it hasn't.' Soon we were laughing about it and reminiscing about old times.

That weekend City didn't have a game for whatever reason so on the Saturday morning I went into town for the first time since getting out. Everything looked the same, the Arndale, the Underground, the shops, the faces. It was about 10am when two lads came in saying there was a firm down at Victoria station but he didn't know where they were from. We went round to see if Donald was in the Underground and he was. We got a few more lads together and made our way via Shambles Square and the back streets into Victoria. We sent the scouts ahead to see if they were still there and they met us outside saying there were now around eighty to a hundred of them, all big fuckers. We still couldn't work out where they were from so we split up to make it look as if there was more of us than there actually was. We came into the station and walked right amongst them and they didn't bat an eyelid. One lad looked at us and Donald went up to him and asked him where they were from. 'Widnes' he replied. They had a Scouse accent, so Donald asked him who they supported. 'Widnes Rugby League' came the reply. Donald went straight to the point: 'do you want a battle with Man City? Go and get your boys out of the café and bar and tell them that we are waiting for them'. He shot over to the bar area – and locked the door behind him as his mates came over to the windows, looking out at us shitting themselves. It was obvious they didn't want to know so we backed off and made our way out of the station.

As we were leaving, one lad who was at the back, turned around and saw there was another firm on the other side of the platform. He reported to us and we went and had a look but assumed they were just more rugby league fans and not worth bothering with. Then someone else we knew came running over, telling us they were Swansea City en route to Tranmere Rovers and were hopelessly lost. 'Wrong stop at the wrong time', we thought! We marched quietly over the platform bridge and onto the platform where they stood. As we came nearer to them, one called out, asking us who we were. We just gave it the 'come on' and they started bouncing around and we went for them. They were trying to come towards us but it was the usual 'two steps forward and three steps back'. One lad stood his ground, he was only a small lad, but he ended up getting smacked to fuck but as soon as he hit the deck he was back up for me, a right game fucker he was and he cracked me back, which I wasn't expecting but two more right handers from me and he was back down - where he stayed as he took a good number of kicks from three or four of us.

A few other Swansea were on the end of a hiding, the rest were legging it across the tracks to the safety of the other platforms across the way. I was buzzing, it was my first ruck in months as I'd been banged up - I was hyper that day. After around five or ten minutes we heard the dibble were on their way so we split up and made ourselves scarce. None of us were injured or nicked, it was a result and I was back in the swing. I couldn't wait for Tuesday to come as City were playing away at Blackpool in the cup – it couldn't come soon enough for me!

BLACKPOOL

Even though it was a night match we set off in the van at 11am and arrived in Blackpool an hour later and went straight into the pubs along the front. We weren't the only ones with the same idea as all we could see were blue and white shirts and scarves everywhere. We knew they had a decent firm as one of our lads had worked on the Pleasure Beach and knocked around with a few of them on his days off. Their trick was knowing that away fans arrived early and drank heavily, so by the time any action came, they were sober, handy lads fighting against half pissed lads, caught off their guard. We continued drinking through the day just going from pub to pub whilst at the same time making our way to the ground. At one point lads were lagging behind and throwing up in back streets as they'd drunk too much.

As it got nearer to kick off, it was pure City everywhere, without a tangerine shirt in sight. Of course not many of us had tickets for the game and we ended up next to the ticket office. Some lads looked through the window and then at the side door - which was slightly a jar. They just ran in and came straight out with a load of tickets in their hands. We looked through the window and didn't think the staff even knew what had happened! The next thing we clocked was a nice little scam being pulled by other lads. If you stood by another window, it was possible to see the pile of envelopes with tickets inside them with the names in full view. All you had to do was remember the names and address and ask for the tickets and the staff gave them to you! After watching two lads do this, Billy followed suit and we ended up with an envelope containing eight tickets. We didn't want to go into the ground yet, we were still looking for Blackpool but there was nothing down for us. Donald then suggested we went into their end and we made our way to the turnstiles. Donald created the perfect decoy by chatting to the bloke on the turnstile whilst the rest of us crawled underneath the revolving mechanism of the turnstile.

We all got in and within minutes City scored and we went bananas! As we were celebrating we were attacked by their firm - we hadn't been in there long enough to suss out that they had moved directly behind us – and they caught us totally by surprise. One lad, James, was cracked on the head and went down but was straight up again, head down and charging at them, we needed to have a few moments where we could just group together and face them, which we finally did. It was pretty hairy and lasted a while, the dibble were all at the other end of the ground watching the City fans in the away end. Blackpool were a tough bunch but we began to get the upper hand, picking them off in twos and threes and they were backing off, I managed to crack one lad on his jaw and he slipped on the terrace and screamed as he went on the receiving end of many pairs of shoes. The dibble arrived but they didn't have enough numbers to deal with it so they had to back off until reinforcements arrived. They were just picking us off and throwing us out – only one lad got nicked all night!

Outside we were lined up but just walked through the police line and away from the ground. There wasn't enough of them outside to deal with us so they simply walked along behind us, keeping us in check. We walked up the front and ended up in the Manchester pub – a where else were going to head for? The dibble were happy to sit outside and keep an eye on us whilst we got the beers in. We were there for most of the game and the landlord came out later and gave us a huge hot pot to share. Donald organised a whip round for him but he wouldn't take it, so as we left we placed it on the bar. On leaving, the dibble were still outside, freezing their balls off whilst we'd been nice and warm inside, silly twats. We were going in search of their firm, sending the younger scouts out ahead but they kept returning with no information. We decided to call it a day and return home, calling in at one more pub for a final drink, not too far from the station.

After a while this lad we called 'Mad Dog' came in - we called him that as he was small and stocky and walked like a Staffordshire bull terrier. He told us he had just had a chat with a Blackpool lad who had told him that their firm were drinking in a pub not too far from where we were. Again we sent a scout out with Mad Dog to check if the information was correct. Moments later they returned to confirm they were in the pub which was just five minutes away. Off we went, following the two of them and found that the pub was surrounded by waste land containing all sorts of stuff we could use as ammunition – broken bricks and rocks, pieces of wood and metal. We ran quietly towards the pub and the silence was soon broken by SMASH, SMASH, SMASH – as the windows were put through. We followed up by running straight into the doors and whacking them over the heads with the stuff we had picked up but not thrown through the windows. It happened that quick they just didn't have time to react. One of their lads had a load of blood all over his face, like in a horror movie, whilst another lad had a cut stomach and his white shirt was turning blood red as he held the wound. One or two of our lot received cuts and wounds but nothing like what they received. We could see the landlord calling 999 so didn't hang around for too long, leaving almost as soon as we'd arrived.

We headed back to the promenade and the dibble turned up. They knew we had turned over the pub but couldn't do anything about it as we were not there when they arrived. We just stood on the front taking the piss out of them. Eventually they had enough and escorted us to our buses and followed us out of town and on to the motorway. I gave a wry smile to myself as we passed the slip road for 'Kirkham' – this time last week I was banged up in there, now I was a free man and had been out and about trashing Blackpool town centre and their fans. It was a good result all round.

*   *   *

Unfortunately my new found freedom didn't last too long though as the following week I was nicked for shop lifting and credit card fraud. I received another stretch inside, this time 10 months. Again I found myself back in Strangeways and within a week I was following the route back to Kirkham again. I signed up to play for the prison football team and we had a good side. A few weeks later, someone came in saying that new arrivals had turned up and two footballers were amongst them – one ex-United and a current Liverpool player! At the next meal time everyone was surrounding them, welcoming them and wanting to be their new best mate - they were Jan Molby and Mickey Thomas. After that football training was amazing as they were taking it! Molby reckoned I wasn't a bad player, which was a great compliment. I spoke to him a few times before he ended up getting shipped out to another prison because Kirkham was an open prison, it was piss easy for the press and photographers to get into the grounds and take pictures of him.

They didn't seem to be bothered about Mickey Thomas as he

was no longer a top player so he was able to stay. Soon Thomas was training and picking the side alongside the Physical Training Instructor. He worked us hard – but fair - in the gym. He really got us fit and because he wasn't a screw we wanted to do it for him. He suggested to me that I played left back, but I had never played there before and was right footed! He suggested I tried it out the next time we practised. He had us playing two-touch football, control and pass, and we soon got the hang of it. We played our first game and won 4-0 – they just couldn't live with our level of fitness. I got to know Mickey quite well – lets face it, we had plenty of time on our hands to get to know each other, he was doing 18 months for fraud. He'd be in our cell, chatting about all the stories of the changing room and staying in hotels, he always had us laughing, but he wasn't up himself either and always saw himself as being no better or worse than the rest of us in there and was always willing to help people out where he could. It was funny when a few of the lads came to visit me and Mickey would be in the next seat or sat behind me. They would be doing double takes and saying 'Is that who I think it is' and I'd be introducing them to Mickey and he'd be signing autographs for them.

The last time I saw him, just before I was released, I was called by some lads to see him – he threw a bucket of cold water over me, it was his farewell present to me! I had his phone number but ended up losing it, though I did write to him once he got out but I never heard from him, which is fair enough as you have to try and get on with your life once you are back out. I can say, however, it was really good to meet and get to know him, he really was a gentleman. I never imagined I'd meet anyone famous in prison and I met two footballers. It is one of my best memories from being inside.

Yet Thomas and Molby were not the only celebrities I came across during my stints inside. During my first stay at The Strangeways Hotel - and indeed my first time in an adult jail - it was far more relaxed than the young offenders prisons I'd been placed at - no making your bed along with daily inspections for a start. The downside, though, came when I learnt that we were to be banged up for twenty-three hours a day and if we were luckily enough to get a day without rain or snow, we got an hour's exercise walking around in the yard.

One day we were walking around when a mate of mine nudged me and said 'Fucking hell, do you know who that is over there'. To be honest I didn't recognise him, but my mate said it was the drummer from the band The Housemartins (who had been sent down for arson). I knew and liked The Housemartins but wouldn't recognise the drummer from anyone. Just before the end of the hour, we went over and had a chat with him, nothing too heavy, just introducing ourselves and asking if he was OK etc. Unfortunately he was on a different wing to us and the next time we saw him during exercise everyone had cottoned onto who he was and he was surrounded by hangers on so we left him alone - yet just before the time was up, he came over to us asking us questions about ourselves. A few days later, he came to see us as he had been given a transfer to another prison. He gave us his radio (radios were like gold dust inside) and we couldn't thank him enough. We shook his hand and wished him luck, he really was a top bloke and every time I hear 'Happy Hour', I always think of Hugh the drummer.

I Predict A Riot

Well if you think I didn't last long outside last time – less than two weeks – it was an even shorter period of time before I was back behind bars again. In fact, I didn't get beyond the gates at Kirkham before I was re-arrested! I had a previous fine of £300 outstanding and I was up before a judge and banged up for forty days. I was trying to explain to this twat of a judge that I'd just been in for the best part of six months but he wasn't interested. So it was back to Strangeways and hopefully transferred again to be back amongst friends in Kirkham. However, the transfer didn't happen, as they intended on keeping me in Strangeways for twenty days, after which I would be released. However, this proved to be a very eventful twenty days indeed!

I was put in B-wing which was a bit of a disappointment as I got to hear a few of the lads who were nicked in Operation Omega were in C-wing. A vicar came to see me and I told him what had happened and whilst he was sympathetic, he couldn't do anything about it. My auntie came in to see me and during the visit you could have heard a pin drop in the room, normally everyone would be chatting away so much that you had to raise your voice to be heard. On my way back to the wing I could sense something wasn't right. Inmates were complaining that they hadn't had exercise for a week, the food was like shit and we had to eat in our cell – people were getting angry. One night, two lads in opposite cells were just verbally abusing each other at the top of their voices. You could see the hate in their eyes, but not at each other – their hate of the system. All these small injustices added up, it was like a time bomb waiting to explode.

As I said, there were a few blues in C-wing and I tried to get in there to see them but was stopped by the screws and eventually locked in my cell to keep me away from the area.

One night, it was time for slop outs and the screws only opened a few doors and left the rest of the cells still with their buckets of piss and shit that now couldn't be emptied until the morning. Everyone was banging on the doors and going fucking mental all night. In the morning when they let us out, the contempt for the screws was obvious. Later that day it was time to watch our weekly film, the atmosphere was electric and I thought if something was likely to happen it was there and then, but it never did. I went back to my cell and had a chat with Glen who I shared it with. The following day was Sunday and Glen asked me if I wanted to go to the chapel. I said I couldn't be mithered, but he talked me into it. Most lads went there because it was a place where you could chill out for a bit and meet mates from different wings.

Normally there would be around forty to fifty here for the service – that day there was around four hundred, it was packed to the rafters with only enough screws on duty for about fifty of us. We were sat near the front and I recall Glen looking around and telling me there were only ten to fifteen screws present. As the last cons came in and sat down, the vicar stood up and was about to open his book when a lad at the front jumped up, pushed the vicar to the floor, grabbed the microphone and said 'let's party boys'. Although I felt sorry for the vicar, nothing could stop us going off on one and smashing the chapel up. All we could see were the screws fucking legging it for their lives as they were over-powered. One screw lost his set of keys and we were running around opening wings and doors. I was scared to fuck, but you just went with the flow, you couldn't stick your head above the mayhem and suggest what we were doing was wrong!

Some lads got into the drug store and were distributing all sorts of pills to everyone. Obviously there will be bits of this story I can't go into, there was a lot that happened that was covered up. Once everyone was free from their cells, a big mob made their way to the nonce's wing – where the sex offenders and rapists were housed. The screws had already got a few of them out before the mob reached it but once the screws saw literally hundreds of cons charging towards them, they fled the area. There were lads running around with knives stabbing nonces, some were holding nonces up by their throats, throwing them over the balcony. When I look back, everyone knew it was going to happen, even the screws knew it was going to happen or why else did they move those few nonces beforehand?

One screw was cornered and given a severe beating, he was trying to be brave and put a stand on, but his head ended up being kicked around like a football. When hundreds of cons are running round smashing the gaff you don't try and be a hero – you get the fuck out of there and run for your life. It was the sheer anger that had boiled over that sparked off the rioting. We were treated like animals so why the surprise when we behaved like animals?

I thought of trying to get into C-wing, to meet up with the lads I knew, but there were just too many people running around and it was best to stay with a large mob than go off on my own. I could see cons swallowing all sorts of pills as I was walking around with Glen, you could just see the hate in everyone's faces. Glen had just about served his sentence and was not far from being released so he had put up with all this crap from the screws for a few good years. We ended up running up the stairs and onto the roof and within minutes everyone was piling up the stairs attracting a large audience on Bury New Road. It was a nice sunny day and I took my top off as we came up. Some were throwing slates off the roof at those below and after a while, I threw my final slate down and told Glen I was going back down and he should too – after all he was due out soon. Glen was happy staying on the roof, so I shook his hand and made my way back down onto the landing.

As I came down, I knew some of the hardcore cons would stick it out for as long as they could and I also suspected Glen would be one of them. I was onto the landing and the screws were behind a locked gate on the other side. They were shouting at us to give ourselves up and we would be OK. I decided then that the best thing to do was to turn myself in and I was led away and eventually we were taken on a coach and shipped elsewhere, though they wouldn't tell us where we were going. I was handcuffed to this quiet lad who turned to me and said that he felt sorry for those sticking it out and that they would get a hiding from the screws. I told him it would be ok and they would be down from the roof later that night or in the morning... it would be 44 days before the last con gave himself up!

As the coach pulled away from the prison, the press were crowding around and taking pictures. We still had no idea where we were going but then we saw the signs for Liverpool and, as we got nearer, we assumed we were heading for Walton. Great, I thought, spending a couple of weeks with a bunch of mickeys! As we entered the city and we were all talking about Walton, this screw turns round and says 'you think you are going to Walton then? You are going somewhere even worse than that!' we all thought where in Liverpool could be worse than Walton? Then one lad calls out, 'oh no, not fucking Bridewell, fucking hell, we're for it now, they'll murder us in there' and the screw started laughing. A few of us thought this lad must be winding us up so we took no notice of him.

On arrival at Bridewell, we were left handcuffed on the coaches for ages. The place looked like a right shit hole, it resembled an old castle with blackened bricks. Eventually they took us off the coach two at a time and led us through to a holding bay that stunk of piss – the toilets were hummed, it looked like there was shit smeared across the walls. The place made Strangeways look like a 5-star hotel! They made us take a shower and you can imagine what state they were in and as we were getting out we heard a scream, followed by another one, a lad was shouting 'bastards, stop it you bastards'. We were drying ourselves off when a screw came in and said 'you finished in here?' He could see we had and turned back into the room he came from saying 'you ready for the next two?' We heard a voice call out 'bring them through'.

We were ushered into this room and there was four screws there, all big cunts, all well over six foot tall. I was told to get over to the bench, I could see they had chains coming out of the wall and I looked at them and said 'fuck off, you don't think I'm daft enough to get on there do you?' The next thing I got a whack on my back and I went down. The floor felt wet and as the first kick came my way I was rolling on the floor trying to get into a ball shape. They picked me up and put me up against the bench and told me to turn around, I was in agony as I turned and then they grabbed the chains and put them on my wrists. I was punched again in the stomach – I wanted to scream but didn't want to give them the satisfaction nor could I anyway as I was in that much pain. Then they unchained me and one of them said 'there, just to leave you in no doubt as to what the score is in here'. I got off the bench and could hardly move. The cunts were just laughing at me. I got onto the landing where the other lads who had gone through the same treatment were waiting. We all looked at each other thinking what sort of a nightmare is this? Eventually we were taken to our cells and were locked up for the night – I know I wasn't the only one who didn't sleep a wink that night.

In the morning they gave us bread and jam for breakfast, the bread was like cardboard. The bastards just took the piss all the time I was in there. For dinner, they gave us stone cold chips with a pie that stunk to fuck and was bone hard. It was like that for days until finally a screw came into my cell and told me to pack my kit – I was out of there! Someone had said they'd heard they were letting everyone out who only had a short amount of time to serve and I couldn't have moved quick enough getting my belongings together. I said my goodbyes to the other lads I'd travelled with and was taken down to the reception area where I overheard some screws saying that a fresh batch from Strangeways were on their way over, so they were clearly moving me on to let someone else in – I didn't give a fuck about them, as far as I was concerned, I was on my way out, that's all that mattered to me.

I was given my belongings and discharged via the front entrance – the Scouse twats didn't even give me any money to get home and neither did they give a shit when I asked them how I was going to get home! Fortunately my auntie was there in her car waiting for me as I walked through the gates. On the way back to her house she was telling me how Strangeways had been big news and that there were still a handful up on the roof demonstrating. I couldn't believe it, especially as I watched it on the news at her house and there was Glen still up there doing his bit for the cause!

CITY IN EUROPE

ALTERNATIVE ULSTER

Yeah yeah yeah - fuck off all you munichs and scousers laughing at this chapter's title - I couldn't give a fuck what you think. My adventures watching City in Europe have been limited for obvious reasons and apart from the 2003 - 04 season with a short run in the UEFA Cup, it had largely been restricted to pre-season friendlies until this past season.

My first two trips were to Cork in the Republic of Ireland and Belfast (via Holyhead and a night in Dublin) and whilst both were memorable trips, there was sadly no off field action to write about.

The highlight of the Cork trip was seeing the then manager Alan Ball wearing a brown flowered shirt, blue trousers and black and white shoes. There wasn't much of a stadium, just grass banks to stand/sit on, so we were able to move around and sit near the substitutes. We had Niall Quinn in stitches as we took the the piss out of Ball's fashion sense. A lad I knew turned out to be staying in the same hotel as the players and we managed to blag a lift on the team coach back to the hotel after the game with them and still ribbed the fuck out of Ball although he did take it in good spirit - not that he had any choice in the matter!

Previously, the trip to Belfast had proved to be a bit of an eye opener as the army were still on the streets at the time, which was something I had never seen on mainland Britain before. We were given a tour of the Loyalist estates, checking out the gable end murals on the walls. We ended up in a Glasgow Rangers bar on the Shankhill Road and we were introduced to a bloke in a wheelchair who told us he had been kneecapped by the IRA for being in the wrong place at the wrong time. The hotel we stayed in had a big fence all around it at the back, the manager said that behind the fence was a Nationalist estate and that we should definitely avoid going there and he also told us to be careful about what taxi firm we used and how to tell the difference between taxi firms on either side of the divide. Fuck me, it was a lot different from being back in Manchester calling a Cresta cab from North Manchester into town at night!

We ended up in one pub but began to be very wary of where we were, it was in the city centre but didn't know whether the pub was on one side or the other or neutral. We sat in the corner, heads down and not letting our accents give us away. Eventually we made our way back to the Shankhill Road and onto familiar territory. Even here though, you had to be careful. Some pubs were UVF (Ulster Volunteer Force) whilst others were UDA (Ulster Defence Association) and whilst on the 'same side' there was animosity between the two groups. In one bar at the end of the night, the landlord asked everyone to stand up and sing the national anthem - a cue for some of the lads to jump on stage and lead the punters through the song! After closing time, we ended up in a UVF club which was full of big lads wearing UVF t-shirts and badges and although we were quite tense, the place was very relaxed. Our hosts made sure we got back to the hotel in the right taxi and on entering our room of four beds, discovered there were now ten of us in there - plus a bird that one lad had brought back with him!

On another trip to Belfast, we bumped into fellow City fan Nick Leeson (who had become infamous after being jailed abroad for his role in the Barings bank fraud case) at Belfast airport. We ended up having a few pints with him at the airport along with a fair few laughs and then he paid for our taxi into Belfast city centre! Nice on Nick.

HAMBURG AUGUST 2002

At last, a decent friendly, for years City had played at Tranmere Rovers, Port Vale, Stockport and Scunthorpe - all clubs within an hour radius of Manchester. What the fans wanted was a real trip to somewhere tasty - both on and off the pitch! With former Hamburg star Kevin Keegan now City's manager, a game was arranged between the two clubs, resulting in over five thousand blues travelling to northern Germany for the game.

We went by plane and were soon checking into our hotel in a Turkish part of town. What a shit-hole it was and there wasn't enough room for everyone which left a few lads going mad at the manager. Luckily there was a bar next door so we all made our way in there to decide what to do. We had arrived on the day of the game but hundreds had been here since the night before when it had kicked off. Hamburg's second team, St Pauli (whose supporters are left-wing anarchists!) had played a friendly against the Dutch team FC Breda. St Pauli's stadium is right on the edge of the red light district which - naturally - is where City fans assembled for the night. Before not too long, the German police had closed off the square where City had gathered and would only allow blues inside the square which contained many pubs! The SV Hamburg fans took exception to this and, wound up by the constant chanting and singing by the City fans, began to throw bottles over the police lines into the square and they then very quickly retreated under a hail of bottles being thrown back. At one point, St Pauli fans arrived and chased their local rivals from the scene. The Reeperbahn belonged to City that night and even the 'ladies of the night' were going home early with very little business coming their way after hours of being hassled and verbally abused by pissed up blues!

So on the day of the game, both sets of fans were expecting things to hot up for the 4pm kick off game. Yet it was a relatively peaceful game (probably due to the fact that German stadiums have beer tents right outside the stadium and you can drink alcohol and watch the game at the same time - UK government take note!) and after the game (which we lost 1-0) we made our way to the local train station to head back into the city centre. Again, things were quiet until we pulled into one station and I was talking to a friend when a big German cunt making his way off the train cracks my mate full in the face. That was it - it went off big time. We piled off the train and jumped the Kraut bastard, knocking him to the ground and following up with plenty of footwork before the police came at us with batons, forcing us back on the train. But then we started laying into Hamburg fans on the train. It took ages before it finally set off and three stops later we got off. There were now only four of us and we hadn't a clue where we were. We ended up getting on the wrong train and being followed by a load of skin heads before getting a taxi back to the city centre and into the square that City fans had triumphantly taken the night before.

After a while there, we made our way back to the shit-hole of a hotel and met up with the rest of the lads sat outside the bar next door. As one lad went in for drinks, a couple of others went for a piss downstairs. I was just relaxing in the late evening sun when someone shouted 'fuck me' and grabbed a load of bottles and started throwing them. I jumped up, turned around and saw around thirty Turks steaming towards us. A few blues ran inside the bar whilst a few of us stood our ground. Those who had gone inside then came back out with more bottles and anything else they could throw at the Turks. They had come armed and were throwing things at us, one lad was dodging a bottle and tripped on the pavement, cracking his head open. In the end, the waiters behind the bar came out and helped us chase them off. What started that incident off I don't know, maybe they just fancied a pop at English football fans, who knows, but they didn't come back either way.

In the morning, we were again at the bar when the police were called by the hotel staff. One of the rooms had been completely trashed. The wash basin was hanging off, pipes had been pulled away from the wall - the room looked like a demolition site. The police were taking statements trying to work out who was in what room and also asking why there was blood all over the hotel steps which was from the night before. Eventually after two hours, the police arrested two lads and told everyone else to pack their bags and leave for the airport. I heard a few days later that the police wanted £30,000 damages from the two arrested lads or they would not release them from jail!

EUROPE FOR REAL!

City were a regular feature in European competitions in the late 60's and throughout the 70's - winning the European Cup Winners' Cup in 1970 and stuffing the likes of AC Milan in 1978. However, defeat to Borussia Monchengladbach in March

1979 proved to be the last game the club played in Europe for 24 years.

The barren run came to an end when City qualified for the UEFA Cup through the Fair Play League for the 2003/04 season. So the munichs mocked the back door entry but we didn't give a fuck what they thought, we never made the rules, we just went along with them and were happy to take the place as England's representative.

We were in the draw for the first qualifying round and were very disappointed to draw Total Network Solutions from North Wales - about fifty miles from Manchester and no passport required! A 5-0 home win in the first competitive game in the new stadium at Eastlands made the second leg a formality. City took 9,000 fans to Cardiff's Millennium Stadium whilst TNS had around 1,500 fans. Not the slightest bit of football hooliganism took place that day. A total waste of time if you ask me!

The first round proper saw us pitted against the Belgium side Lokeren and after a tight 3-2 home win, we were off in our thousands to the lowlands and hopefully a bit of continental action.

We took the train to London and Eurostar to Brussels. I saw a real old head, a lad called Gilly. You knew it must be a special occasion if you saw Gilly - he was the equivalent of the relative you only saw at weddings and funerals. The journey down was made quicker by the usual reminiscing of the 'good old days' and all the battles over the years were dissected over again. We finally arrived at the town of Lokeren and instantly recognised faces at the station and followed the noise of the City fans in the town and came across thousands of blues in the main town square - clearly there were far more fans than tickets. For what seemed like the next hour, we were just shaking hands and greeting lads we had long forgotten about, lads who had come out of retirement for City's first venture into Europe in twenty four years, every Tom, Dick and Harry was there. Fuck TNS, this was the real thing! There were fans lined up all along the square, grandfather, father and son - three generations following their club together.

Of course, it wasn't long before the Belgium dibble became

interested and they started to film us in the square. For me it was a case of turning my back to the camera and keeping a low profile. We also decided to make our way to the ground. Gilly was telling us proudly how he had managed to buy a ticket whilst we were in no doubt that we would get in - what we never expected was just how easy it would be. We bumped into a tout we knew, who told us there was no turnstiles at the stadium, just a line of stewards you had to pass. Well fuck me, there was thousands of blues walking down the street towards the ground. We came up to the line of stewards and the flow of fans behind you simply carried you beyond them. Some blues held up Manchester bus passes or beer mats - I just carried on walking through the line and was then inside the stadium. We all looked at Gilly and took the piss out of him, still proudly holding up his ticket to any steward who was bothered enough to see it!

The end we were in was a joke, it was a temporary affair like the Gene Kelly stand we had at Maine Road and everyone was stood up for the whole game. Officially there were 4,000 of us, I would hate to have to guess how many blues were behind that goal with other groups dotted around the stadium. City were awarded a penalty and Anelka duly scored from the spot to put City 4-2 up on aggregate (which was the final score) and we all went wild.

In the corner of the stand to our right it began to kick off as a group of Lokeren fans began to steam into a handful of lads. We went ballistic behind the goal, running into that corner and trying to climb the fence to get at the Belgiums. The dibble were on the outside of the fence beating us back and eventually came on our side of the fence to move us back. One policeman dropped his truncheon and a blue went to pick it up and was subsequently beaten by another policeman which set those City fans in the vicinity off and it was like that around 10 minutes, we were charging over the seats at them, with loose seats being slung at them before they charged us back. Finally the police decided the best cause of action was retreat. What pissed us off even more was that City fans on the other side of the away end started chanting 'You're not fit to be a blue' which is absolute bollocks. We thought that City fans were being attacked by

Lokeren fans and we were trying to stick up for them - yet then our own fans say we are not fit to be a blue... all I can say is I'm glad none of them said it to my face as it would have been the last thing they did!

Eventually the word got around that it wasn't City fans being attacked by Lokeren fans but fans from their local rivals Ghent and things calmed right down behind the goal. The rest of the evening passed by without incident and we were just left to get on with the evening, boozing away in town.

*   *   *

In the next round we were drawn against unknown Polish side Groclin and had it all to do in the second leg following a 1-1 draw at home in the first leg. The game was played in a poxy little ground and City only received just over 1,500 tickets in a 6,000 capacity. However, as with Lokeren, I turned up without a ticket and still managed to get in with little trouble, I simply walked into a section for Groclin fans whilst all the stewards were busy at the City end! At halftime I recognised an English police spotter but ignored the cunt as I wasn't doing anything wrong. It was a bit of a family section we were in and we just watched the game rather than looking for a fight. Unfortunately both the game and City were shit and we went out of Europe on away goals after a 0-0 draw. We made our way to a pub nearby and when we saw the City team coach come our way we blocked the road and set about kicking the coach, letting the players know we were not happy with the performance, only it turned out to be a City supporters coach rather than the team coach! We went looking for the home fans - we'd heard the Poles were supposed to be hard bastards but with it being such a small town, there was no one to fight. A shit result both on and off the pitch.

A few days after I got home there was a knock on the door and two dibble, one holding a set of papers, stood outside.

'Hello Mr Sullivan' the one with the papers said.

'Fuck off' I replied.

The dibble continued, 'You had better read these, you are to attend court next Thursday - it will take you that long to read them' before informing me 'we have enough on you for a banning order and jail' the cunt had a big smile on his face. I wanted to crack him there and then, but just then my girlfriend came to the door to see what was going on. The dibble, smiling even more now, told her 'he's been a naughty boy has Mr Sullivan and he's going to get a banning order, possibly jail if we are lucky'. They got into the car and he wound the window down and reminded me again about Thursday. You can imagine the shit I got from my girlfriend once we were back in the house! Later that night she told our daughter what was going to happen, it was horrible, I couldn't even face her.

On the Thursday I went to court and the case was adjourned for two weeks and this kept happening for months with nothing ever getting resolved. By now the Euro 2004 championships in Portugal were about to commence. Because my case had not been completed, the daft twats had not put my name on the official list of banned fans and after checking with my solicitor, he said legally I was free to go but if the dibble did see me at the airport they would probably arrest me. I was crapping myself at the airport but managed to fly out without any hassle.

I tried my luck again a few months later for England's first World Cup 2006 qualifying round in Azerbajhan. One minute I'm walking through the terminal at Manchester airport - the next thing I'm laid out on the floor with a gun pointing at my head, cuffed and dragged off to the cells in the airport. I had to sign a form agreeing for my passport to be confiscated and was held there from 10am until 8pm, then released and told to appear in court the following morning. This proved to be just a formal hearing to prevent me from travelling abroad until my original banning order case was finally completed - yet this took a further 15 months to happen and during that time the bastards held my passport.

So finally it comes to court again and the lad who was up before me was given a banning order. His crime? Sticking two fingers up at opposition fans a football match. Fuck me, what is the world coming to when you get banned from attending matches for sticking two fingers up, a complete fucking joke. We were up next and the judge adjourned the case until the following day. In all it took four and half days, such was the evidence they had against me, from City and England games, though mainly England. The judge, in summing up, trotted out the usual platitudes about me having been in and out of trouble since the age of 13 and now having a daughter blah blah blah. Once more I was told 'It is time that I started to grow up'. I just looked at him, urging him to spare the lecture and just give me what he was going to give me, when the twat says he is going to adjourn the case until the morning for sentencing. The following morning I faced him again and he said he still hadn't reached a decision and would adjourn the case for a further three days.

The problem I had now was I was due to appear in court the next day in Preston on counterfeit charges. I was found guilty and the magistrate gave me twelve years! My solicitor, aghast at the sentence, stood up and pleaded for a rethink on the sentence as I had only been caught with four forged £20 notes. The magistrate had been under the impression it was a lot more than that and after checking the records, she reduced the sentence to nine months and after another ear-bashing, I was cuffed and taken away. I really do not know why they bother with the stupid fucking lectures. Do they really think we are listening?

After two days I was driven to Strangeways and back in court the following day in Manchester. The judge appeared and saw that I was now handcuffed to two officers whilst stood in the dock which didn't make a good impression. Once again the lecture came out - I stared at the ceiling - he went on and fucking on for ages. I'd rather be in a cell full of whinging smack heads doing cold turkey than listen to this boring cunt. I was almost falling asleep at times, yawning like fuck in the process.

Just when I thought he was finally going to sentence me, the twat drags up my record. 'I see this is not the first time you have been found guilty of football hooligan related offences' he informed the court. Then he drags up offences such as assaults on police officers and informing me that 'your record is bad'. And on he went again 'I don't know where to start, if it's not one offence it's another - you have certainly been around haven't you Mr Sullivan? I shall take into consideration that you have been out of trouble for a while, however you are currently serving nine months aren't you? So I shall give you a further nine months. I could give you more but I won't. I am also going to put conditions on you upon release - namely preventing you from watching Manchester City FC and England. You will have to report to a specific police station each time either team plays a game of football. If you break this condition you will be brought back here in front of me and I will not be so lenient next time.'

He looked at the security guards and ordered them to take me away. In my cell, my brief was pleased with the sentence, saying that out of the three of us in court, my charges were the worst yet with eighteen months, I got the lighter sentence. I could have had a bigger sentence and banning order.

*   *   *

On release, which was early, I was given a tag - anyone who has had a tag will tell you what a nightmare it is wearing one. Every time I was out I was asking people the time, making sure I was back home in plenty of time. I managed to keep to the terms and conditions of the tag for the three months I had to wear it, but once it was removed, I still had to report to the local police station on the days City or England were playing.

A week before the World Cup finals in Germany in 2006, I was going to visit a friend who was going over to Germany to support England when I received a knock on the door. Prior to this a bunch of Jehovah fucking Witnesses had called round, so I ignored the knock on the door. I went into the kitchen and the next thing I hear is a 'bang bang bang' on the window and a call 'Police - open up!' Then the same thing happens on the kitchen window. The fuckers had turned up in force - in total there were four vans, three cars and two dogs with the dibble wearing riot gear! I open the door and recognise a dibble from the Football Intelligence Unit saying 'Well Mr Sullivan, you haven't handed in your passport - you are nicked'.

I was staggered. 'You're having a laugh, you took my passport when I was nicked at the airport ages ago and I'm not going anywhere until I've called my solicitor'. My solicitor arranged to meet me at the Grey Mare Lane cop shop in Beswick. Once there, this plod kept saying he couldn't believe I was only given the small ban I'd received and not a longer one. I told him I didn't give a fuck what he thought, it was what the judge thought that counted. The dibble replied 'Sign this, you are in court tomorrow and the judge will extend the ban'.

My solicitor turned up, I signed the papers and was bailed to appear in court the next day. My solicitor said I'd be OK as long as I turned up in court. I turned up as required and the case was adjourned for a week. A week later and the case was heard. The dibble threw everything they could at me and my solicitor threw everything back at them including telling them that they still held my passport so he couldn't understand what this whole case was about . The judge didn't look that interested and as a result he did not extend the ban, but just put a condition on me that I signed on at the police station on the morning and evening of every England game during the tournament. He justified not extending the ban by telling the dibble that I had not broken any existing conditions. The bastards were gutted!

I kept to the new conditions, signing on twice a day on the day of the games, but was not happy about it. My solicitor told me to make sure I did that each time England played, reminding me that had the judge taken a bit more interest, he could have extended the ban or even sent me down until the World Cup was over as I was still out on licence. After the competition, I asked my solicitor to ask the court to give me my passport back so I could take my girlfriend and daughter on holiday. I had no chance - apart from the court, I would have to seek approval from the prison governor as well as the home office. It just wasn't going to happen and it was two more years before I got my passport back. It was like another fucking sentence I was given. And even now my ban is up and I am in possession of a passport, I still feel like I am tagged. If I go to a football match - even with my daughter - there is a camera in my face - it isn't nice, yet I see some fans being filmed kicking off and nothing happens to them.

The dibble have people who are marked, they want them to do something so they can be nicked and sent down - others they are not arsed about. As you know, I've been done for assaulting police officers - as well as football hooliganism, theft and fraud - it's a case of 'I fought the law and the law won' and they are still after me, watching and waiting for me to slip up so they can have me again. But I won't give the bastards the satisfaction, so keep on filming me all you want to! But as I said, it does get to me when filming me with my daughter... what the fuck do they think I am going to do? Even in August 2008 when City played EB Streymur from the Faroe Islands in the UEFA Cup qualifying round and City's home leg was played at Barnsley I was being filmed with my daughter... wankers! How long is this going to continue?

*   *   *

During my final spell inside Strangeways, I questioned all I had been involved in. Was it worth it? Well it certainly was a buzz and until the dibble got wise and filmed everything going on, there was rarely a problem. Football violence will never reach the heights it did in the 80's - certainly never in the stadiums itself and it's less to do with all-seater stadiums and more to do with CCTV and access into grounds becoming much more difficult. The days of firms turning up and paying cash on the turnstile or jibbing their way in are a thing of the past on the whole.

Someone once asked if I regretted what I did. Certainly not when I was younger, in my teens and early twenties. What hit me hard this last time was missing my daughter. When I was single and without responsibilities I didn't give a fuck and being inside was a bit of a laugh and a break anyway - but having my daughter visit me while I was inside was hard to take. I would have to put on a smile and brave face for her visits because I didn't want her to see me upset and then I would cry in my pad after she visited me and I'm not ashamed to say that. There have been plenty of so-called hard men who have done the same, anyone denying it is talking shit.

Since coming out, I've kept my head down and after a further year, had the conditions on me attending games lifted. I am a season ticket holder along with my daughter in the Family Stand and value the time we spend together watching our beloved Manchester City FC. I remain the sweet and tender hooligan!

WHAT IS A FOOTBALL THUG?

Over the years I have come across many different types of firms and individuals. Some are top lads who you could trust with your life, knowing that they would stand with you and fight, whilst some are a complete fucking joke. There are many out there who talk a good talk, but there are far fewer that walk the walk. Anyone who has really been involved in football hooliganism will know where I'm coming from and to be honest, anyone who hasn't been involved but likes to talk about it knows fuck all about the subject.

As I've said before, I'm not particularly proud of my achievements but neither do I regret what I have done. I did what I did and at the time it felt right. Over the years I have been beaten to fuck - by other firms and the dibble – stabbed, had bottles cracked on my head, been hospitalised and had lads threatening to come round my house and smash me and my gaff up, but you wont hear me complain about that. I chose to get involved. As football fans often sing *'que sera sera'* 'whatever will be, will be' - I just got on with it. If I didn't like it or I'd had enough then I would have got out of it, but I didn't because it was a buzz.

It's hard to explain to someone who wasn't involved, it's the not knowing what will happen from day-to-day that kept me going, no two days were ever the same. Yet I will sit in a pub on match days and hear lads brag to their mates how they were 'sticking the fingers up' at opposition fans behind the safety of a barrier or two, with the police and stewards in the middle or how they threw a coin or a rock across the road into an escort. One lad was treated like a hero because he was banned from all grounds for a few years – and what heinous crime had he committed that deserved a ban? He was caught singing 'munich' songs! It's a bit like teenagers and sex. Those talking about it were not actually doing it. Those doing it just quietly got on with it. I don't know who is worse – the gobshites spouting this shit or their mates happily taking it all in. I have no time for either of them.

What's even more amazing is the dibble and the courts think they are onto it. They issue all these figures each year saying how many hooligans have been banned and had their passports taken off them when England play. Then government ministers stand up in Parliament and tell fellow ministers what a great job the football intelligence unit is doing. Yes the figures may be up each year, but for what? Having one pint too many? Singing munich songs or throwing a coin? Even ticket touting gets you in court! My, my, aren't the police doing such a fine fucking job in catching Category 'C' hooligans?

The judges then think they have real hard cases in front of them, get all excited and ban them from all grounds at home and abroad. The lad then goes to his local pub (dressed in Burberry or Stone Island, looking like he has shopped in Selfridges, a fucking joke!) and gets a standing ovation and instant status (which includes free drinks all night from easily impressed twats thinking they are in the presence of a demi-god, who they don't want to get on the wrong side of - someone now officially branded / labelled a 'football hooligan') when all he has done is got caught throwing a coin at away fans from twenty yards away with a police cordon in between. Congratufuckinglations. No wonder attendances at grounds are going down - it's not just the price of a ticket but at the current rate of arrests and banning orders, looks like there will be plenty more empty seats up and down the leagues over the coming years.

*   *   *

On the flip side, I would just like to say I will always remember the 'good old days' with the Mayne Line Service Crew. There were battles and robbings and we were the ultimate force. We were the first mob to travel by coaches and the first to introduce calling cards. Donald even organised coaches for the scousers when they were in Europe, mainly Everton. I often wonder what became of all the lads I ran with - those who stood their ground and fought for the cause, game fuckers who feared no one and gave their all week in, week out. There were so many pure characters to remember and good times to savour. In more modern times I've gone to City away games on a coach and the characters are no longer there - even worse, you can't even have a fucking drink on the coach and they don't stop at the services to allow you to rob them anymore! Everything is more organised, sanitised and controlled. The fans today are no longer free spirits travelling the length of the country doing as they please, whereas we took what we wanted, when we wanted it.

I'd like to finish by recording my appreciation to Donald Francis and everyone else mentioned in the book who stood firmly with us and fought with us side by side. This book is a true account, devoid of sensational bullshit. Nor is it an attempt to glamorise what went on or enhance my ego or any of those mentioned. We simply did it - and for all mentioned within the pages who did the Mayne Line Service Crew proud - the pleasure, the privilege was mine.

Before I sign off, I just want to say to my mate's son Callum, from Moss Side, Steven Reid from Liverpool and another lad Josh from Moston. Always remember don't get into trouble - it's not worth it. Keep your head for what you want in life, use your brains and not your fists. Always remember you've got a mam and dad that love you, whereas I never had that and if I'd had what you've got, I wouldn't have ended up this way.

Think of your mam and dad and make them proud - whenever you're thinking about trouble just pick this up and read it.

Thanks for everything,

Tony.